Broadcast News in the Digital Age

Written by two award-winning broadcast journalists, this book offers a practical, hands-on guide to the modern digital TV newsroom.

Pulling from extensive industry experience, the authors provide a comprehensive look at the key journalistic skills needed to excel in broadcast news today, including storytelling, writing, story pitching, video production, interviewing and managing social media. The textbook is organized into five sections: building a foundation, storytelling and writing, producing, live performance, and ethics and career progression. The authors also provide step-by-step instructions on how to efficiently multitask while staying true to journalist ethics. Each chapter includes clear learning objectives, review questions and practical assignments, making it ideal for classroom use. QR codes integrated in the text allow students to easily see and hear examples of the stories they are learning to write.

Broadcast News in the Digital Age is an engaging, student-friendly guide for those seeking to become successful writers, producers, anchors and journalists in today's newsrooms, both on-air and online.

Faith Sidlow is an award-winning broadcast journalist with three decades of experience in television and radio news. She is an associate professor of broadcast journalism at California State University, Fresno, where she teaches broadcast and multimedia journalism. Faith worked as a reporter, anchor and producer for the Fresno NBC affiliate for 28 years. Her early broadcast career included radio reporter and board operator at KPBS-FM; San Diego reporter for KNX News Radio, Los Angeles; and research intern for CBS News in London.

Kim Stephens is an Edward R. Murrow and Emmy® award-winning journalist and college professor. She's worked as a news anchor, producer, reporter, weather anchor, telethon host and community event emcee at KERO, WBIR, HGTV, WVLT, KNTV, KMPH. Kim is also an adjunct professor teaching broadcast news writing, on-air performance and broadcast reporting and production at California State University, Fresno.

FAITH SIDLOW AND
KIM STEPHENS

Broadcast News in the Digital Age
A Guide to Reporting, Producing and Anchoring Online and on TV

NEW YORK AND LONDON

Cover image: © Faith Sidlow and Kim Stephens

First published 2022
by Routledge
605 Third Avenue, New York, NY 10158

and by Routledge
2 Park Square, Milton Park, Abingdon, Oxon, OX14 4RN

Routledge is an imprint of the Taylor & Francis Group, an informa business

© 2022 Faith Sidlow and Kim Stephens

The right of Faith Sidlow and Kim Stephens to be identified as authors of this work has been asserted in accordance with sections 77 and 78 of the Copyright, Designs and Patents Act 1988.

All rights reserved. No part of this book may be reprinted or reproduced or utilised in any form or by any electronic, mechanical, or other means, now known or hereafter invented, including photocopying and recording, or in any information storage or retrieval system, without permission in writing from the publishers.

Trademark notice: Product or corporate names may be trademarks or registered trademarks, and are used only for identification and explanation without intent to infringe.

Library of Congress Cataloging-in-Publication Data
Names: Sidlow, Faith, author. | Stephens, Kim (Television news anchor), author.
Title: Broadcast news in the digital age : a guide to reporting, producing and anchoring online and on TV / Faith Sidlow and Kim Stephens.
Description: London ; New York : Routledge, 2022. | Includes bibliographical references and index.
Identifiers: LCCN 2021033494 | ISBN 9780367683405 (hardback) | ISBN 9780367683429 (paperback) | ISBN 9781003137016 (ebook)
Subjects: LCSH: Television broadcasting of news--United States. | Television--Production and direction. | Broadcast journalism--Technological innovations.
Classification: LCC PN4888.T4 S54 2022 | DDC 070.1/95--dc23
LC record available at https://lccn.loc.gov/2021033494

ISBN: 9780367683405 (hbk)
ISBN: 9780367683429 (pbk)
ISBN: 9781003137016 (ebk)

DOI: 10.4324/9781003137016

Typeset in Joanna MT
by KnowledgeWorks Global Ltd.

We dedicate this book to our families who have supported us throughout the writing process and throughout our lives.

Contents

Acknowledgments xiii

Building Your Foundation Part 1 1

Meet the Newsroom Team One 3
Assignment Editor (AE) 4
Broadcast News Producer 4
Digital Content Producer 5
Reporter/MMJ 6
Photographer 7
Editor 7
News Anchor 8
Weather Anchor 9
Sports Anchor 9
Director/Production Crew 10
News Director 11
Questions 11

Finding and Pitching Good Stories Two 12
Know the News 12
Deciding a Story's Newsworthiness 15
Pitching Your Story 21
Reminders for Finding and Pitching Good Stories 32
Questions 32
Try This 33

Broadcast News Writing Fundamentals Three 34
Why We Write Like We Speak 36
Conversational Writing 38

Now, New, Next	41
Names	44
Pronunciation and Pronouncers	45
Let's Not Get Sued	45
You're Under Deadline	46
Reminders for Broadcast News Writing Fundamentals	47
Questions	47
Try This	47

Tips and Tricks to Good Writing   **Four**   49

Words Matter	49
Grammar, Spelling and Punctuation	50
"No, No, No" Words	57
Reminders for Good Writing	62
Questions	62
Try This	62

Real World Lessons   **Five**   63

Know Your Community	63
Beat Check	64
The Law	65
The Military	67
Law Enforcement	68
Emergency Responders	69
Legislative Officials	70
Politics	71
Brands	72
Reminders on Real World Lessons	73
Questions	73
Try This	73

Interviewing   **Six**   74

Why We Interview People	76
How to Prepare for an Interview	77
Conduct the Interview	79
Challenging Interviews	84
Video Chat Interviews	85
Reminders for Interviewing	89

Questions	90
Try This	90

Telling the Story Part 2 91

The VO Seven 93
The Lead	93
Writing to Your Video	95
Reader	99
Graphics	99
Timing Your Video	103
Reminders for Writing the VO	104
Questions	104
Try This	104

The VOSOT Eight 105
Who are the Best Interviews?	106
What is a VOSOT?	106
How to Write a VOSOT	107
The Soundbite	108
Finishing the VOSOT	112
Important VOSOT Scripting	113
Ethical Writing and Editing	114
Reminders for Writing a VOSOT	115
Questions	115
Try This	115

The Package (PKG) Nine 117
Journalist's Toolbox and "Go" Bag	118
Equipment	120
Time Management	121
Package Basics	125
Package Workflow	127
Shoot	128
Log	135
Write	140
Voice Track	148
Edit	150

	Writing the Web Story	150
	Reminders for Writing a PKG	152
	Questions	153
	Try This	153

Shooting and Editing Video **Ten** 154

	Shoot Like a Photojournalist	154
	Lighting	162
	Sound Matters	165
	Shooting Interviews	168
	Editing Efficiently	172
	Reminders for Shooting and Editing	177
	Questions	178
	Try This	178

Producing for Broadcast and Digital **Part 3** 179

Producing the Broadcast Newscast **Eleven** 181

	What is a Newscast Producer?	182
	Day in the Life of a Producer	184
	Newscast Themes	185
	Building a Newscast	187
	Rating Periods (or Sweeps)	197
	Running a Live Newscast	198
	Breaking News	199
	Reminders for Producing Broadcast News	202
	Questions	202
	Try This	202

Producing for Digital and Social Media **Twelve** 203

	What is a Digital Producer?	204
	Getting Permission to Share Pictures and Video	206
	Writing the Web Story	207
	OTT (Over-The-Top)	210
	Social Media	211
	What About the Haters?	218
	Trends and Analytics	219
	Reminders for Producing for Digital and Social Media	222

	Questions	222
	Try This	222

The Art of Live and Recorded Performance — **Part 4** 225

Storytelling—Taking it to the Next Level — **Thirteen** 227
- Story Focus 227
- Literary Devices 230
- Content Wins 233
- Drone Journalism 235
- Reminders on Storytelling 236
- Questions 236
- Try This 236

Live Reporting — **Fourteen** 238
- Good Live Shots 240
- Setting up the Live Shot 245
- When Things Go Wrong 246
- Writing the Live Shot Script 249
- Anchors Asking Questions 249
- Breaking News 250
- As-Live/Look-Live 252
- Digital Live Shot 253
- Reminders for a Great Live Shot 253
- Questions 254
- Try This 254

Newscast, Sports and Weather Anchors — **Fifteen** 255
- What the Public Sees 255
- Anchor or Influencer 257
- Building Credibility 258
- Voice Health 261
- Facial Expressions 265
- Clothes, Hair and Makeup 267
- Live on the Anchor Set 274
- Sports Anchor 276
- Weather Anchor 279
- Community Engagement 282

Social Media	284
Personal Protection	285
Reminders in Anchoring	285
Questions	286
Try This	286

Part 5 Local Journalists and Journalistic Practices — 287

Sixteen Ethics, Law and Deciphering Fake from Fact — 289

Ethical Considerations	290
Codes of Ethics	291
Legal Considerations	296
Fake News	300
Reminders about Ethics, Law and Fake News	302
Questions	302
Answers to Ethical Questions	302

Seventeen Getting That Job — 305

Building Your Digital/Social Media Brand	307
Internships	308
Networking	310
Applying for a Job	312
The Demo Reel	315
Do You Need a Website?	318
Resumes to Impress	320
The Job Interview	321
Negotiating a Contract	323
Starting Your News Career	324
Agents, Consultants and Recruiters	327
Why Your Mentors Love Their Jobs	328
Reminders on Job Opportunities	335
Try This	335

Key Terms	336
No No No Words	341
Works Cited	344
Index	347

Acknowledgments

"We can just bang it out!"

That's what we said when deciding to write this book. Both of us had the beginnings of this book in our computers and heads for years. We taught a version of each chapter in each of our classes for years. One day we decided why not pool our class notes together and "bang out" a book.

As long-time journalists we are accustomed to and driven by deadlines. We are both able to write quickly. That's a news script. A book? Well, what's *your* idea of quick? We started one month before the COVID-19 pandemic hit. Add family member health challenges, children's weddings and virtual teaching, and we still forged ahead.

Broadcast News in the Digital Age really started when we first began our careers in the 1980s. We learned by doing. We made a lot of mistakes live on the air along the way. Our hope is to help students make fewer mistakes by knowing more about our world and the role of the journalist.

The mentors in this book are people we've worked with, attended conferences with or watched and learned from through the years. Some are former students who have gone on to have successful careers in the journalism industry. We hold all of these colleagues in high regard, not only for their dedication to the industry, but for their work ethic and heart inside and outside of the newsroom.

We thank each and every one for taking the time to share memories, advice, tips, stories for the QR codes and scripts and log sheets to help readers visualize each lesson. We also thank those colleagues who reviewed our early drafts and made comments and suggestions that helped improve this book. We are eternally grateful. And we thank our students who have taught us so much about pride, perseverance and grit.

We couldn't have accomplished any of this without the help of the following: Adrian Luevano, Al Tompkins, Alex White, Alicia Acuna, Allizbeth Clavijo, Anthony Greene, Bob Butler, Boyd Huppert, Brandon Mercer, Brett Akagi, Bryan Lenocker, Carmaine Means, Chad Hypes, Chad Nelson, Chris Alvarez, Cyndee Hebert, Da Lin, Desiree Hill, Dion Lim, Donald Munro, Elisa Navarro, George Hsu, Greg Vandegrift, Jake Milstein, Jeff Lenk, Jobin Panicker, Joe Little, John Colucci, Kevin Olivas, Kianey Carter, Les Rose, Lisa Argen, Luis Godinez, Marion Coomey, Marti Skold, Michael Carr, Michael Golden, Nancy Bauer Gonzales, Nick King, Randy Forsman, Robin Slater, Ryan Hudgins, Sarah Light, Scott McGrew, Stan Heist, Theresa de los Santos, Tim Buchanan, Tracie Potts, Victor Hernandez, Wayne Freedman and Will Tran. These mentors are incredible people who work every day to fertilize the nation's state of journalism. Not everyone's picture is included in this book. That in no way negates the acumen of their craft or power of their mentorship.

We thank the Taylor & Francis Group along with Routledge for their interest and support, with special thanks to Priscille Biehlmann for helping us through every challenge along the way and to copy editor Emily Boyd for her keen eye and attention to detail. Kim thanks her bosses at Sinclair and KMPH for allowing her the time outside of the newsroom to pursue her passion of teaching the next generation. We also thank our colleagues in the Department of Media, Communications and Journalism at California State University, Fresno for supporting this process with special thanks to Fresno State President Dr. Saúl Jiménez-Sandoval and Dr. Honora Chapman, dean of the College of Arts and Humanities for creating an environment that encourages creativity and intellectual and personal growth.

And, of course, neither of us would have been able to complete this book without the unwavering support of our families. They understand our passion to help our students as they have overheard many a conversation through video chat at our dining room tables after we taught our classes online in that very same location. Breakfast, lunch and dinner plates, files and notes beside us, milking every moment out of our busy schedules.

Speaking of which, Kim would like to thank Faith for being so understanding when at 6 p.m. Kim had to sign off to go to bed to wake up at 2:30 a.m. the next day for her morning news shift. Many times, she'd wake and find Faith still up and they'd do a little work in the middle of the night. And Faith would like to thank Kim for her endless energy and encouragement throughout the process.

We both find teaching the next generation to be an honor. We also cherish our nation's First Amendment right to a free press. Our hope is that future journalists, who read and learn from this book, feel enriched, empowered and enthused to continue to promote ethical, visual storytelling and to keep local news alive.

Building Your Foundation
Part 1

Meet the Newsroom Team

One

In This Chapter

Assignment Editor (AE)	4
Broadcast News Producer	4
Digital Content Producer	5
Reporter/MMJ	6
Photographer	7
Editor	7
News Anchor	8
Weather Anchor	9
Sports Anchor	9
Director/Production Crew	10
News Director	11
Questions	11

The newsroom is a place where change is constant. The coronavirus pandemic and quarantine orders of 2020 jump-started another big change to the way the newsroom works with many working from home. **Producers** put together the newscast from home. Reporters used cell phones to shoot stories out in the field and did live reports, never going into the TV station.

These forced changes prove what was once thought to be impossible (putting on a **live** newscast from home) and is more common post-pandemic.

In this newsroom tour, everyone is in the building to meet you and share a little about what they do. They each welcome you with pride and excitement to tell you why they are in this business, what their day is like, what advice they'd like to share and how they support your decision in learning how to be a valued member of this news team.

Every newsroom has a different physical layout, but for the most part, they are made up of a bunch of desks and cubicles.

DOI: 10.4324/9781003137016-1

Each cubicle quadrant is organized by position. The producers and writers are in one area. The reporters and anchors are in an area close to the producers. The photographers are likely near small editing rooms. At one end, past the sea of cubicles, is a raised long desk. That's where we'll begin this tour—at the assignment desk.

ASSIGNMENT EDITOR (AE)

> **Mentor Moment: Victor Hernandez, Chief Content Officer, WBUR, Boston**
>
> "Strong communication skills, a digger/investigative thinker, digitally savvy and astute, someone who can comfortably operate free from praise and notoriety. It's often known as the thankless job of the newsroom. Being resourceful is about 85% of the role."

The assignment desk is the heart of the newsroom. It's where you'll find the police and fire scanners, calendars, planners, schedules and story files including everything the newsroom is working on today and months from now.

The assignment editor has an important job making community connections, the kind built on trust to know who will pick up your call in the middle of the night during breaking news or who will talk to you "off the record" to get you information "on the record."

"I became instantly addicted to the fast-paced environment of the broadcast newsroom where seconds, literally, meant the difference between making **slot** for the lead newscast story or missing and suffering dire consequences. It was an adrenaline junkie's dream," says Victor Hernandez, chief content officer at WBUR Boston.

On any normal day, the assignment editor is the big picture captain connecting all members of the team in their storytelling responsibilities ensuring all newscasts are covered. This position can be a stepping stone to a management position.

BROADCAST NEWS PRODUCER

> **Mentor Moment: Kianey Carter, Senior Producer, KNXV, Phoenix**
>
> "You are the leader of a 3-ring circus. The go-between for the desk and the reporter. The go-between for the directors and the anchors."

Producers create newscasts that each have a different purpose depending on the timeslot. They choose which stories to run, when to run them, and which anchor should read them. They must always think about the viewer.

The smart producer must go beyond cutting and pasting these stories from the feeds and dig deeper, using local and station resources to create and write a newscast that helps inform the local news audience, always giving perspective. During the newscast, when any well-laid plan can change in a moment, the producer times the show, cues the live shots and decides what to do in the event of breaking news. This position is a newsroom team leader who stays calm under pressure and can be a direct line to newsroom management such as an **executive producer** or **news director**.

DIGITAL CONTENT PRODUCER

> **Mentor Moment: Sarah Light, Digital Content Producer, WNCN, Raleigh**
>
> "To be a successful digital content producer, you have to be able to multitask and have excellent news judgment. There are many aspects you have to pay attention to. The ability to separate each project and publish stories with accuracy is fundamental. You might be in the middle of writing a story, but if breaking news happens, you have to be ready to stop what you're writing and work on what's happening in the now."

This position works with reporters in the field, helping them to break their news story on social media hours before a TV news broadcast. They also work with the assignment editor and producers to break their news stories on the station's website and social media feeds hours before a TV news broadcast.

"As the digital content producer, you hold a lot of power because you get to choose what is posted on social media. The ability to be nonpartisan in this type of position is vital to being successful," says Sarah Light, digital content producer at WNCN-TV.

REPORTER/MMJ

> **Mentor Moment: Jobin Panicker, Reporter, WFAA, Dallas**
>
> "On a professional level, I am doing exactly what I hoped to be doing: storytelling. There are few other jobs out there that allow me to be creative and connect with people. I truly enjoy the hard work of crafting beautiful stories about people."

Pack that bag with an extra set of clothes and toiletries. Throw in some extra lavalier microphones, backup batteries and SD cards, and make sure the phone is charged. A good reporter is ready at the drop of a hat. This position also builds and fosters sources, people who can be called, no matter the time on the clock, because there's always a deadline for new information.

This is a hectic and invigorating field that calls for keeping a cool, unbiased head, knowing who to call in a pinch, making deadlines, ad-libbing for a **live shot** in which little information is available, and becoming an expert in something learned that day.

"It's not an easy job," says Boyd Huppert, reporter at KARE11 in Minneapolis. "Therefore, a strong work ethic is paramount. Good people skills are key as well. Make people feel comfortable, and they will open up to you."

One day a reporter may cover city council, the next day a rocket crash, a family's bone marrow drive to save their dying child, and then a protest. Good reporters already have knowledge of these topics by staying up on local, national and international news.

Nowadays, many reporters are multimedia journalists (MMJs) also known as multi-skilled journalists (MSJs). They are a reporter, photographer, digital content producer and editor all rolled into one. Most entry-level reporter positions are MMJs.

Good reporters listen more than they speak. They think visually, always looking for ways to use pictures and sound to tell the story and engage the viewers. Constant self-analysis and critique are important to learn and grow.

"I chose broadcast journalism because I wanted to spend the rest of my life doing things I love: writing, connecting with people and keeping them informed," says Tracie Potts, NBC news correspondent.

PHOTOGRAPHER

> **Mentor Moment: Carmaine Means, Photographer/Drone Pilot, CNN, Chicago**
>
> "I started working professionally at ESPN when I was still in college at Columbia. I had two mentors. One was Jackie Denn, who was the first woman photographer hired at ABC. My other mentor is Mabel Miller. She is another African American woman who worked at WGN and NBC. Seeing the two of them, particularly Mabel, was extremely inspiring to me because I didn't see any women like myself."

A camera is what used to set TV apart from radio and newspaper. Now, many radio and newspaper reporters shoot video to use on social media, web and streaming services. Usually, the TV camera is bigger and more complex, but these days, it may just be a cell phone.

Pictures tell the story. Many great stories can be told with natural sound and interviews and no reporter **voice track**. All compelling stories need purposeful video and sound that matches the words and focus of a story.

The photographer knows the camera, microphones and light kit and how to fix them in a crisis, how to shoot quickly and efficiently, how to edit the story in the camera while shooting and how to work collaboratively with a reporter. Many times, the photographer and reporter are one and the same—an MMJ.

Each photographer should also have a resource list such as video to grab in a pinch on a certain topic and names and numbers of people to call for information or access.

Photographers and reporters should also periodically sit down together and review past stories to critique themselves. It's the best way to grow and get better.

EDITOR

Creativity and a broad knowledge base are crucial in video editing and graphic design. This job is far more than cutting video or creating compelling graphics. Here, too, is a place where news and community perspective are important. When someone says, "Get me a shot of a house," you have to find the right kind of house.

Editors add color, texture, dimension, excitement and relevance to stories. Editors must know software and technical devices because, in the crashing moment of breaking news and deadlines, the "Wow" factor is still expected. Editors must look for compelling, unique videos from all sources that come into the newsroom. The editor can be a critical team player when finding new video and sound and making the producer aware of it.

NEWS ANCHOR

> **Mentor Moment: Dion Lim, News Anchor, KGO, San Francisco**
>
> "It's true some anchors just read and look pretty. But here's the reality—as popular as these anchors can be, the most successful ones are journalists at heart, who live the mission of wanting to give a voice to those who do not have one, using their platform to make change."

The news anchor is the face of the TV station, which is a huge responsibility.

News anchors convey stories through words, tone, facial expression, body language and emotion. There's a lot that goes into looking natural because, let's face it, being on TV and talking to a camera with lots of eyes, make-up, hairspray and lights on you is not natural, and few anchors feel comfortable early on.

News anchors also cover stories. Some anchors have a weekly franchise such as the health, education or political beat. Others produce their own segments, such as sports, business or what's trending.

Homework comes with this job, no matter how many years' experience. Anchors study current event and memorize faces of important people so they can ad-lib easily and confidently.

News anchors are leaders in a newsroom, role models in the community and far more than a good haircut. There's a lot of balance and grace that comes with this job.

"I saw a half hour special done by one of the local news stations when I was growing up in Michigan," remembers Scott McGrew, a news anchor at KNTV-TV in San Jose. "I was fascinated. No office, get to ask a lot of questions and go interesting places? Yes please."

WEATHER ANCHOR

> **Mentor Moment: Lisa Argen, Meteorologist, KGO, San Francisco**
>
> "Getting comfortable relaying science and weather takes time—even years. It takes familiarizing yourself for many seasons to get it right."

The weather person or meteorologist is also a highly visible role. Some markets that experience a lot of weather require this person to have a degree or seal in the science of meteorology. Other markets don't require that degree, but all markets do require this person to energetically and conversationally show the viewers the weather that's coming or is happening right now.

This person must be a master ad-libber and well-versed in geography. There are no scripts. The weather person must be comfortable using the **chroma key**, also known as the green screen. It takes practice to point to a blank green screen while looking out of the corner of your eye at a nearby monitor to see the superimposed weather maps. The chroma key is mostly used by weathercasters but is also used to display virtual news sets or other video behind an anchor or reporter.

There can be a lot of stress in getting a forecast right. Sometimes a weather system changes quickly from sunny to stormy or vice versa. The science a weather person uses can only predict so much. Sometimes they get it wrong.

Argen says missed forecasts aren't all bad. They can lead to a better understanding of prediction tools when it really matters. They can also lead to a human moment when you simply admit you missed it.

SPORTS ANCHOR

> **Mentor Moment: Nick King, Sports Reporter/Anchor, 3TV CBS5, Phoenix**
>
> "Covering sports is an absolute thrill ride. One of the most attractive parts of this business is the opportunity to experience something new every single day. No two games are the same. No two people playing, coaching, watching the games have the same life stories."

The sports anchor is a jack of all trades—a photographer, producer, writer, editor and anchor. The gift of ad-lib is also important here in describing video and highlights on the air. Many newsroom sports departments have two people—the weekday and weekend sports anchor. They shoot, edit and anchor the high school games, local college sports and big national stories that come down on the network feed.

This job is also much more than reading numbers on the screen. The viewers can do that. The sports anchor provides context to the statistics and focuses on the humanity of the stories.

When they aren't covering specific sports events, they are creating stories about the people involved in those sports, teams, towns and schools.

DIRECTOR/PRODUCTION CREW

> **Mentor Moment: Randy Forsman, Newscast Director, KCRA, Sacramento**
>
> "The control room environment can be fast-paced and stressful at times, but as long as you remember that you're the one in control, you ultimately can decide how stressful you'll let it be. Once you learn the flow and the rhythm of a live newscast and learn how best to utilize the strengths of your production team, you'll learn that there is no better feeling. It's cliché, but once you get the hang of it, it's like riding a bike."

The **director** is the captain of the newscast who literally calls the shots—the camera shots, the anchor microphones, the video, the live sources and when to go to commercial break. This person must be calm amidst chaos, lead by example and help everyone do their job to keep the live program afloat and problem-free.

The director is the liaison between the news staff, engineers and master control operators. These departments, under the direction of different bosses, must work on the same team during that live broadcast.

"The director and producer play important roles in tandem with one another," Forsman says. "One analogy I love to use when explaining what I do is that the director is the one driving the car, and the producer is the one with the map telling the director where to go."

NEWS DIRECTOR

> **Mentor Moment: Chad Hypes, News Director, KTVL, Medford**
>
> "I always tell people that my day is a mix of high school principal and college professor. I am constantly coaching/teaching/training people throughout the day. It starts with reporters/producers in the morning getting the day planned out. Then I work with the noon director/editor to make sure we have everything we need. Then I spend some time with the anchors/meteorologists to talk about that morning's show and tomorrow's newscast. In the afternoons, I do it all over with the evening team to make sure we are good to go for the evening shows."

This is the newsroom boss—the one who hires and fires. The news director works directly with the station general manager because news is often the biggest department and expense.

At some stations, the news director is hands-on. At other stations, the boss is barely seen by the ranks and is more involved in budget and interdepartmental endeavors. Either way, for the newsroom, the buck stops in this office.

QUESTIONS
1. How are the roles of producer and director different?
2. Which job is the main liaison between the engineering and news departments?
3. What job is considered glamorous but can also be quite stressful?
4. What two jobs are most tied to upward mobility into management?
5. Why is the ability to stay calm a positive characteristic for all of these jobs?

Finding and Pitching Good Stories

Two

In This Chapter	
Know the News	12
Deciding a Story's Newsworthiness	15
Pitching Your Story	21
Reminders for Finding and Pitching Good Stories	32
Questions	32
Try This	33

For journalists just starting out, finding a story can be intimidating. Questions are commonly asked such as:

- Where do I find stories?
- How do I talk to strangers?
- What if I'm uncomfortable talking with strangers?
- How do I know what a good story is?

Here's a secret. Nearly everyone feels that way in the beginning. You may have a curiosity about things and a desire to learn and explore but are afraid to take the next step. You may not think you have permission to ask those questions.

We are here to tell you that you have permission. In this chapter, we'll show you how.

KNOW THE NEWS

First, you need to be an active viewer of the world. You need to pay attention to what's going on in your circle of friends. What are they posting? What are they most concerned about? What are they complaining about or celebrating?

DOI: 10.4324/9781003137016-2

Then, expand that circle to what's going on in your immediate community, including family. What are they talking about or doing or changing in their lives?

Go further to look at what's going on at your school or workplace. If your school or workplace has a newspaper, newsletter, website or active social media page, what are the topics being shared and covered?

Keep looking outward to see what's going on in your section of the state, the whole state, and beyond. The only way to do that effectively is to truly pay attention.

Not all stories will be of interest to you. You may know very little about some of the major stories and events. That's why you must study.

Fox News correspondent Alicia Acuna remembers when she was first hired by the network and placed in the Denver bureau. She immediately went from doing local news in a medium market to covering major national news stories including the Jon Benet Ramsey murder case and jury selection for the Terry Nichols trial in the Oklahoma City bombing case.

"I was 27 years old, terrified, and because of the way schedules worked in Fresno and Bakersfield for the 10 months where I was prior, I had never been in the courtroom," Acuna says. "My first judge was Richard Matsch, who was a federal judge at the head of the Oklahoma City bombing trial. I was scared to death. So, you study. I had to study, study, read, read, read and make sure I had my recall on just about anything. It was fear that drove me."

No one told Acuna to study. She did it on her own so she'd be prepared. This is an important lesson. You must take it upon yourself to understand things.

KTNV News Director Nancy Bauer Gonzales couldn't believe the number of people in her Las Vegas newsroom who didn't know who Tommy Lasorda was the day the former Los Angeles Dodgers manager died.

"It shocked me," Bauer Gonzales says. "I was like, am I going to have to explain? When we were young and we got into news, and we didn't know something, we'd be really embarrassed and we'd run for the dictionary. Now they have the internet. They have no excuses. All they have to do is type it in."

Yes, asking questions is important, but don't be lazy. Do some legwork on your own to earn confidence and respect.

Here are a few suggestions to stay on top of what's happening. Follow and read social media feeds from:

- news professionals and community organizations
- city and state services such as the police, fire, highway patrol, sheriff's departments and emergency agencies
- city, county, state and federal government leaders
- public services such as water, garbage, gas and electricity companies
- school districts, community colleges and area universities.

Read signs posted at your local grocery store and mall, and, yep, you must watch, read and follow the news.

> **Mentor Moment: Chad Hypes, News Director, KTVL, Medford**
>
> "It's important to stay engaged with news and the newsroom. I'm not saying you have to eat, sleep, breathe news 24/7, but you must stay engaged. Everyone needs to check out occasionally, but you can catch up in a few hours before your next shift. It's easier than ever with apps and alerts. There is no excuse for being out of the loop because you were off. People in the newsroom aren't going to call you on your day off just for fun. You owe it to the viewers, your colleagues, and yourself to take this profession seriously. That means staying up to date with what's happening in the news and at your station."

It's becoming more common to not own a television, with viewers watching the news on digital or mobile devices. Most stations stream news on their website, **OTT** (Over-The-Top streaming devices) and apps. They also post stories and live video on their social media pages. You need to pay attention to those. If you have a smartphone, you can keep up with the news.

News isn't handed to us. We get it by doing research, asking questions and using handy resources such as our phone to Google Tommy Lasorda. This is purposeful journalism—journalism created with intention. We are rewarded when we pay attention, problem solve and ask questions with an open, curious mind.

How do you know "what's news?"

"Whenever one of my reporters finds themselves in a story idea slump, I encourage them to put their devices away and attend community events," says Victor Hernandez, chief content officer, WBUR in Boston. "Listen to real people. Interact with them. Ask for a follow-up coffee meeting to understand their issue more. Oftentimes, these interactions will lead to new sources, story possibilities and angles worth pursuing."

Hernandez says too often young reporters get stuck on their social media all day. They need to get out and authentically connect with real people.

"An easy slump-breaker is to hit the streets and actually speak, better yet listen, to your community," Hernandez says.

It's also important to expand your focus from that which is popular and voyeuristic to more substantial content. Some stories are pure entertainment. There's little substance behind the words. They are stories about who's dating whom, who's dissing whom, the designer outfit someone's wearing or which person just got voted off the latest reality show. This is fun information. Some organizations, mainly in larger markets, air programs that cover only that genre—entertainment with little substance.

There is a place for entertainment stories in some newscasts. On social media, entertaining posts get a lot of interaction. On TV, it could be the final story of the newscast, otherwise known as a **kicker**, to leave viewers in a good mood and help them transition into the next program.

But the rest of the newscast and a news organization's mission is to focus on other newsworthy information that is important, timely, relevant and interesting, and can be told in a compelling way with words, pictures and sound.

DECIDING A STORY'S NEWSWORTHINESS

Ask any beginning journalist what are the key questions to answer in a story and the response will be who, what, when, where, why and how. True, but we are here to remind you of a few more. Many news stations and digital publications still use news values to determine whether they should cover a news story.

News values are the criteria that are used to rate the newsworthiness of a story based on the interest it carries for the audience and why the audience should care. This holds true for all forms of journalism: TV and digital. When TV news **ratings** are high, it indicates viewers like what they are watching.

In the digital age, the audience influences whether a story should be covered based on user generated data otherwise known as **analytics**. When people click stories on the website, they are telling the digital editors that story has news value. Each TV ratings point and web click turns into income through advertising revenue. The goal is higher ratings and more story clicks, likes and shares.

News values include prominence, human interest, unusualness, impact, conflict, relevance, timeliness and proximity.

Who Is This Happening To?

A person's name, standing in the community, even celebrity, plays a big part in deciding whether a story is newsworthy. If something happens to a well-known person in the community or that person's family, it is likely a story. **PROMINENCE** is the price one pays for being well known. If police arrest an 18-year-old for reckless driving, it may not be a story unless the teenager happens to be the son of the city's police chief. If a news anchor is arrested for shoplifting, that's a story. If an average person is arrested for shoplifting, it's not an obvious story.

> **Mentor Moment: Cyndee Hebert, Managing Editor of News Content, WTHR13, Indianapolis**
>
> "There was a police officer accused of molesting a relative. Because it's a police officer that's important and why you do the story. But you have to protect the victim's identity. We reported the name of the officer but didn't say he was accused of molesting a relative. Instead, we said he was accused of child molestation."

Another way of looking at the "who" brings in the **HUMAN-INTEREST** aspect of the story. If a Girl Scout selling cookies outside a grocery store ran to help a shopper having a heart attack, that's a story. If a four-year-old is selling lemonade on the sidewalk to raise money for her preschool friend who's getting cancer treatment, that's a story. If a homeless man found a bag of money and brought it to the police station and then met the person who lost that money, that's a story.

Those are stories that make you feel something; stories that show humanity. This could also include the "Hey Mable!" story. A story that is so unusual or incredible that the viewer yells to his wife, Mable, to stop what she's doing and come watch this story.

Maybe that's the guy walking a tightrope 15 stories above downtown Honolulu. Maybe it's the little girl with spina bifida taking her first steps. Or, maybe it's the 80-year-old woman arrested for stealing money from her dead son's bank account and his body is still inside the home.

The producer at one station didn't think twice about running this next story. He knew the **UNUSUALNESS** of the story would be of interest to viewers.

> On a warm September night in California's Central Valley, an intruder broke into a house and rubbed spices on the body of a man who was sleeping on a couch. The intruder used a sausage to hit another man in the face.
>
> Local TV stations reported the story the next morning. A Fresno County sheriff's deputy gave this statement to the media: "It seems the guy ran out of the house wearing only a T-shirt, boxer shorts and socks, leaving behind his wallet with his ID."
>
> It turns out deputies arrested a 21-year-old man, and found $900 that had been taken from the house. But they couldn't find the sausage, which they said the dog ate. Here's the quote of the day: "That's right. The dog ate the weapon," the deputy said.[1]
>
> No charges were filed in the case.[2]

What/Why Is the Story Focus?

One way to get to the "what" of the story is to see whether it's connected to a larger topic in the news right now.

What is its **IMPACT**? If a person sneezed at the airport and someone called the police and made a commotion about it, this could be an impactful story because it happened amid a big virus health scare. Any other day of the week, it's simply rude and gross.

If a person threw a bucket of water on the school superintendent in a show of anger over the school district's old water fountains, that could make what is normally an uneventful meeting a newsworthy story because of the **CONFLICT**.

If protesters go to a city councilmember's house and berate him because they disagree with a controversial vote, that may be a 20-second story with video (otherwise known as a **VO**). But, if the councilmember shoves one of the protesters, again sparking conflict, that is a story. And if you have video of the shoving, that may be the lead story of the newscast.

We often say there are two sides to every story, but in reality, there are often many more. Make a list of everyone who could be a potential stakeholder in your story and talk to them. Find out what they're at odds about. What is the source of their conflict? Is there a neutral party who can help provide insight, analysis or background? You'll want to interview that person, too.

Just because there's conflict does not mean it's an automatic story. For example, if a parent calls you saying her son's teacher is rude, that's not necessarily a story. And, just because a viewer gave you video of a fight at a supermarket, that may not be a story either. More questions must be asked. Context is important.

What is the **RELEVANCE** of the story to your community, region or the world? If two people get into a fight because one of them sneezed in the other person's face, this would be relevant during the coronavirus pandemic.

If a statue in the community is vandalized, it would be relevant in light of the recent Black Lives Matter movement for equality, justice and liberation.

When Did This Happen? Or When Will It Happen?

Timing is everything. You've probably heard that phrase. In news, **TIMELINESS** certainly holds true because of the way it could directly impact your viewers. For example, in some drought-stricken communities, people are only allowed to water their yards on certain days and times.

A newscaster reading the story at 8 a.m. could say, "You have two more hours to water. If you can't get it done by ten, you'll have to wait until after six tonight."

That's what we call conversational writing.

Many news managers will tell the morning producers to not run a story from last night's newscast because it's old news. However, if something new is happening today with that story, then it has a place in the morning newscast. It all depends on the writing.

This speaks to the now, new, next aspect of newsworthiness. If you can explain why it matters to the viewer right now or that it will soon affect the viewer, then it has a place.

Where Is This Happening?

If five businesses in your community got burglarized overnight, that's a story because of **PROXIMITY**. If the burglaries happened in a different state, it's likely not a story because it doesn't affect your community. However, in the gray area of news, the out-of-state burglaries could be a story if the person arrested is originally from your area.

Proximity has fluid boundaries. You must write about stories that are in your local viewing area or are about people from your viewing area. A homeless dog that walks into town every day to visit with shopkeepers might be a heartwarming newsfeed kicker, but it will be much more interesting to your viewers if it's a local dog.

We're not limited to one news value when gauging a story's newsworthiness. If there is a big car crash on a highway in a different state, it likely does not affect your viewers. If that crash happened on the main highway in your community, it is clearly newsworthy not only because of the "where" of the story but because of the "how."

The viewer needs to know if the road will be open for tonight's drive home from work or tomorrow's rush hour commute.

If there's a medical breakthrough in cancer treatment or a new concussion treatment, the story may not affect everyone. If you can apply this to something local or regional, then the likelihood of that story's newsworthiness is greater.

A lot of stories journalists tell are recycled ideas, brought back year after year. For example, we see the fireworks safety story every

Independence Day. A good reporter finds a *new* way to tell the story. An enterprising reporter finds a timely story on the topic that's never been told and an interesting character around which to base the story. Strive to be that reporter.

> **Mentor Moment: Victor Hernandez, Chief Content Officer, WBUR, Boston**
>
> "Most news stories are boring and predictable. How can you tell the same stories and issues with a different approach? What will be unique and interesting about how you can present the information and perspectives of those central to the issue? Can it be shot differently? Can you speak with different, under-represented voices for this story? Can you leverage innovation to help move the story along and engage an audience on connected devices? How do you plan to produce a fresh experience on the story that is likely to also be covered by market competitors across the street?"

Visuals

Visuals should be central to all of the stories you tell. What opportunities does your story idea offer for still photos? For video? We want to see people *doing* things or the visual aftermath of something. If there are no visuals, the story may still be important but we now must think of a way to help visualize it. Graphics, animation, stand-ups, courtroom sketches, etc. Maybe it would be a better social media/digital story.

Because we tell stories with pictures and sound, we must know where we can get the visuals. Do we have access to video from network feeds or a network of photographers? Do we have permission to use video from someone who posted it on social media? If you cannot get video or create graphics to correspond with your story, you may not be able to air that story on TV.

Some stories are fabulous radio or social media stories and not so fabulous for the visual medium of TV. Think about the visuals when you pitch your story.

PITCHING YOUR STORY

Now that you can answer those news value questions, there are a few other aspects you must think about.

> **Mentor Moment: Victor Hernandez, Chief Content Officer, WBUR, Boston**
>
> "Brevity is key. You have to make your seconds count. Come out with a memorable open, use visuals if you can, storyboard the pitch, capture the imagination of who you are trying to win over with your pitch and do so in the shortest amount of time necessary. Remember, a story pitch isn't about explaining the full story A through Z—it can be a tease or a preview for what the journey will likely provide."

Pitching a story is not just throwing out a cool idea during the newsroom pitch meeting. Pitching a story is showing your news team the research you've already done on that idea, the people who are willing to talk about it, and the visuals that will help turn the idea into a meaningful story.

Creating a Solid Pitch

Here's a common example of how this plays out. You want to cover a festival. You could quote the press release, which says the festival has been going on for a decade and has music, crafts, food and an antique car show. You could go to the festival and shoot generic video and give the facts and figures of how long the festival has been going on, how much it costs and the hours. That's not very memorable. Or, you could concentrate on a character and tell a more lively, memorable story through the eyes of that person. People want to relate to someone before they can believe, sympathize and identify with a stranger. It's human nature.

How do you pitch that? You research who will be showing an antique car and meet up with a few of those people and learn the history of the car, their love for it and what they went through to get it.

Maybe your interview is with the car owner in his garage surrounded by tools and other antique loves as he's getting ready for the festival. The video and natural sound could be amazing.

Then, you transition to the festival, show that one car among the others, meet a few other car owners, and get beautiful pictures of antique cars with their chrome sparkling in the sun.

There's music at this place, too, according to the press release. You could do a feature story about an old-time fiddle player. How do you pitch that story? Start by researching old-time fiddle music. Just like with the antique car owner, you should find out if there is a club in your area. Does the club have 25 members? 250? Is there a national group representing the preservation of old-time fiddle music? Will they be at the festival?

Just as in the example of the antique car owner, maybe you meet with this fiddler before the festival and see that musician in his or her real environment. Then you meet up with the fiddler at the festival and see the musician in that wider environment. Interview another musician, a few people who are watching and tapping their feet to the beat. This side of the festival story is memorable even though you showed just one aspect of it.

You may ask how you research the car owner or the fiddler? Won't it take a long time? How can I access this information? You could call the organizer whose contact information is on the press release. While waiting for a callback, you could also type a few keywords into your computer or phone.

For example, if you live or work in California, go to data.ca.gov, the State Level Open Data Pilot Portal for the state of California; randstatestats.org and look at categories of interest for your county or neighboring counties. Learning a few tricks to best use search engines can make researching stories fun and quick. Those tricks can make you a go-to person in the newsroom—one who's often asked, "How did you get that information?"

Tapping into other resources can turn you from a so-so storyteller into an exceptional one.

The Pre-Interview

After you research the topic, it's a good idea to pre-interview by phone potential subjects to get information about the story so you are well versed when you pitch the idea to your producer or assignment editor.

Take it one step further, and set up appointments to interview people on camera. In the news, you will notice the "bird in the hand" mentality will serve you well. Just remember that even if you make a solid pitch, your story may not get the green light because of breaking news or other conflicts. You should let potential interviewees know the story could get postponed if breaking news happens.

Many assignment editors and reporters have a great story idea and a wonderful pre-interview but are not able to set up the on-camera interview because the person never returned their call. Waiting for a callback, an email or a DM (direct message) on social media is excruciating when you're on a deadline. Wait a few hours. Wait a day at the most depending on your deadline.

If you still don't get a response, call the person. Yes, by phone. Wait less time for a response the second time you reach out. If you don't hear back, you must find a different interview and move on. Don't rely on one person or source. You must always have a backup plan. Maybe you call a few people and go with the person who gets back to you first. You need to be persistent to be successful.

Communication Skills

Marion Coomey, a media production professor at Ryerson University in Toronto, says despite all their technical and social media skills, many of her students have no idea how to search out and then call interview subjects for news stories. She says many students are terrified to make cold calls.

"I had one student say: 'Well, what if someone actually answered? What would I say? I'm going to phone at 10 o'clock at night when I know she's not there and leave a message instead.'"

This wasn't the first time Coomey had to talk a student through the simple, basic steps of making a phone call to a stranger.

"I realized they may know how to text and tweet, but they've either lost the ability or never learned how to communicate clearly and effectively in 'real time' over the phone," Coomey says. "They tell me when they use social media, they can rewrite and edit what they say before posting, but in a live phone call they're afraid they will sound awkward or stupid or just not know what to say."

It's best to talk with a variety of people, not just officials such as the CEO, a police officer or a school principal. These interviews are often one-sided press availabilities with little human interest or emotion.

Compelling Interviews

We want a personal perspective with our on-air TV interviews. Not like this hypothetical example of an interview with a highway patrol officer after a 25-car crash in the fog on a local highway:

> ADOT: "At 0-600 this morning, a red Nissan rear-ended a big rig in the number three lane going southbound at mile marker 253. What transpired next is a chain reaction of vehicles hitting the Nissan and big rig. When we arrived on scene, we dispatched fire crews to extricate the big rig driver. A third alarm was called to render aid at the back of the crash."

That's not an exciting or conversational interview. It would be better to use that as background information for the story. The best interviews are from people who share a personal connection to the story.

You have several choices for interviews in this scenario: someone who just got out of one of the crashed cars; someone who stopped on the other side of the highway to help; or, someone at a nearby rest area who needed to pull off the road and calm down after seeing the crash. These people help share the humanity of the story.

When is it OK to break a newsroom rule and use an interview from an official? If the highway patrol officer told you in an on-camera interview, "In all my 30 years on the road this is the worst crash I've ever seen." That is a compelling interview with an official that can be included in the story because it includes humanity, emotion and personal perspective. Do you see the difference?

Figure 2.1 shows how we would write that story.

Notice how this is a more impactful story with the personal angle? The script is also written to the most compelling video of the smashed cars. That is how all of our stories should be written. You must look at the video before ever writing one word of copy.

Making the Pitch

Back to the story pitch. You are about to see an example of a story pitch form. It's designed to get you thinking about all that's required to professionally and successfully pitch a story to your assignment editor or

[ANCHOR ON CAM]	**{ANCHOR ON CAM}** FLOWERS MARK A SIDE OF THE HIGHWAY WHERE A CRASH HAPPENED NEAR THE TANK STREET TURN-OFF OF HIGHWAY 22.
[TAKE VO] [CG: FREEBURG, HIGHWAY 22]	**{TAKE VO}** IT WAS HARD FOR DRIVERS TO SEE THIS MORNING IN THIS THICK FOG. THE FIRST FIVE CARS CRASHED INTO THIS BIG RIG AROUND SIX A.M. THEY DON'T LOOK MUCH LIKE CARS ANYMORE. HIGHWAY PATROL OFFICERS SAY THE CRASH STARTED WITH THE DRIVER OF THIS RED CAR NOT ABLE TO SEE THE BACK OF THIS GREY BIG RIG IN THE THICK FOG. THEN, A CHAIN REACTION OF 25 CARS SLAMMED INTO ONE ANOTHER.
[TAKE SOT] [INCUE: "In all my 30...." [OUTCUE: "...like this. Ever. "] [TRT :10] [CG: FRANK SMITH, HIGHWAY PATROL]	**{TAKE SOT}** ("In all my 30 years on the road, this is the worst crash I've ever seen. The fog always comes in right here this time of year, but we've never responded to a crash like this. Ever.")
[TAKE VO]	**{TAKE VO}** SOME PEOPLE ARE IN THE HOSPITAL WITH A FEW BROKEN BONES BUT EVERYONE SURVIVED. IT TOOK SIX HOURS TO CLEAR THE HIGHWAY. THE ROAD IS OPEN NOW. FOG IS FORECAST FOR TOMORROW MORNING AS WELL. SO, PLEASE BE CAREFUL.

Figure 2.1 Script Example with Compelling Interview

producer. Don't worry. Once you're in a newsroom, you won't have a formal form to fill out. You'll have this one memorized.

Why all of these questions? They help the assignment editor, producer and reporter find the **story focus**, which many beginners fail to do. This pitch form helps with that.

> **Mentor Moment: Victor Hernandez, Chief Content Officer, WBUR, Boston**
>
> "The biggest mistake I see early-stage journalists make with their stories is the pressure to 'kitchen sink' their pieces. That is, they involve too many voices and interviews, too much disjointed information, too many jarring visual elements."

Focus Statement

Use the form in Figure 2.2 to develop your story pitches and focus statements.

You'll notice the pitch form asks for a focus statement at the top. This is where you define what your story is about.

Try to think of your story concept in the subject-verb-object format. The same applies to your focus statement. Who is your actor? It can be someone who did something or to whom something happened. It can be someone who intervened. That's how we analyze what we have or hope to have. We start by finding the most interesting aspect of the story. The part that makes you *feel* something or say, "Wow," when you read about it or see it.

Remember your focus when you pitch your story, conduct interviews, shoot video, log, write and edit. The focus statement will help keep you on track.

Additional interviews allow you to get many angles of the story. They could also help create a compelling social media post in which a short interview is used on social media teasing ahead to more of the story on the newscast. Of course, each story topic is different, but the goal is to offer varied sides of a story and stay impartial. It's OK to let your interviewees share their opinion and bias. But you, the reporter, must only state the facts.

Sometimes you won't get three interviews, but your goal should be more than two for objectivity, variety and diversity. You don't need to use soundbites from all of your interviews in your story, but it's helpful to use information from additional interviews to verify, attribute and crosscheck your story.

Some stories are told with a lot of interviews. We call that an **MOS** or man-on-the-street. You might hear the term **POS** for

1. **What is your focus statement?** What is the most interesting aspect of your story? Write it in terms of subject, verb, object or actor/action/object. (Example: Student struggles to pay tuition; grandmother gets vaccine; farmer loses crops, etc.)

   Focus Statement:..

2. **Research your subject:** Use Google, social media, online newspapers, library databases. Write three facts about your subject of topic:

   - Fact 1:
   - Fact 2:
   - Fact 3:

3. **Who will you use to personalize your story (first interview)?** (You must have at least one person/personal angle as the focus of your story, a real person and not an expert or official. This is the person who is the most impacted—the person who lost his/her job, the student who sends 5,000 texts a day, the fiddler who's playing at the festival.)

   - Who (name):
   - What is his/her relationship to the story?
   - Where is s/he located?
   - When did this person do something related to the story?
   - What is a meaningful details about this person?

4. **Who will you interview second (not an official)?** Make sure that you include diverse voices in your story.

   - Name
   - Relationship to your story

5. **What is your third interview?** (An official is OK, or you may use a "real person.")

   - Name
   - Relationship to your story

6. **Where will you shoot your interview?** Think of a location that will be visually appealing and relevant.

Figure 2.2 Developing your Story Pitch and Focus Statement (*Continued*)

- Main interview location:

- Interview #2 location:

- Interview #3 location:

7. **What interesting video could you get that will enhance your story?** What camera angles and shots will you shoot? List three close-ups that you plan to get.

    - Close-up #1

    - Close-up #2

    - Close-up #3

8. **What interesting natural sound could you get to enhance your story?**

9. **What data or statistics do you have that could be visualized with props in the field or photos, graphics or maps?**

10. **What *extra* equipment will you need** (in addition to tripod, wireless lavalier mic, batteries and SD cards)?
    - steady bag
    - spare batteries or charger
    - SD cards
    - XLR cable
    - camera light, light kit or reflector
    - GoPro

Figure 2.2 (*Continued*)

person-on-the-street. An MOS is several interviews, three to five, usually short, from a wide variety of people. These interviews are rarely set up in advance.

Think of it as a verbal survey to convey public opinion on an issue.[3]

As you are about to read from this next mentor, not everyone is a fan of the MOS.

Mentor Moment: Joe Little, MMJ/Director of Storytelling, KNSD, San Diego

"OK, fine. They want you to go do an MOS package. Great. Go out and find one MOS. Go find one person on the street, and then stick with that person for five minutes. Shoot everything. They want you to do an MOS package on the new iPhone 27 that's coming out. And there are hundreds of people in line, and they think they have to have a new phone. Don't interview 20 people. Go find the one person in line who's the loudest, most obnoxious person you could find, or go find the person in the front of the line or the person at the back of the line. But find that one person and stay with them. Go on the journey with them. Maybe there's a secondary character, but give me a primary character that I can root for or hate or laugh with or cry with. This is so important for so many reasons. One, it's a better story. It allows me to build a relationship. It gives me a focus. Reaching your time management goals? Begging for 10 interviews and then shooting them is a time suck. And anyone who tells people to go do an MOS package should go in the mirror and punch themself in the face several times."

Once you've decided whom you will interview, you now need to decide where you will conduct the interview. Your assignment editor may have already made the decision for you. But if this is a story that you're pitching, and you're taking ownership, you'll want to set up the interview in a location that is visually appealing and relevant.

For example, if the story is about a water park, it would be good to be at the park at the bottom of a slide where people come splashing down, or as you float in the water.

If the story is about a mural, do the interview with people painting the wall behind the interviewee. Or better yet, do the interview while the interviewee is painting. We call that an **active interview**.

If the story is about illness prevention, you could either be in a doctor's office or in the cold and flu aisle at the drugstore. You'll need permission to shoot inside a doctor's office, store or anywhere on private property. Call ahead. If it's a local store, the owner may give you clearance quickly. If it's a national chain, permission could take days.

You also need to think about interesting or unusual video that will help tell the story. It can be difficult to find compelling video for court and city government stories. What do you do?

Look for the human angle. Take the story out of the meeting or the courtroom. *Who* is impacted? Tell the story from that person's perspective.

Another important element is sound. Good audio is just as critical as good video when it comes to producing a quality news story. In fact, some reporters and editors will tell you that audio is more important than video. When you're setting up your story, take both into consideration using your focus statement to guide you.

As you're filling out the pitch form, think about other ways you can enhance your story. What data or statistics do you have that could be more easily visualized with graphics or maps?

Finally, in addition to your camera, what other equipment will you need for your assignment? Plan ahead if you think you'll need a wireless microphone or a GoPro camera. Tools such as a small, lightweight camera with a wide-angle lens will add to your story and will give viewers a point-of-view perspective. A wireless microphone will allow you to do active interviews—recording the interview in a natural setting.

Once the editorial meeting is over, you should know what your job is for the rest of the day. The assignment editor or lead producer has written the story slugs on the whiteboard in the newsroom or in the electronic day planner, assigning each reporter or photographer to a story.

In some newsrooms, the assignment editor decides the story format and the newscast in which each story will air. In other newsrooms, producers decide that or it's a combination of the two who do this as a team. Each newsroom handles these responsibilities differently.

Next, it's the assignment editor's job to help the crews get the interviews and video they need. Maybe it's making a few phone calls to set up another interview. It might be pulling up past scripts to help you, the reporter, get texture and perspective for your story.

The assignment editor and newsroom archive system can be a wealth of information. It's a good habit to look at the files (physical or digital) for each month of the year where media releases, notes, contacts, copies of previously reported stories and reminders of upcoming stories are kept. This information helps you find an upcoming trial date, background on a story, sources who may be willing to talk and important historical perspective for the "why care" aspect of a story.

For example, you may be assigned to cover that protest scheduled to take place in front of the councilmember's house. You are handed a fact sheet with background on the issue that protesters are angry about.

"Go out and spray it down. Get a soundbite," the assignment editor tells you. In other words, you've been asked to get a short interview, a sound**bite**, and some supporting video.

The assignment editor also works with each producer (broadcast and digital) to ensure they have what they need. If they need a reporter to go live, the assignment editor sets that up. The assignment editor is the direct link between the news crews out in the field and the producers back in the station.

Deciding If a Story Will Run

Now that you have covered the story and are finished writing and editing it, the newscast producer or executive producer will decide if it will run in the newscast. Just because you think you did a great job on this story does not mean it has an automatic place in the newscast. You cannot take this decision-making personally. The producer is the one who knows best if a story fits and flows. Here are five simple questions the producer asks in deciding if a story should air:

- How is the story *written*? Are the words precise, well placed, well used, focused, grammatically correct and written to the video?
- Is the story *factually correct*? Is it accurate and factual?
- Is the story *relevant*? Is it applicable to something happening in the community or world right now?
- Is the story *unbiased*? Is everyone and every fact treated fairly?
- Does the story *flow*? Do the pieces of the story tie together?

The key to remember is that this is a business and a lot of other decisions are happening in the newsroom and the station that have nothing to do with you or your story.

If your story is not placed where you want it in the **rundown**, if your producer is not as in love with your story as you are, if your managing editor asks for changes, or if your story is floated or dropped, *do not take this personally*. Ask questions, and if there's anything you could have done differently, learn from it. If it was out of your hands, let it go and inform your interviewees so they can watch the story at a different time.

REMINDERS FOR FINDING AND PITCHING GOOD STORIES
- Make friends with people who aren't like you.
- Subscribe to *everything* (e-zines, listservs, newsletters, magazines).
- Follow news leaders, journalists and areas of interest on social media.
- Listen to talk radio.
- Read (kiosks, flyers, local newspaper editorials, inserts, bulletins).
- Be on the lookout for a story every time you walk out the door.
- Remember to answer the who, what, when, where, why and why care? How does this story affect the viewer?
- Have a clear story focus when pitching your story. Are you proposing to do a story about the downhill ski club in summer or the campus basketball team after the season is over?
- Find a character to interview who can connect with the viewer and help make the story relevant.
- Put yourself in the shoes of the viewer. Think like the viewer. Question the facts like the viewer.
- Look for diverse voices.
- Look for ways to take a national or international story and relate it to your local community.

QUESTIONS
1. What are the five main questions you must ask yourself to know if a story is newsworthy?
2. What are the four elements of a good story pitch?
3. What questions should you ask to determine whether a story is ready for air?
4. Why is showing the human side of the story recommended?

TRY THIS

1. Fill out the pitch form in Figure 2.2 with a story you will do in this class.
2. Look at five stories on a news website, and write a focus statement for each story.

NOTES

1 The Fresno Bee, "Man rubbed with spices, other beaten with sausage," September 7, 2008.
2 Galvan, Louis., The Fresno Bee, "Alleged sausage attacker set free - DA decides not enough evidence to try man held in bizarre robbery case," September 11, 2008.
3 Prato, Lou (1999) Easy to do, but often worthless, American Journalism Review. Retrieved from https://ajrarchive.org/Article.asp?id=3299&id=3299

Broadcast News Writing Fundamentals

Three

In This Chapter

Why We Write Like We Speak	36
Conversational Writing	38
Now, New, Next	41
Names	44
Pronunciation and Pronouncers	45
Let's Not Get Sued	45
You're Under Deadline	46
Reminders for Broadcast News Writing Fundamentals	47
Questions	47
Try This	47

You know how to write. You've been doing it for years. Up until now, you've been writing book reports, essays and term papers. Maybe you've written stories for your school newspaper or yearbook. You've been writing for the eye.

Now, with this book, you will learn to write for the ear. You will learn to write like you talk because that's what we do with our broadcast audience. We have a conversation. We write in active voice to grab and hold the attention of our listeners. We use short sentences. Sometimes we write in incomplete sentences when we're trying to make a point. Write as we talk.

In this chapter, you'll learn the difference between the kind of educational writing you've done so far and the broadcast style you are about to learn. You'll learn a new terminology that is used to describe the kind of story you are writing.

There are four basic story formats in broadcast news.

A **Reader** is a story that has no video. The anchor reads the story on camera for the entirety of the story. This story usually runs between 20 to 25 seconds.

DOI: 10.4324/9781003137016-3

A **VO** is a short story (20 to 30 seconds) with video. VO stands for "voiceover." That means the anchor is seen on camera reading the first line (also known as the **lead** of the story) and then, while the anchor reads the rest of the story, the viewer sees video on the screen. The anchor is "voicing over" the video.

A **VOSOT** is a story that combines a voiceover (VO) with an interview clip. That interview is called a **SOT** which stands for "sound on tape." The story begins with the anchor on camera reading live the lead sentence or two, and then video is seen on the screen as the anchor voices over that video. This is followed by the SOT, a short portion of the interview—about eight to 15 seconds long. Once the SOT ends, the anchor reads live over more video.

It is important to know that a VO is its own story. A VOSOT is its own story. The two may be about the same topic but they are considered two separate stories. A VO about a festival may air in one newscast. A VOSOT about that same festival may have similar pieces of information, but it is written differently to include a clip from an interview and will run in a different newscast. The two stories are not interchangeable.

A **PKG** (short for **package**) is a self-contained story that includes video, multiple interviews, natural sound, reporter stand-up and recorded reporter voice track. For this style of story, the anchor is seen live on camera saying a few words to introduce the story and the reporter. Next, the video rolls, and the viewer sees the pre-recorded story.

This story style traditionally takes a more in-depth and textured approach to a story, weaving together natural sound and interviews. The reporter may be seen in a stand-up in this story showing or demonstrating something. Packages end with a tag-out—the reporter saying his or her name, location and then the TV station name. That's the close of the story. Sometimes an anchor will say something live on camera after that package, which is known as an anchor tag. Each newsroom has its own style.

Before you write a broadcast news story, you must give it a title, known as a **slug**. The slug is seen by the whole newsroom in the digital day planner and in the newscast rundown. It's a short name because there's a short amount of space in each rundown line.

Brevity makes for clarity when someone needs to find a story quickly in the rundown or announce to the team what story is being added or dropped at a moment's notice. But, in the effort to be brief, the slug must still have some specifics to it. A story about a fire can't just be slugged, "Fire." It needs to have a specific word such as "Cedar Recycling Fire," which includes the location, street, city or business. That way it will be easier to find in the archive system.

> **Mentor Moment: Chad Hypes, News Director, KTVL, Medford**
>
> "If you don't love and respect this job, you won't last. If you are in it for the money or the face time, save us all some time and look elsewhere. This job is hard, but it can also be rewarding. You get back what you put in. You have to be coachable, you have to listen, and you have to want to learn. You should learn a lot at your first job. It will go by quickly so you have to work to get a little better each day. Learn as much as you can. Volunteer to learn a new skill, do something that makes you uncomfortable, try something different and don't be afraid to fail. This business is full of people sitting around waiting to be told what to do. The ones that step up and get things done are the ones that stand out."

WHY WE WRITE LIKE WE SPEAK

With our broadcast audience, we get one chance to tell the story. One chance to get the viewer's attention and share important information. If they don't understand something, viewers can't go back and read the story again like they can when reading a print or web story.

Remember, we communicate with our TV viewers by writing for the ear. The viewer hears the story once, so we need to be clear. The best way to know how a story sounds is for you to write your story and then read it out loud. Better yet, read it out loud as you write it. And listen. When you listen to what you read, you may hear words that are unclear. To the eye, the words may seem fine, but to the ear, you may realize you missed typos or words that need to be changed to make the story accurate or sound more conversational.

Here's an example of a digital or print format, which is different from broadcast format. Notice the dateline at the top of the story and the long, summary lead that includes all of the facts of the story in one sentence. This is known as the inverted pyramid style, often used in print stories. The digital story is written in sentence case.

> PIXLEY, Calif.—The shootout with police Thursday that killed three officers stunned a small community of 180 people, disrupted classes at a nearby elementary school and overwhelmed the local and county police force. Investigators say the shooting began as they served a search warrant at a small house on the edge of town.

The following example is a TV news script. Notice the anchor read at the top, and the story is written in short, conversational sentences, with one thought per sentence.

> [ANCHOR 1-SHOT]   {ANCHOR 1-SHOT}
> THREE POLICE OFFICERS ARE DEAD IN THIS MORNING'S SHOOTOUT IN PIXLEY.
> SHERIFF'S DEPUTIES SAY A MAN STARTED SHOOTING AT OFFICERS AS THEY SERVED HIM A SEARCH WARRANT.

You may be wondering why the TV example is in capital letters. We are not yelling. This is how we will write our broadcast scripts in this book, to help you see the difference between broadcast and digital news stories.

Quick history sidenote: In the 1850s when the teletype was created, it could only accommodate a small set of characters, so all capital letters were used. This machine was used for communication in the military, then the news and other important communique like telegrams. Newsrooms received their Associated Press newswire on teleprinters in all caps so the standard continued for continuity when newsrooms wrote their own scripts.

In 2016, the National Weather Service stopped using all capital letters in its weather alerts because it had become a general consensus at the time that all capitals signified yelling.[1] Some newsrooms now use mixed case in scripts and the teleprompter. Many digital news producers prefer this. It makes copy editing quicker and easier between TV and digital scripts. Some news anchors say all capital letters are easier to read in the teleprompter. Others say the opposite. So, while all capitals were the norm, that is changing.

CONVERSATIONAL WRITING

Many broadcasters say we should write stories for Joe Six-Pack or a sixth-grade audience. On one hand that may sound demeaning. We should not assume our audience is uneducated, dumb or drunk.

> **Mentor Moment: Kevin Olivas, News Recruiter, Sinclair Broadcast Group**
>
> "You need to be an excellent writer. Short, declarative, conversational sentences—the way that you would talk to a friend."

That doesn't mean using slang or jargon or that we should disregard grammar and punctuation. And, it doesn't mean smart language or an occasional "SAT word" is off-limits. It just means less formal.

"You don't write in cop-speak," says Cyndee Hebert, managing editor of news content at WTHR 13 in Indianapolis. "You don't want to write technically. You want to write how you would be talking to somebody."

> **Mentor Moment: Da Lin, MMJ, KPIX, San Francisco**
>
> "I love this field because I get to meet interesting people and learn something new every day. I also like writing. And this field requires a lot of critical thinking and writing."

Contractions

There is a lot of gray area in the study of broadcast news writing. Just as we said a few sentences ago, we write conversationally. Using contractions is a common part of modern conversation and is often preferred in broadcast scripts. However, some contractions can be confusing when heard. For example, HE WAS TOLD HE CAN'T GO OUT AND PLAY.

It's clear when you read that with your eyes. Now, read it out loud. The "t" in can't may not be heard well and if the audience can't hear the "t," then the whole meaning of the sentence changes. So, in cases like this, we write out the contraction for emphasis. For example, HE WAS TOLD HE CANNOT GO OUT AND PLAY.

It's OK to use contractions in your web story.

Commas, Quotes and Attributions

Have you ever tried to read a teleprompter? It's that device on news cameras that allows the script to be reflected onto glass in front of the camera lens so the news anchor is looking directly at the camera and the viewer and reading the script at the same time. The art is in looking like you're talking, not reading. It's our job to write so the anchor sounds like he or she is simply talking. To do so, punctuation matters.

In that long term paper from last semester, did you include complicated sentences with commas or quotation marks? The semicolon has a great purpose in long, involved sentences, too. Some titles may include a / (slash), & (ampersand) or # (number sign, hash or pound sign).

In broadcast TV news writing, we use very few commas and write out all of those symbols. Yep. We write "dollars" not the $ symbol; "hashtag" and not the # symbol; and if we're talking about a web address, we write "dot com." We do this so the person reading the script, talking to the viewer, is able to speak clearly with no question about what's in the script.

NO: THE COVID RELIEF PACKAGE WILL COST $4B.
YES: THE COVID RELIEF PACKAGE WILL COST FOUR BILLION DOLLARS
NO: FOR MORE INFORMATION ON WOMEN'S HEART HEALTH, GO TO SOCIAL MEDIA AND TYPE IN #WEARRED.
[CG: #WearRed]
YES: FOR MORE INFORMATION ON WOMEN'S HEART HEALTH, GO TO SOCIAL MEDIA AND TYPE IN HASHTAG WEAR RED.
[CG: #WearRed]
NO: YOU CAN CHECK OUT THEIR WEBSITE FOR DETAILS ON THAT. IT'S BEAUTIFYFRESNO.ORG
[CG: beautifyfresno.org]
YES: YOU CAN CHECK OUT THEIR WEBSITE FOR DETAILS ON THAT. IT'S BEAUTIFY FRESNO DOT ORG.
[CG: beautifyfresno.org]

Quotation marks are perfectly fine to use in your web writing. For example:

In "Return of the Jedi," Luke Skywalker confronted Darth Sidious with this famous quote: "I'll never turn to the dark side. I am a Jedi like my father before me."

Here's how we handle the same quote in a TV script: HE SAID, IN HIS WORDS, I'LL NEVER TURN TO THE DARK SIDE. I AM A JEDI LIKE MY FATHER BEFORE ME.

Or you may paraphrase: HE SAID HE'D NEVER TURN TO THE DARK SIDE BECAUSE HE IS A JEDI LIKE HIS FATHER.

Now, let's talk about abbreviations. We don't abbreviate for TV scripts. We write it out for the anchor to easily read. The only exceptions are Mr. and Mrs.

> St. becomes STREET or SAINT
> Ave. becomes AVENUE
> Dr. becomes DRIVE or DOCTOR

But what about acronyms like ESPN or FBI? For broadcast script writing, a dash must be put in between each letter that is pronounced.

> E-S-P-N
> F-B-I
> NINE-ELEVEN
> NINE-ONE-ONE

These last two numbers mean very different things. When not written out clearly, the wrong one can be said. We definitely don't want that.

Occasionally, you will combine both the words and the letters. For example, NAACP would be written N-double-A-C-P. Likewise, the NCAA could be written N-C-double-A if that's how you want it pronounced.

For web writing, abbreviations and acronyms should be written according to the AP Stylebook.

Numbers

We just wrote out NINE-ONE-ONE. It's much clearer to read in a TV news script than 911. We follow the basic Associated Press formatting when it comes to numbers. Write out one through nine; 10–999 all get numerals. Then, we start using a combination of numbers and letters. We don't use commas in broadcast script writing for numbers. If a number is big enough to have a comma it must be written out.

> 1,000 becomes ONE-THOUSAND.
> 3,200 becomes 32-HUNDRED.
> $1.6 becomes MORE THAN ONE-AND-A-HALF-MILLION DOLLARS.

When rounding won't change the meaning of the story, it's OK to round a number up or down. It's also more conversational. If you must be specific then write ONE-POINT-SIX-MILLION DOLLARS.

Write out phone numbers as they are. Like this: 559-555-3242.

Let's not use a number for an address unless it's important to the story. Most viewers don't know exact addresses, but they do know areas of town or cross streets. If something happened in the 44-hundred block of Smith Avenue, you'd instead say it happened around Smith and Maple.

When it comes to someone's age, we don't need that number, either, unless it's important to the story. For example, AN 81-YEAR-OLD MAN JUST FINISHED HIS CLIMB OF EL CAPITAN IN YOSEMITE. HE IS THE OLDEST PERSON ON RECORD TO DO SO.

Why would the age of the man be used in that example? Because the correlation of the age and the feat are unusual and impressive.

Some scripts may use the word "elderly" instead of the man's age. That is a word you should think about before using. Some newsrooms request the use of that word only if a person is 80 or older. Anyone younger is considered a senior, grandparent or retiree, whatever applies to the story. The IRS considers 65 to be elderly. Do you know anyone that age? Maybe your mom or dad? We bet they'd not think too kindly to being called elderly because that word alludes to a person being incapacitated by age, illness or injury. Clearly, the mountain climber is far from incapacitated. If age has no place in the story, then don't include it.

For web writing, numbers are written numerically according to Associated Press style.

NOW, NEW, NEXT

Many newsrooms live by this mantra. The script should always say what is happening now, what is new in the story and what will happen next. That's what we call active writing. Our story leads must be active and they must pull in the viewer. We must always find a way to make the story relevant.

If it's something that happened yesterday and you can't find any new aspect, then why is it a story today? If a house burned down yesterday, it's still ashes today. Not a story. But, if this was the third time that house burned in the last few months, then today's updated story could be about how the city is changing its policy on boarded-up homes. Instead of letting homes sit and be used and destroyed by squatters, after a certain amount of time they will be bulldozed and cleared. That is now a today story from something that happened yesterday.

Always look for the today angle. That means you will need to ask questions. That means you will have to search on the web or in your TV station's archive system for similar stories at that location. Get history. Get perspective.

We've long heard that a good news story includes the who, what, when, where, why. But that's not all. We also need to include the "how" and "why should the viewer care?" Answering those questions will give much-needed perspective to the story.

A story about a car crash at an intersection is just a crash. But if that intersection has been the site of three crashes in the last two weeks, that perspective is necessary and worth a follow-up story. Same with that house that burned three times.

Subject/Verb Placement

When the subject of the story is placed close to the action of the story, the sentence is easy to understand. It also becomes a more active form of writing.

> **NO:** THE INVESTIGATION INTO THREE SMITHVILLE HIGH SCHOOL FOOTBALL PLAYERS ACCUSED OF SEXUAL ASSAULT CONTINUES THIS MORNING.
> **YES:** THE INVESTIGATION CONTINUES THIS MORNING INTO THREE SMITHVILLE HIGH SCHOOL FOOTBALL PLAYERS ACCUSED OF SEXUAL ASSAULT.
> **NO:** THE SEARCH FOR TWO MISSING AMERICAN SOLDIERS IS OVER.
> **YES:** THE SEARCH IS OVER FOR TWO MISSING AMERICAN SOLDIERS.

Keeping the subject of the story close to the action is a simple way to keep a sentence active. However, we want to make sure we are using active voice and not forced present tense. Have you ever heard a newscaster say?

> **NO:** A FIRE BREAKS OUT AT JULIA'S RESTAURANT ON THE MALL.
> PEOPLE RUN IN PANIC.

That is a forced present tense. It works just fine for a tease. It is not a good way to lead the story because it's not the way we talk.

Instead, you could say:

> A POPULAR DOWNTOWN RESTAURANT IS SMOLDERING TONIGHT.
> **OR**
> A FIRE TORE THROUGH A POPULAR DOWNTOWN RESTAURANT.

That was the beginning of the story. Now let's go to the end.

Ending a story with "The investigation continues," is a waste of three words. It's a waste of three seconds. It's a waste of the last few moments you have in a script. Instead, we challenge you to find a way to say what's next in the story. That final line can say what's next *and* summarize what the story was about, just in case your viewer got distracted and lost concentration: THE FIRE MARSHALL IS NOT YET SAYING WHAT SPARKED THE FIRE THAT DESTROYED THIS POPULAR DOWNTOWN RESTAURANT.

What Time is It?

Time matters. We need to know when our story will air because that TV news air-time could affect how we write a story. For example, THE FESTIVAL STARTS AT EIGHT THIS MORNING is fine for a story that runs at seven in the morning. It's not OK for the 9 a.m. newscast. The sentence would need to be rewritten.

In keeping with our active writing, we do not want to start a story with the word yesterday. If you can find a today or now aspect to the story, then *that* is your lead. You may then use the word "yesterday" later in the script.

Here's the deal. We want viewers to watch our newscast. We want them to feel like we are the most connected and up-to-date source of news in the market. That's why we write actively, giving the *now* and the *what's next* aspect of the story so our viewer can be informed and forewarned.

Why, in tonight's 11 p.m. news would we do a story about a car crash that shut down traffic for hours at 8 a.m. that same day? To help the viewer know if their commute *tomorrow* morning needs to be adjusted. Just make sure you lead with the "what's next" theme of the story and not the 15-hour-old part of the story.

Another aspect of time includes days of the week. If today is Tuesday, February 11, and you're writing a story about something that happens on February 13, it's best to write Thursday instead of the date in your TV news script. Here's a question for you. Do you know what the date is right now as you are reading this? Most people don't know the date, but they know the day of the week. So, if something is happening within the five to seven days of the broadcast, then it's best to say the day rather than the date.

We write dates in web stories because those stories have a much longer life online.

NAMES

Writing names of people for broadcast news is much the same for print. We say the whole name first and then every other reference includes only the person's last name: **JACK WEBB** IS IN JAIL ON CHARGES OF THROWING A PIPE BOMB IN THE MEDIA NEWS WRITING CLASS. COURT RECORDS SHOW **WEBB** DID THIS ONCE BEFORE IN A MATH CLASS.

If Jack Webb had a brother who was somehow a part of the story, then you may need to use both full names to avoid confusion.

If Jack Webb's job title was an important aspect of the story, then you would put the title before the name. Here are some examples:

- Digital: Jack Webb, Concord police chief, is in jail.
- Broadcast: CONCORD POLICE CHIEF JACK WEBB IS IN JAIL.

When it comes to saying the names of children, most newsrooms use the child's full name and then every other reference includes the first name. That's not a hard and fast rule. It's a newsroom choice.

For example, FOUR-YEAR-OLD FINNLEY COOPER HAS A BUCKET FILLED WITH 600 DOLLARS. FINNLEY IS RAISING MONEY FOR A FRIEND WHO IS SICK.

Notice how $600 was written in that TV news script. Remember, we don't use dollar signs in broadcast scripts. We write out the symbols for clarity.

In web writing, it would be Finnley Cooper, 4, has a bucket filled with $600. Finnley is raising money for a friend who is sick.

PRONUNCIATION AND PRONOUNCERS

So far, we've used words that are easy to pronounce, but when things get challenging, it's up to us to include pronouncers in the broadcast script. It's always best to err on the side of caution, so put in the pronouncer. If the anchor doesn't need it, then he or she can take it out.

If you've ever looked at pronunciation cues in the dictionary, you've likely seen symbols that may be confusing like ăĕĭŎû. We do not do that in broadcast writing. We write out pronouncers as they sound. The syllable with the emphasis is written in capital letters.

LADY GAGA (GAW-gaw) THOUGHT SHE WAS SHAKING THE STAGE WITH HER MUSIC. THEN SHE REALIZED HAWAII'S KILAUEA (kill-uh-WAY-uh) VOLCANO WAS ERUPTING DURING HER CONCERT.

Also, if there is a symbol in the name, you must write out the name:

A$AP (AY-sap) ROCKY WILL SPEND THE NEXT WEEK IN A SWEDISH PRISON AFTER AN ASSAULT CONVICTION.

There is no need for pronouncers in web writing.

LET'S NOT GET SUED

Ever heard the phrase, "Innocent until proven guilty?" It's not just something said on your favorite TV crime drama. It's real. No matter what, in the U.S. legal system, people are considered innocent all the way up to the verdict when a jury or judge rules guilt or innocence. Remember that when reporting your stories.

The police may say, "This guy robbed the place and is now under arrest" or "This woman was driving drunk and caused that crash," but *we* cannot write our scripts like that. **We cannot convict people in our stories**. Sadly, that happens when words are put in the wrong place in a script. This is true for both TV broadcast scripts and web stories.

> **NO:** THEY WILL TESTIFY ABOUT WHAT THEY SAW AND HEARD WHEN WILLIAMS SHOT AND KILLED A MAN LAST YEAR.

The person who wrote that script just convicted Williams. It doesn't matter if there's a video of the shooting. It doesn't matter if tons of people say they saw it. This must be rewritten.

> **NO:** THE FOOTBALL PLAYERS LURED THE GIRLS INTO THE BOYS' BATHROOM AND ASSAULTED THEM AFTER THE GAME.
> **YES:** THE GIRLS SAY THE FOOTBALL PLAYERS LURED THEM INTO THE BATHROOM.

We must always attribute. We must always identify the person or agency that said something happened. "According to the bank manager," "Investigators say," "Witnesses report" are **attributions**. Try to be as specific as possible. It's better to write, "Police Chief Jonathan LaBelle says," instead of, "Police say." We, the reporters, are rarely the ones who witnessed something and can say it as fact, so we need to report who said what happened.

It's rare that a person will sue a reporter or TV station for defamation, but it has happened. It takes deep pockets to defend a defamation lawsuit, and in many cases, the TV station settles out of court rather than going through the expense of a trial. But this isn't about money. It's about doing the right thing. We do not convict people. Period.

> **Mentor Moment: Kevin Olivas, News Recruiter**
>
> "Verify. Verify. Verify. Don't assume anything. It's lazy. It's a disservice to the storytelling profession, to accuracy, and ultimately, to the audience."

YOU'RE UNDER DEADLINE

Once you've nailed these writing tools, you need to remember to make deadline. In this business, you do not have the luxury of much time. The faster you write the better. Write, then edit your words. Don't let yourself stare at a blinking cursor waiting for genius to flow from your head to and through your fingertips. Get the words out. It doesn't matter if they don't make sense at first or that they don't answer every who, what, when, where, why of the story. Get the words out. Then edit your copy. You have a newscast in a few hours or a few minutes.

REMINDERS FOR BROADCAST NEWS WRITING FUNDAMENTALS
- Write clearly, using conversational, active voice.
- Write clearly so the news anchor can read the words easily.
- Write out symbols, numbers, acronyms and contractions.
- Know your newsroom's style for broadcast scripts. It may be capital letters or sentence case. Use sentence case for web stories.
- Use pronouncers for tricky words, names and places for broadcast stories.
- Always attribute.

QUESTIONS
1. Why do we write conversationally for broadcast news?
2. Why should the subject and action be close together in a sentence?
3. What's the best way to attribute information?
4. What are three differences between digital and broadcast news writing?
5. Why should we find a different way to end a sentence other than "the investigation continues"?

TRY THIS
Watch a current local newscast.

1. Give an example of conversational writing.
2. Give an example of source attribution.

Rewrite these sentences in broadcast style based on what you learned in this chapter.

1. 8 cars crashed in the fog around 6 o'clock PM on Interstate-5.
2. THE INVESTIGATION THIS MORNING INTO THREE GELSTINE HIGH SCHOOL FOOTBALL PLAYERS ACCUSED OF SEXUAL ASSAULT CONTINUES.

Add a pronouncer for the underlined name/location.

3. HURRICANE LANE IS CREDITED WITH STOPPING THE LAVA FLOW OF HAWAII'S <u>KILAUEA</u> VOLCANO.

NOTE

1 National Weather Service will STOP YELLING and Use Lower-Case Letters in Alerts, *Weather.com*, 11 April 2016, web. https://weather.com/news/news/national-weather-service-to-use-lower-case-letters

Tips and Tricks to Good Writing

Four

In This Chapter	
Words Matter	49
Grammar, Spelling and Punctuation	50
"No, No, No" Words	57
Reminders for Good Writing	62
Questions	62
Try This	62

WORDS MATTER

We have a few seconds to grab the attention of our audience or lose it. Our words matter. We want to use a few words to be succinct. We want to use strong words to be clear and straightforward. We want to use words that show no bias and are ethically, legally, culturally and colloquially appropriate.

Remember, we want to write conversationally. For example, when we get information from the police about a crime, we must translate the police jargon into more conversational language. When we get information in a news release promoting an organization or event, we translate the promotional spin into unbiased facts.

At the same time, it's important to remember the ABCs of news writing: accuracy, brevity and clarity. An important component of this is grammar, spelling and punctuation. In order to be accurate, you must use correct grammar and spelling. To be understood, correct punctuation is critical for TV and digital scripts.

Word usage involves using the right words at the right time—using the correct word in a phrase and making proper distinctions among words that are often confused. Many people tend to associate word usage with grammar, but that's not quite the case. Word usage is more

DOI: 10.4324/9781003137016-4

a matter of vocabulary as well as a complicated intersection with everyday expression.

People sometimes use the wrong word in everyday speech simply because they don't know the meaning or because they're trying to use a word that makes them seem more educated or smart.

It's best to stick with words you know. If you find a word that's unfamiliar to you, look it up.

> **Author Note: Kim Stephens**
>
> "My co-anchor and I were ad-libbing about Christmas decorations, and I said I felt like 'such a schmuck' for not having our outside lights up yet. After the newscast, I received a phone call from the local rabbi who told me 'schmuck' means penis in Yiddish, and I may want to choose a different word to describe myself. Another time, while ad-libbing, I called a problematic situation a SNAFU. My general manager called me into his office after the newscast to remind me the military meaning of that acronym is 'Situation Normal All F'd Up.' Oops! I've never said that again, either."

GRAMMAR, SPELLING AND PUNCTUATION

Spelling

Spelling matters. Misspelled words can cause an anchor to stumble when reading a script. Also, many closed-captioning systems use the scripts from the newsroom software system. A misspelled word in a script becomes a misspelled word on the TV screen.

Also, watch for words that are easily confused. These are words that look or sound alike but are spelled differently or have different meanings. These words can create a problem for several reasons. First, when we're writing in auto-pilot, we use words without thinking. For example, *hear* and *here*. Even your professors, teachers and news directors catch themselves writing the incorrect word.

Second, most journalists are under the pressure of a deadline. Rushing to submit your story increases the odds of making mistakes. That's when we see mistakes using words such as *their*, *there* and *they're*. Remember, *there* is a place; *their* belongs to someone; and *they're* is a contraction for they are.

Third, spellcheck doesn't work for confused or misused words. The words are spelled correctly. They are just used incorrectly. Spellcheck will not catch a misused *their* or an incorrect *your* or *you're*.

Finally, always double and triple-check the spelling of people's names in both digital and broadcast copy. In broadcast, viewers will see names in the **lower-thirds** on the screen and in closed-captioning. A misspelled name is an easy way to lose credibility with your audience.

That's why you'll keep hearing us say, "Read your story out loud." If we don't read our email, story or social post out loud before we send, submit or post it, we may not catch the mistake. Our brains tend to adjust for errors when we review our copy silently. The best way to catch mistakes and typos is by reading the script out loud.

Another issue is misused words. These are phrases that are confused more over meaning than sound. Until you are certain that you're using the correct word, look it up.

Affect is usually a verb meaning to impact, influence or change something.
Effect is usually a noun meaning the result of something.

Capital is wealth and is also a state's governmental center.
Capitol is the building where the state or nation's government leaders meet.

Further is a metaphorical way to describe time moving on.
Farther describes physical distance.

Imply means to say something in an indirect way; to insinuate or hint at.
Infer means to come to understand something by hearing or reading it.

Its is a possessive pronoun meaning belonging to something or someone.
It's is a contraction for "it is" or "it has."

Less is used for a singular noun for a mass of something, like salt or money.
Fewer is used when talking about things that are countable, like cookies.

Robbery is when someone takes something from someone by force.
Burglary is when someone takes something from an unoccupied place.

Take implies moving away from something.
Bring implies moving toward something.

That is used to describe or define something.
Which is like saying "by the way" when describing something.

Who refers to the subject of the sentence (replaces he or she).
Whom refers to the person something is happening to (replaces him or her).

Your is a possessive pronoun meaning ownership.
You're is a contraction for "you are."

Proper Verb Tense

We need to talk about verbs. They are one of the most important parts of speech to master in both speaking and writing. A verb expresses action or state of being and tells what a noun or its substitute is doing. A verb can sometimes stand alone as a complete sentence. Verbs also have a tense, voice, mood, person and number. Use of verbs helps you write in the active voice.

Al Tompkins of the Poynter Institute says verbs matter. "The verbs you choose will tell me what you believe occurred. When you choose an action to describe what you believe occurred, that gives us a window into what you believe." Did America invade Iraq or did America rescue Iraq? Both verbs frame the story differently. The first one paints the U.S. as an aggressor; the second one as a rescuer, Tompkins says.

It's also important to pay attention to the placement of verbs. If you write a sentence using passive voice, "Iraq was invaded by America," that doesn't carry as much weight as when it's written in active voice,

"America invaded Iraq." When you write in the active voice, it's immediately clear who the actor is. If you use passive voice, we don't know who's doing what until later. Passive voice is perfect if you want to absolve someone of blame: "No assignment was submitted," is a much nicer way of saying, "You didn't submit your assignment."

Verbs are formed through conjugations in different tenses. A tense refers mainly to time—when the action takes place. In the English language, there are at least six ways to express time frames. Most verbs form their conjugations simply. Others are more complicated—the irregular verbs. These are the ones most frequently missed by writers.

Again, reading your copy out loud is going to help you catch errors when it comes to writing conjugations for irregular verbs. However, there are some that many of us have been using the wrong way since we were children because our parents or even our teachers used them incorrectly.

For example, you and your friend, Amelia, have lunch together once a week. If you tell your professor that you and Amelia have *ate* together many times, that would be wrong. You should say that you and Amelia have *eaten* together many times.

With irregular verbs such as *to eat* you will need to change the beginning of the verb when you go from present to past (eat/ate). Sometimes the perfect tense of the verb will change (have eaten/has eaten). And sometimes nothing will change.

Let's look at a few irregular verbs that are often conjugated incorrectly (see Table 4.1). We'll use three different tenses: present, past and present perfect (something that happened in the past but the time is vague).

The best strategy for knowing which conjugation to use is to browse the list, say the word in each tense out loud, and memorize. For example, say out loud, "Eat, ate, have eaten." Now use these three tenses in a sentence. I eat in the dining hall; I ate in the dining hall; I have eaten in the dining hall. I go to the store; I went to the store; I have gone to the store.

Mentor Moment: Nancy Bauer Gonzales, News Director, KTNV, Las Vegas

"To learn the craft is the most important thing. To learn how to write. If you can write and spell and string four sentences together, you can go anywhere."

Table 4.1 Irregular Verbs

Present	Past	Present Perfect
drink	drank	(have) drunk
drive	drove	(have) driven
eat	ate	(have) eaten
fly	flew	(have) flown
go	went	(have) gone
sing	sang	(have) sung
cling	clung	(have) clung
pay	paid	(have) paid
swim	swam	(have) swum
swing	swung	(have) swung

Punctuation

Punctuation is important because a misplaced or missing comma or apostrophe can change the meaning of a sentence or word. As with misspelled words, punctuation in the wrong place can also cause the news anchor or reporter who is reading the copy to stumble. Fortunately, broadcast writers don't use a lot of punctuation because we write in short, conversational sentences. But when writing for the web, punctuation rules apply.

There are too many rules to discuss all of them here. We're going to limit it to a few rules about commas and semicolons, and we'll also look at possessives to determine when and where to add an apostrophe. But remember, when writing for TV, for the ear, you want to avoid writing in complex sentences offset by commas. Leave that for the web story where more complex sentences are welcome. If you find yourself writing with a lot of commas and semicolons in your broadcast script, your sentences are probably too long and complex.

And always keep your AP Stylebook or dictionary by your side, or bookmarked on your computer, for quick reference.

Commas

You may remember your elementary school teacher telling you to insert a comma whenever you hear a pause in a sentence. In broadcast news writing, some reporters and anchors may use ellipses instead of commas, to emphasize pauses in the copy. That's fine as long as you remember to convert those ellipses to commas in your web stories and social media. In digital copy, ellipses (…) denote omitted information, something you want to avoid.

Here are a few rules to remember about comma placement for your web story:

1. Place a comma after an introductory phrase or word.
   Once the semester starts, Joe is going to move all of his books into his car.
2. Place commas around explanatory material (clauses that are not essential to create a complete sentence).
   Riley, a golden retriever, loves to go to the beach.
3. Interruptions in thought must be offset by commas.
   Joe Rodriguez, who is the university president, will not be able to attend.
4. Place a comma between sentences of equal weight joined by a conjunction (and, but) to form a single sentence. Use a semicolon when using words such as "however" or "therefore."
   He is known for his fancy desserts, and his son makes an awesome quiche.
   He is known for his fancy desserts; however, his son makes an awesome quiche.
5. Never use a comma between two closely related sentences causing a comma splice. You may use a semicolon in your web writing (not broadcast) or you can add a coordinating conjunction such as "and" after the comma. But do not add the "and" without first adding the pronoun (in the following example, "he").

   NO: Fernando has a 4.0 GPA, he hopes to get a scholarship. **(comma splice)**
   YES: Fernando has a 4.0 GPA; he hopes to get a scholarship.
   NO: Fernando has a 4.0 GPA, and hopes to get a scholarship.
   YES: Fernando has a 4.0 GPA, **and he** hopes to get a scholarship.

6. Use a comma after "said" or "says" when introducing a direct quote, but you may use a colon (for web writing) if it is a quotation that requires a formal introduction.
   Jordan Singh said, "The polling place is in the middle of a gated community making it difficult for voters to gain access."

My father always used his favorite quote from Albert Einstein: "If you can't explain it to a six-year-old, you don't understand it yourself."

7. Use a comma (in web writing) before and after the year following a month in a date.

    The Notre Dame fire started on April 15, 2019, causing the building's famous spire to collapse.

8. Use a comma to separate two adjectives of equal weight.

    White, puffy clouds filled the blue sky after the thunderstorm.

9. Use commas to denote direct address.

    Harry, the deadline is Tuesday at 6 p.m.

10. Never, ever use a comma (or a period) after a quotation mark. The comma or period *always* goes in front of the quotation mark.

> **NO:** "The fire was small enough that it didn't impact us", said June Preciado, the homeowner.
> **YES:** "The fire was small enough that it didn't impact us," said June Preciado, the homeowner.

Apostrophes

Some other common punctuation mistakes involve apostrophes. Use an apostrophe for contractions, possessives and to set off a single letter. Be careful to distinguish between contractions and possessives because some possessives, such as *its*, *theirs*, *ours*, do not get an apostrophe.

1. Use an apostrophe to shorten and combine two words.

> **NO:** Each house of Congress can write it's own rules.
> **YES:** Each house of Congress can write its own rules.
> **YES:** If someone speaks up, it's usually because they want media attention.

2. Use an apostrophe to denote possession.

> **YES:** Parents are organizing a rally outside the *governor's* mansion.
> **YES:** The *Giants'* playoff dreams ended when Washington beat the Eagles.

3. Use an apostrophe for clarity when a single letter or number is made plural.

> **YES:** My favorite team is the Oakland A's.
> **YES:** Learn the ABCs of growing herbs in a window garden.

4. Do not use an apostrophe when making a year plural.

> **NO:** Ed Burns set his series in the 1980's.
> **YES:** Ed Burns set his series in the 1980s.
> **YES:** Ed Burns set his series in the '80s.

"NO, NO, NO" WORDS

One of the most important tips for good writing is knowing which words to not use. The following sub-sections contain words we do not use in news writing because there are more conversational choices and better legal options. We are including a short list here, but in the appendix of the book, we include a more extensive list. Seriously, get these words out of your news vocabulary.

Allegedly

This word does not protect you legally and is not conversational. It's much better to attribute to a reliable or official source instead.

> **NO:** THE MAYOR ALLEGEDLY STOLE FROM THE CITY BUDGET
> **YES:** THE CITY MANAGER IS ACCUSING THE MAYOR OF STEALING MONEY FROM THE CITY BUDGET.

Attributing sources is crucial in the news. If you were to take out the word "allegedly" in the previous example, you would be saying that the mayor is a thief. You have no right to say that yet. You *can* say it if the mayor is convicted of the crime in a court of law.

Suspect

This is also a common word used in crime stories, but it's often used incorrectly. A suspect is a *named* person who is *known* to be connected to a crime. Many times, a reporter will simply call the unknown hooded guy who stole a woman's purse a suspect. That cannot be true because the police do not know who the purse thief is. It's much better to describe the situation and the people.

> **NO:** POLICE ARE SEARCHING FOR THE SUSPECT WHO STOLE A WOMAN'S PURSE AS SHE SHOPPED ON FIFTH AVENUE.
> **YES:** A PURSE SNATCHER RUINED A WOMAN'S DAY, STEALING HER PURSE AS SHE SHOPPED ON FIFTH AVENUE.

Even if you know who the person is, it's still better to not use the word "suspect" so your script can be more conversational.

> **YES:** A MAN WHO GOT OUT OF JAIL LAST NIGHT IS BACK IN CUSTODY FACING CHARGES IN ANOTHER PURSE THEFT. POLICE ARRESTED JIM BROWN TWO BLOCKS FROM WHERE A WOMAN SAYS HER PURSE WAS STOLEN.

You could use the word "suspect" in this story because the police know who the accused robber is—Jim Brown. However, we were able to tell the story clearly and conversationally without using the word.

Victim

This word in and of itself is a disenfranchising word. It takes away a person's empowerment. If a crime happens to someone, that person's control and sense of safety are taken away. Giving them a negative, stripping label on top of that is unkind, especially when this crime happened to them without their authority, willingness or say so. There are other ways to describe the person and what happened.

> **NO:** THE ROBBERY VICTIM SAYS SHE WAS WALKING TO HER CAR WHEN HER GROCERIES WERE TAKEN FROM HER.
> **YES:** THE MOTHER SAYS A ROBBER TOOK HER GROCERIES AS SHE WENT TO UNLOAD THE FOOD AND PUT HER BABY IN THE CAR.

Apparently

This word is more aligned with hearsay, innuendo and supposition than facts. It conjures notions of gossip. If you replace it with a source, the story will have much more credibility.

> **NO:** THE JORGE JEWELER'S MANAGER WAS APPARENTLY MUGGED AND ROBBED AS SHE TOOK THE DAY'S EARNINGS TO THE BANK.

When said this way, it makes it sound like the manager faked the mugging and stole the money herself.

> **YES:** THE MANAGER OF JORGE JEWELERS SAYS SHE WAS MUGGED AND ROBBED AS SHE TOOK THE DAY'S EARNINGS TO THE BANK.

Undetermined

That's what you'll find in a police department news release. "It's not known," is a more conversational way of replacing this word.

> **NO:** THE BANK ROBBER GOT AWAY WITH AN UNDETERMINED AMOUNT OF CASH.
> **YES:** RIGHT NOW, POLICE ARE NOT SAYING HOW MUCH MONEY THE ROBBER GOT AWAY WITH.
> **YES:** BECAUSE THE BIG RIG FIRE MELTED PART OF THE ROADWAY, POLICE ARE NOT SURE WHEN THEY'LL BE ABLE TO RE-OPEN THE HIGHWAY.

Resident

A resident is a person who lives somewhere. This is common law enforcement jargon, which is fine for that job, just not for ours. Instead, we replace it with more conversational phrasing.

> **NO:** THE EARLY MORNING FIRE FORCED ALL OF THE RESIDENTS OUT OF THEIR HOMES.
> **YES:** EVERYONE WHO LIVED HERE RAN OUTSIDE IN THEIR ROBES AND PAJAMAS TO GET AWAY FROM THE FLAMES.

Occur

This is another common jargon word in law enforcement. In news, it's our job to translate and make our stories read more conversationally.

Simply replace this word with another meaning the same thing: "happen" or "happened."

Wounded

Here's another easy replacement word. Just say "hurt."

Female/Male

Woman, lady, man, child are all better choices in making your scripts more conversational.

Collision/Accident

These words are OK, although "crash" would be better in terms of making the story more conversational and accurate. This brings us to a teaching moment. When a car crashes, it's important to ask other questions about speed and impairment. If it is determined that the driver was impaired (high on drugs or drunk) it's not an *accident*. Driving while high or intoxicated is a choice. This is a mindset that many in law enforcement hold in partnership with Mothers Against Drunk Driving (MADD).

In an open letter to The American Bar Association and American Judges Association, MADD CEO Adam Vanek wrote,

> MADD believes that drunk and drugged driving incidents are crashes not accidents because they are the result of choice, not chance. This seemingly insignificant change in lexicon reinforces that drunk and drugged driving are 100 percent preventable crimes 100 percent of the time. In 1997, the Department of Transportation also stopped referring to drunk driving crashes as 'accidents' and encouraged publications to do so as well.[1]

Handicapped

Unless you are talking about a parking spot that is labeled "handicapped" (most states now label these spots "disabled parking"). Associated Press prefers the term, "handicapped-accessible parking." The term "handicapped" may have been a common and acceptable word in the 1950s, but today's society is more welcoming and accepting of people's abilities and capabilities. You need to question whether an individual having a disability is relevant to the story. Does the fact that the person uses a wheelchair have any bearing on the story of her graduation? Does the fact that the person is autistic have any bearing on the story of a child getting help after falling off the park slide?

A person's challenges may play a part in the story, but we'd still never call those challenges a handicap. Maybe he is a college graduate who was told he'd never move again, but he defied the odds and finished his studies to graduate. Maybe the girl knows what it's like to be bullied so she went to help the child who was being teased. You'll never know these fantastic human stories if you don't ask.

By the way, if a person without a "disabled" parking placard gets a ticket for parking in a "handicapped-accessible" parking spot, it's OK to use that phrasing.

Due to

"Because" is a simple replacement to write more conversationally.

Murderer

This is another word that is often used incorrectly. Homicide is the legal term for slaying or killing, according to the AP Stylebook. It is a legal charge. A homicide should not be described as murder until a person is convicted of that charge. Instead say the person was killed. Once a homicide moves to the courts, then the term murder may be used to describe the charge, such as, "He pleaded not guilty to one count of first-degree murder."

Incident

Replacing this word allows you to write more specifically. A fight that led to a shooting isn't an incident. It's a fight that ended with two people getting shot. When a gunman shoots an FBI agent who is serving a warrant, that's not an incident, that's an ambush.

Soap poured into the university fountain isn't an incident. It's a sight to see that has students frantically taking selfies surrounded by bubbles before the grounds crew turns off the power and drains the fountain.

Evading

Who evades? Someone with something to hide. Instead of doing a story on a white Bronco evading police, why not say, "driving slowly along the 405 Freeway trying to get away from police." Evading is another word that may be used frequently in common language, and certainly on TV dramas, but in news, with the goal of being more conversational, it's best to replace it with "running away," "speeding away" or "hiding."

REMINDERS FOR GOOD WRITING
- Use conversational words.
- Know the difference between words that are often confused such as further/farther and fewer/less.
- Read your scripts, emails and social posts out loud, checking for grammatical and punctuation errors. Rewrite any phrases that cause you to stumble.
- Double-check the spelling of all names used in your story.
- Write in short sentences, and vary the length of your sentences.
- Try to keep only one thought in each sentence.
- Make sure irregular verbs are conjugated properly.
- Use correct punctuation for web stories.

QUESTIONS
1. Why should we avoid using the words "alleged" or "allegedly" in news stories?
2. What is required to call someone a suspect? Why is it recommended to use a word other than "suspect"?
3. What's the difference between a burglary and a robbery?
4. When is it appropriate to use the word "murder"?
5. Why is it important to read your scripts out loud?

TRY THIS
Rewrite these sentences into proper broadcast style:
1. Jayden Smith allegedly murdered Kayla Pappas.
2. The female suspect fled from the scene. She apparently was wounded in an altercation with another resident at the apartment complex.

NOTE
1 www.madd.org/get-involved/no-accident/

Real World Lessons

Five

In This Chapter	
Know Your Community	63
Beat Check	64
The Law	65
The Military	67
Law Enforcement	68
Emergency Responders	69
Legislative Officials	70
Politics	71
Brands	72
Reminders on Real World Lessons	73
Questions	73
Try This	73

KNOW YOUR COMMUNITY

To report, produce, write and anchor the news, we must understand the world around us. We in the news business know a little bit about a lot of things. Most of those lessons are learned on the job. But that means there is likely to be a mistake or five that end up on the air in that learning process. These are humiliating lessons that can get you fired. So, let's brush up on a few critical aspects of community reporting so you can save yourself from some of those mistakes.

Mentor Moment: Kevin Olivas, Recruiter, Sinclair Broadcast Group

"The job of a journalist is in the United States Constitution. The First Amendment. The founders of our nation put it in for a reason. To have a fully and accurately informed citizenry so they

DOI: 10.4324/9781003137016-5

> can make the best decisions to keep freedom alive. Not one word in the entire Constitution is about CEOs. The job of a journalist is a duty. It can be humbling, gratifying and fulfilling. Without journalism, without a truly Free Press, there is no United States. It's that simple."

BEAT CHECK

One of the first things you may be asked to do as an intern or as a new newsroom employee is to make the **beat check**. Every newsroom has its list of phone numbers or emails to the public information officer (**PIO**) of each law enforcement agency and hospital to check what happened in the last few hours since the last beat check. Each newsroom shift takes care of this at the start of each shift. If someone was taken to the hospital, then the beat check would include a call to the nursing administrator at that hospital.

As you make those calls you will likely hear the police **scanner** nearby. There are certain calls and codes to listen for. Keep in mind, we don't ever report a story simply based on scanner traffic. Anything you hear on the scanner must be verified before you write a digital or broadcast story.

Each station has its own protocol on scanner information, but here's a brief description of what those codes mean. The full list can be found, possibly, at the station's assignment desk. You may be familiar with at least one of the codes from watching TV shows: 10-4. That means "message received."

Be aware that 10-code lists can vary depending on department protocol or the county or state where you are working. It's best to request a list from local law enforcement.

In addition to the 10-code, you may hear a few others that help you understand the nature of an emergency call. Here are a couple: Code 3 means lights and sirens are being used by the police. Code 4 means no additional units needed, or everything is OK.

Here are some others that denote the penal code, and these are consistent across the U.S. For example, 211 is a robbery; 415 is a disturbance; 417 is a person with a gun; a 51-50 is a welfare and institutions code for a mental health case.

THE LAW

Timeline in a Criminal Case

Remember in this country we are innocent until proven guilty. Let's briefly and simply go through the timeline of a suspected crime:[1]

1. Someone commits a crime, and police investigate.
2. Police arrest someone. During that procedure, the person is processed and booked into jail and may immediately get out depending on the bail amount and the city, county or state laws to combat jail overcrowding.
3. The district attorney files a criminal complaint and the person is arraigned. (The time limit varies from state to state.) Arraignment is a process when the person who was arrested is now considered a defendant and goes before a judge to hear the official charges against him/her and is asked to enter a plea to that crime. Usually the plea is "not guilty." Or, the defendant may plead "nolo contendere" or "no contest," which is basically a guilty plea without directly admitting guilt.[2]
4. If the charges are not dropped, the defendant (person who faces charges in a crime) has a preliminary hearing in which the judge decides if there's enough evidence to proceed to trial. If there's enough evidence, the case goes to trial or may be resolved with a plea bargain.

A criminal trial is one in which a person is charged with a crime that is considered harmful to the community at large. In these types of cases, the county district attorney's office is the one filing the charges and acting as the prosecutor.

It's important to note that each county has one district attorney (DA). In most counties that is an elected position. That person leads the entire office of deputy district attorneys. Remember, there is only one DA and many deputy DAs.

Here is a brief timetable once a criminal trial begins:

1. Jury selection (also known as voir dire, to speak the truth)
2. Opening statements
3. Direct examination (witness testimony)
4. Cross-examination

5. Closing arguments
6. Jury instruction
7. Jury deliberation
8. Verdict
9. Judgment
10. Sentencing

It's critical that anyone working in news knows this flow of the law to correctly and accurately tell the story.

Throughout the case, you must remember that the person accused of the crime did not do it. Not in the eye of the law, anyway. That person "is accused of," "on trial for," "taking the stand in the case of." Remember, innocent before proven guilty.

If the jury comes back with a guilty verdict and the judge enters the judgment, then you may say the person committed the crime. After that, the judge will decide the sentencing, which usually happens at a later date.

Here is an example of how simple word placement is key. First, in this example, the newscaster wrongly convicts the man of committing a crime. The lead sentence says he did it—he killed his wife:

> **NO:** A MAN IS IN JAIL TONIGHT FOR KILLING HIS WIFE. POLICE SHOWED UP TO SEAN MENGAL'S HOUSE IN SOUTHWEST LARKSPUR AND FOUND HIM SCREAMING AT NEIGHBORS. HIS WIFE'S BODY WAS FOUND IN THE POOL.

Remember, we do not have the power to convict a person. Only a judge and jury can do that.

The story should be written this way instead:

> **YES:** A LARKSPUR WOMAN IS DEAD TONIGHT. POLICE SAY HER HUSBAND IS IN JAIL FACING CHARGES OF KILLING HER. POLICE SHOWED UP AT SEAN MENGAL'S HOUSE IN SOUTHWEST LARKSPUR AND FOUND HIM SCREAMING AT NEIGHBORS. THEY FOUND HIS WIFE'S BODY IN THE POOL.

Note the difference. It says he's *facing* charges and attributes the statement to police.

Officers on the scene may have told the reporter, "We arrested Sean Mengal for killing his wife," but we journalists cannot say that. We must rephrase.

One more thing. There is a difference between jail and prison. Jail is where people are detained while awaiting trial or are serving sentences for minor crimes. Prison is where convicted criminals serve sentences for felonies and serious crimes, usually for sentences longer than one year.[3]

Civil Law

You may find yourself covering more than criminal cases. Depending on the legal dispute, you may cover civil trials or trials in juvenile court or even traffic court. A civil trial is traditionally a private dispute in which a person or business, the plaintiff, files a complaint against another person or business, the defendant, accusing them of a wrong.

In civil cases, the pretrial procedure is different from a criminal case although the basic courtroom procedure is similar.

THE MILITARY

There are seven branches of the U.S. military. While their collective mission is to protect the safety and preserve the peace of America and its assets and positions around the world, each has a specific role. Each has a specific name. The names are NOT interchangeable.

The Air Force, Air Force Reserve

- Members are known as airmen or airwomen.
- Primary mission is air and space power flying planes, helicopters and satellites.

The Army

- Members are known as soldiers.
- Primary mission is to secure or guard an area or U.S. installation by land.

The Coast Guard

- Members are known as a Coast Guardsmen (irrespective of gender).
- Primary mission is to secure and guard domestic waterways through rescues, law enforcement and drug prevention.

The Marine Corps and Marine Corps Reserve

- Members are known as Marines.
- Primary mission is to be the first to arrive fighting by land or sea.
- Pronunciation is "core." The "ps" is silent.

The Navy and Navy Reserve

- Members are known as sailors or seamen.
- Primary mission is to protect and secure oceans around the world.

The National Guard

- Members are known as National Guard troops.
- Primary mission is to support combat missions, help with humanitarian and domestic emergencies and homeland security.
- Comprised of the Air National Guard and Army National Guard.
- Each state has its own Guard.

The Space Force

This is the newest branch of the military, signed into law in December 2019.

To be clear, you don't ever call a marine a soldier or vice versa. It's common to hear a person refer to any member of the military as a soldier. That is incorrect. Each has its own name depending on branch of service. Collectively, they are servicemen or servicewomen. They are members of the U.S. military.

LAW ENFORCEMENT

Most communities have police officers, sheriff's deputies and highway patrol officers who are charged with keeping the community safe. Each wears a different uniform, drives a different vehicle and answers to a different boss. It's essential you know the difference.

Police Department, Sheriff's Department, State Police

Police officers work for the city police chief. There is only one police chief and that person is usually appointed to that position through the department and possibly the city council. Police officers patrol the city limits.

Sheriff's deputies work for the county sheriff. There is only one sheriff and that person is usually elected to that position during a county primary election. Sheriff's deputies patrol the county limits. There are sheriffs and sheriff's deputies in almost all 50 states. You should know whether your region has a sheriff's department.

Highway patrol officers and troopers work for the state. They are also known as the state police. There is one commissioner or chief of the highway patrol who is usually appointed to that position by the state's governor. These officers patrol the highways as well as city roadways and, in some states, patrol terrorist targets.

We tell you this so you never write a story incorrectly like this:

> **NO:** Sheriffs are investigating the dead body in an almond orchard.
> **YES:** Sheriff's deputies are investigating a body found in an almond orchard.

Because the body in this example is being investigated, it can be inferred that it is dead. That's why there is no reason to precede "body" with "dead."

EMERGENCY RESPONDERS

In an emergency, the local fire department is often the first to arrive. When you cover an emergency, it's important to know which agency helped the person.

Emergency Response Agencies

In some communities, it's easy to distinguish the three fire agencies. Usually, they have different colored fire engines and different bosses. Each has its own chief and funding source: city council for the city fire department, county board of supervisors for the county fire department, and state government for the state fire department. In many communities, there are city ambulance companies and private ambulance companies. Their rigs also look different, and it's important to know the difference.

When reporting a story, you need to be correct in saying whether it was city fire, county fire or state fire involved in the work. If you get facts like that wrong, it can be difficult to earn respect and receive dependable information down the road.

LEGISLATIVE OFFICIALS

You learned this in high school civics class, but it never hurts to have a refresher. This is a simplistic look at our nation's legislative branch so you know who to contact for a story and who's in charge of what in your state and community.

- City Council
- County Board of Supervisors
- State House of Representatives (the Assembly in some states)
- State Senate
- The U.S. House of Representatives
- The U.S. Senate

City Government

The city council is the heart of the local government. The council is made up of elected councilmembers who represent a specific part of the city. The head of the council is usually the mayor. In some strong-mayor cities, there is a council president and a mayor. A mayor can be either elected or appointed by the council. In some communities, these city leaders are called commissioners or aldermen/alderwomen.

County Government

The county board of supervisors oversees the county government and is made up of elected supervisors who represent a specific part of the county. The head of the board is the board chair and is usually appointed by the board.

Some communities have combined city and county government, such as San Francisco and Nashville, Tennessee. In those cases, the mayor runs the consolidated city-county government.

State Government

Each state is run by an elected governor. In that state's capital city, the governor oversees both the state house of representatives (some states call it the assembly) and the state senate. These legislative houses are home to elected members who represent specific areas of the state. The bulk of their work is done in the state capital, but their home is always the area of the state they represent.

Four states, Kentucky, Massachusetts, Pennsylvania and Virginia, use the term "Commonwealth" for their official name, as in the commonwealth of Massachusetts.

Each state also elects representatives to the U.S. Congress. Congress is made up of two entities, the U.S. House of Representatives and the U.S. Senate. Again, while these elected officials do the bulk of their work in Washington, D.C., their home is still in the area of the state they represent. A member of the U.S. House of Representatives may be called "representative" or "congressman" or "congresswoman." A senator is always called a senator.

It's critically important that you know the difference between a state legislator and a national legislator. Why? For the obvious factual reasons but also out of respect. Putting in the wrong title for an elected official is a great way to lose credibility with your viewers, community, co-workers and boss. The same goes for knowing the party of that legislator. It's critical you know if the legislator is a Democrat, Independent, Republican or member of another political party.

POLITICS

Now, let's get a quick lesson in party politics.

The Democratic Party is characterized in graphics on election night by the color blue and the donkey. The correct term is "Democratic Party," not "Democrat Party," which is a disparaging term used by opponents of the party.[4] You would, however, call a member of that party a Democrat. If a state is called a blue state, that means that it historically votes for the Democratic Party in national politics.

The Republican Party or GOP (Grand Old Party) is characterized in graphics on election night by the color red and the elephant. A red state is one that historically votes for the GOP in national politics.

You may hear reference to "purple states." These are known as battleground states or swing states. They are states where the two major parties are competing for a majority, but it's not clear which party has the upper hand.

Parties matter. When you put in the **CG** (graphic on the bottom of the screen with the person's name and title) of a legislator, you better spell his or her name correctly as well as that person's title representing the correct state and party. Each newsroom has a different CG style for these interviews but here are a couple based on the AP Stylebook: Sen. Alex Padilla, (D) Calif.; Rep. Ben Cline, (R) Lexington, Va.

Here's why attribution is important:

> **NO:** LAWMAKERS DID IT BECAUSE IT WILL DRIVE DOWN THE PRICE OF FOOD.
> **YES:** LAWMAKERS DID IT BECAUSE THEY SAY IT WILL DRIVE DOWN THE PRICE OF FOOD.

If the anchor reads the script the "NO" way, it sounds like he or she is blaming lawmakers for fiddling with food prices. By attributing the comment to lawmakers, it makes it clear that the anchor is not making a personal statement.

BRANDS

One final writing tip in terms for "NO, NO, NO" words: Don't use brand names. They denote partiality or even profiteering, which we don't ever want to do in journalism. We must stay impartial in our reporting. There are times a brand name is appropriate, though, when it specifically matters in a story.

> **YES:** WITNESSES SAY THE DRIVER OF THE SILVER FORD BLEW THROUGH THE STOPLIGHT AND CRASHED HEAD ON INTO THE RED TOYOTA.
> **YES:** THE UBER DRIVER IS CHARGED WITH STEALING THE WOMAN'S PURSE.

In those stories, the brands Ford, Toyota and Uber mattered, but when the brand has no bearing on the facts in the story, do not use it.

- Q-tip is a brand name. Replace with "cotton swab."
- Jet Ski is a brand name. Use "personal watercraft" instead.
- Bubble Wrap: "packaging material."
- Jacuzzi: "hot tub."
- Crock-Pot: "slow cooker."
- Vaseline: "petroleum jelly."

- Band-Aid: "bandage."
- iPhone: "smartphone."
- Uber and Lyft: "ride-hailing service."

REMINDERS ON REAL WORLD LESSONS

- Be familiar with your local city/county government officials.
- Know who your state and U.S. legislators are.
- Know what your local emergency services look like (uniforms/trucks).
- There's only one sheriff in town, one DA and one police chief.

QUESTIONS

1. Why do we not use brand names in scripts?
2. What's the difference between a state and federal legislator?
3. Name the different military branches.
4. What's the difference between a civil trial and a criminal trial?
5. What's the difference between the police department, sheriff's department and highway patrol?

TRY THIS

1. Pick four officials who represent your area. Include a picture of that person, title and a few things the class newsroom should know about the person.
2. Many local police departments allow civilians to go on ride-alongs with law enforcement. Submit an application to do a ride-along with your local police or sheriff's department. It's a great way to learn about an officer's job and develop contacts.

NOTES

1 American Bar Association, How Courts Work. Retrieved from www.americanbar.org/groups/public_education/resources/law_related_education_network/how_courts_work/casediagram/
2 Ibid.
3 www.apstylebook.com/ap_stylebook/prison-jail
4 Siegal, A. and Connolly, W. (2015). *The New York Times Manual of Style and Usage: The Official Style Guide Used by the Writers and Editors of the World's Most Authoritative News Organization*, 5th Ed. Crown.

Interviewing

Six

In This Chapter

Why We Interview People	76
How to Prepare for an Interview	78
Conduct the Interview	79
Challenging Interviews	84
Video Chat Interviews	85
Reminders for Interviewing	89
Questions	90
Try This	90

Why are you here? You want to be a reporter, MMJ, producer, assignment editor or photojournalist, but are you cut out for it?

Do you wonder whether you could be a good journalist if you identify with any of the following characteristics?

- You're shy and uncomfortable meeting strangers.
- You don't want to ask people difficult questions when they're experiencing a time of pain and crisis.
- You don't know about a lot of things such as politics, business or the stock market.
- The news makes you sad or mad.

The answer is yes, you could be a good journalist and member of a newsroom because you lead with your heart, feel empathy and don't think you are better than others.

DOI: 10.4324/9781003137016-6

> **Mentor Moment: Chad Nelson, Director of Photography, KARE11, Minneapolis**
>
> "Fear is definitely something that you feel in the beginning. One thing that helped me lose that sense of bashfulness or uncomfortability is I just forced myself to do it. The more you do it, it just becomes natural."

We are in the business of telling people's stories. If you are inquisitive, like to learn new things, enjoy challenges and pushing your creativity, this career is for you. A lot of good news people are shy people. They are introverts. But when they put on the journalist hat, they know they have the right, the jurisdiction, the allowance to ask questions and find answers.

> **Mentor Moment: Alex White, News Producer, KFSN, Fresno**
>
> "Accept that things will be hard and scary at first. You'll have a lot of growing pains and that's part of life. Try to learn from every mistake you make."

Strong writing is the top skill news directors look for in broadcast and digital reporters and producers. Some of the other important *hard* skills include shooting and editing, storytelling, web and social media. News directors also look for candidates with strong *soft* skills such as those who can problem-solve and have a curiosity about life and how things work.[1]

In the modern newsroom many different job descriptions include interviewing people. Conducting interviews isn't just for reporters. Photojournalists are often called upon to shoot a story and interview people without a reporter by their side. Both broadcast and digital producers often conduct interviews in person, on the computer and over the phone. Assignment editors do the same thing, as do news anchors. A newscast director may even conduct an interview digitally or over a station news feed in a pinch. The ability to interview people is a universal skill. So, let's get comfortable with it.

> **Mentor Moment: Victor Hernandez, Chief Content Officer, WBUR, Boston**
>
> "If approaching strangers turns your stomach in knots, then you have to be honest with yourself. You either confront these discomforts or you reconsider what truly brings you fulfillment. Journalism is a critical public service. We get to observe and ask questions, probe and analyze. We ask people to reveal the most intimate details of their life and they trust us to carry out our responsibilities with decent ethics and integrity. The job is daunting and not for everyone. But if you can embrace the discomfort and uncertainty, it's unlike any other profession."

WHY WE INTERVIEW PEOPLE

To Learn Something

We interview people to learn the facts about something, to better understand how or why something happened, or to get background information. The only way we can learn about things is to ask questions.

When covering a car crash, we might start by interviewing an officer at the scene to find out what happened. We would also look for a person involved in the crash or who witnessed it to share a more personal aspect to the story.

If a young woman who grew up in your hometown wins the U.S. Open, you could interview her to find out how it feels to achieve something she always dreamed about.

If you're sent to cover an apartment fire, you could interview a neighbor to find out how he saved people in the middle of the night.

Bring Humanity to the Story

> **Mentor Moment: Boyd Huppert, Reporter, KARE11, Minneapolis**
>
> "I think of a good interview as someone who helps me feel their happiness or anger or sadness."

We interview people to get their perspective on something, to bring humanity to a situation. When we interview regular people, not officials, our stories connect to viewers on a more basic, personal level.

This brings the "why care" aspect to a story. While we might interview officials for background information, we might not use the on-camera portion of the interview in our story. It depends on the type of response you get.

Remember in Chapter 3 when the traffic officer explained his personal reaction to a multi-car crash in the fog? The emotion in that official interview brought humanity to the story.

While we ask officials and experts for important facts and figures, we must also interview regular people who represent our viewers and give voice to the community. These people bring emotion and personality to a story. In many ways, they make a story more relatable. Always work to get a diverse perspective so the interviews mirror the diversity of the community.

In his book, "Aim for the Heart," the Poynter Institute's Al Tompkins says you don't want your stories to be wide and thin. You want them to be narrow and deep.[2] We do that by focusing on a main character.

In the example of a Black Lives Matter (BLM) protest in a big northwestern city, reporters interviewed people holding signs, chanting and walking down the middle of the street. These people all had different reasons and perspectives for being there. Those differences made the story relatable not only to the people of that specific city but also to viewers from around the country. Had the reporters only talked with people of one race or the same person night after night, that would have given only one voice and one perspective to the story, which is not enough.

Sometimes people are such good interviews that newsrooms go to that person over and over again. During the BLM protests in 2020, Kianey Carter, producer at ABC15 in Phoenix, remembers asking her boss why her station regularly interviewed one specific person in the community for Black Lives Matter stories. That person was vocal. He was passionate. He was always available.

Carter told her boss: "I don't appreciate that we continuously go to the same person for any kind of comment from the black community in town. There are a million black people. Why is the same one person the mouthpiece?"

Her boss agreed. The newsroom began using a variety of people in the community for those interviews.

HOW TO PREPARE FOR AN INTERVIEW

Research Your Topic

Research shouldn't take days or even hours like it did when you wrote research papers in other classes. In the news, we are on quick deadlines every day. Rarely do we have time to do highly researched long-form stories.

So, in these **day-turn** stories when you need to quickly educate yourself on a topic and turn the story that same day, ask your colleagues for their perspective. Do a quick search online and through your station archives. These steps are important because, yes, there are some dumb questions. It's better to ask these questions in the newsroom than to your interviewee who expects you to know the basics.

People in the community expect people who work at TV stations to be all-knowing about everything that happens in town. That may not be fair or realistic, but do your best to know *something* about the topic before you start your interview.

This is especially important if you are new to a community. For example, a story about a park may appear to be just a park. But after doing research, you might discover the site was the scene of one of the city's most horrific crimes. That information is important to know.

Prepare Questions

Once you've done some research, you'll have obvious questions right off the bat. The who, what, when, where, why questions must all be asked. Then, you need to dig deeper into the "why care" and historical aspect of the story. In the example of the city park, one of the questions must be, "Can a park like this help erase or ease the horror of what happened here?"

> **Mentor Moment: Chad Hypes, News Director, KTVL, Medford**
>
> "You must research and interview to get to the truth. Talk to experts and ask good questions. The more you know about a subject before doing the interview, the better your story will be. We have a few reporters that started right before the pandemic hit. In nine months, they had to become health, school, business, wildfire, homelessness and unemployment experts. It didn't happen overnight, but it happened because they put in the work."

As you prepare your questions, remind yourself that you need to interview a variety of different people—the officials from the parks department, neighbors, family who attended the park dedication and maybe a child going down the slide, as long as the parent approves of that. It's OK to ask the same question of these different people. You will likely get different answers because they have different perspectives.

If you are working with a photojournalist on this story, it's important to talk before you get there so you can plan how and where you envision conducting the interviews. When we say *where*, we mean in what part of the park. On a bench? On a swing? In the far corner with the playground equipment in the distance behind the interviewee? These things should be planned ahead, as much as possible, so you can get the job done efficiently.

CONDUCT THE INTERVIEW

Introduce Yourself

As soon as you walk up to the story location, introduce yourself. Look the person straight in the eye and stretch out your hand for a firm handshake (or wrist bump or open palm wave if there are concerns about germs[3]). Introduce yourself with your name and the station's name. Thank the person for taking the time to meet with you or if you have not had the opportunity to talk ahead of time, explain why you are there and what you plan to do. Be professional. Be caring. Be honest. Ask yourself how you can make this story real for your viewers, how doing this story can make a difference and how you can tell this story in a compelling way.

Ask Permission to Record

If the interview is virtual (conducted over the internet), ask the person if it's OK that you record the interview. This should not be a surprise. In some states, it's a courtesy so the person is well aware of when the recording begins and when it ends. In other states, you are required by law to get consent from all parties before recording an interview.

If you are shooting your interview in person, there are many technical details you need to consider such as audio, video, framing, sequencing, **B-roll**, etc. We cover all of this in Chapter 10.

First Question

Once you have set up your **tripod** and camera, ensured your shot is properly framed and white balanced and you've done an audio check, begin the recorded interview with an easy question. One of the best is, "Please say and spell your first and last name and your title." This helps put interviewees at ease because they're talking about something with which they're quite familiar. It also helps you double-check that you have the correct information including the correct spelling of the person's name.

Why ask this question if you already know the answer? A couple of reasons. First, as we said, to make the person comfortable. Next, as a stop-gap measure to any unforeseen circumstances. Let's say right after this interview you are planning to put the story together, but breaking news happens and you need to give this story to someone else to write and edit. That person will have the correct information on the recording, no problem.

It's also good to get in the habit of asking questions you think you know the answer to. We always want the information to come from our sources to ensure accuracy and their personal perspective. And, you never know. That introduction may work perfectly in the story.

Sometimes the person you're interviewing will ask for the questions ahead of time. We don't do that. The person is asking to better prepare or to control the message. No. We want the interviewee's answers to be spontaneous and true.

It's OK to say the topic you'll be asking about. That is rather obvious, but it's something you could answer with. If the focus of the interview is about a fire that sparked during a windstorm pushing electric lines into dry tree branches, you can tell the person from the electric company that you'll be asking questions about the fire.

> **Mentor Moment: Scott McGrew, Anchor/Reporter, KNTV, San Jose**
>
> "I suspect there are two kinds of questions you're afraid to ask: the one where you will sound stupid and the one where you're challenging authority. You do both all the time in journalism. You can't possibly know everything, so an interview about a power outage, new drug or forest fire may involve terms and ideas you've never run into before. So, you have to ask the "stupid" question. Authority figures will try to lie, dissemble or hide, and you have to be tough on them."

Listen to Each Answer

If you have a hard hitting or controversial question, ask that *after* you've asked a few easy questions. And remember, the key to a good interview is to *listen*. Just because you have a list of questions does not mean you should rattle them off without listening to the answers the person is giving. Avoid thinking about your next question while the interviewee is talking.

> **Mentor Moment: Tracie Potts, Washington Correspondent, NBC News, Washington DC**
>
> "You've probably seen TV shows or movies depicting the 'hard hitting investigative reporter,' asking the tough questions, running after people with a microphone. That certainly does happen. As the 'Fourth Estate'[4] our role is to hold government accountable. But not every interview is like that. The scientist with a fantastic discovery, who has a hard time explaining it in layman's terms, needs a reporter to patiently walk them through the impact of their research. A grieving mother, if she's willing to talk, may just need someone to listen."

In the case of the park, what if you were interviewing a neighbor who said this is a nice place, even though she fought against it being built. Because you weren't listening, you didn't hear her answer and instead of following up and asking why she fought against it, you ask your next question on your list about something else. You just missed a prime opportunity to dig deeper.

Listening could bring about a different line of questioning. It could turn the focus of the story in a different direction. You must always be prepared for that and to possibly throw away your original questions.

You must stay in control of the interview. Don't allow yourself to be used. Remember everyone has an agenda. They're either trying to make themselves, their company or their institution look good. They may use "the party line" or "talking points," which means to stick to the organization's agenda. These responses may not be answers to your questions at all. You must listen and stay focused to ensure you're getting the information you need.

Ask follow-up questions and don't ever be afraid to ask for an explanation if you are not quite understanding something or if you feel like you are getting the runaround.

> **Mentor Moment: Kevin Olivas, News Recruiter, Sinclair Broadcast Group**
>
> "You have to know which voices are legitimate and which are not. You have to play gatekeeper. It's one thing to give someone a voice who needs to be heard. But you have to be savvy enough to call them on it if they are purposefully spewing misinformation or disinformation or decide up front if they really should be in your story. That is more of an issue now than it was in the recent past."

Some topics are challenging to understand. Maybe you're doing a story on a cogeneration plant and you only just found out what that kind of energy creation is when the story was assigned to you. And just because you read a few things online you are still wishing you paid more attention in science class. *Don't ever leave an interview without fully understanding what was said.* You must keep asking questions until you understand.

On topics like this, it's acceptable to ask the person to describe the subject as he or she would explain it to a child. That doesn't mean "dumb it down." It means simplify it.

Be Quiet

It's important that we clearly hear the interviewee during the interview. That means keep your reactions to a minimum, and if you react, try to do so silently. A lot of beginners will interject, "Oh wow," or "Uh huh," throughout an interview as a way to show interest. Please don't do that. Nod your head, use facial expressions, but let the audio be untainted while the other person is speaking.

NBC news correspondent Tracie Potts says, "Don't over talk, and don't cut people off. Remember, they are the highlight of the story, not you." Also, she advises to not be afraid of silence.

"A moment of uncomfortable silence can prompt greater insight. Often, I've found that the best sound happens after a person stops for a beat, thinks, then tells you what they really think," Potts says.

Open-Ended Questions

"Are you having a good day?"

"Yes."

That is what we call a closed question. You got a one-word answer, which doesn't give you any information. Go back and ask again.

"Why is this a good day?"

Now you will get details, humanity and perspective. This takes a little training. The good news is, you can begin practicing this now. When you ask questions in your daily life, try to make them open ended. Then, you'll be in the habit of doing that for work.

Some of the best questions aren't even questions at all. Retired NBC reporter Bob Dotson calls it the Non-question question.[5] It's basically a moment when the interviewer refers to something the interviewee just said—not in the form of a question. Frankly, it's a conversation, like we all have every day with family and friends. It's information give and take.

In an interview with the Poynter Institute, Dotson explained it this way. He was interviewing a man, Taylor, about music. Dotson made a comment instead of asking a question.

"I said something like, 'I used to love to sing myself but I never got around to it,'" to which Taylor said, "I would have started earlier, but I was homeless."

That opened up a whole new subject and background about his interviewee that Dotson wasn't aware of. He said it became a giant surprise in the story. Dotson is always looking for surprises like that.

One Last Thing

Before the interview ends, it's perfectly acceptable to ask if there's anything else the person would like to add. Or, if you are working with a photojournalist, ask your colleague if there's a question he or she would like to ask. It's a kind gesture to the person you are interviewing. It gives that person an opportunity to re-answer a question in a different way or say something you didn't think to ask about. It's also a good way to engage the photographer who is shooting the story. Remember, you're a team and both of you should be collaborating on the story at all times.

This is also a good time for you to repeat a question that didn't get a clear response. Maybe there was a plane flying overhead or a fly was buzzing around. Maybe the person was a little flustered or unclear about an answer.

We never tell our interviewees what to say, but we can ask questions a couple of different ways to possibly get a cleaner, more descriptive or tighter answer the next time around.

Boyd Huppert and Chad Nelson of KARE11 in Minneapolis call their interview technique "the dance." They prefer to conduct active interviews, which are more of a conversation with a person who is doing something at the same time. It takes coordination and communication.

Nelson says Huppert knows when Nelson misses a shot because of where Nelson's camera is pointed. So, Huppert will draw out the question until Nelson is in place, or he might say he didn't hear the answer. Most interviewees will repeat the answer to the question.

"Boyd always jokes that he's the most hard of hearing, and Chad is the dumbest person on earth," Nelson says with a smile. "If I miss a shot, I'll ask a question because I know what will happen if I ask that question. It's like, how does that mouse work? Or, where are you in that photo? And they're going to point at it either with their finger or with a mouse. And now I have those two things to go with the emotional sound that I needed. And the person never felt like I coached them and never felt like I told them what to do."

CHALLENGING INTERVIEWS

Yes, there are days we have to ask hard questions. But it's our job, and this is where that humanity comes in. We do our best, in a kind, empathetic manner. If we think we're about to get the runaround, we listen with discernment.

Grieving Families

Very few journalists feel comfortable covering the story of someone who died and having to talk with the family. It doesn't ever get easier because it's always heartbreaking. It helps to have a plan. First, do not ask someone who is grieving, "How do you feel?"

You could get the obvious answer back. "How the (bleep) do you think I feel? My — just died."

The person gave you an emotional soundbite, but this interaction did not likely leave that interviewee with a positive feeling about you or the station.

A reporter from *The New York Times* received a similar response when she asked a family member how the attack that killed his brother in Iraq made him feel.

"'That is a question I don't want to answer,' he said. 'How many different types of dead are there?'"[6]

There are other, softer ways to go about this. Instead, you could ask, "How would you like (name) to be remembered?" Or, "What would you like the community to know about (name)?"

These questions are much more likely to get an airable response, and the person answering may have a more positive memory of this heartbreaking situation.

Dealing with Deception

What if you feel you are being lied to? If the interviewee intentionally gives you false information, you might give the verified facts and ask for a response. If that person refuses, explain that lack of response or purposeful use of misinformation will likely be reported in your story.

If the person gives you incorrect information because he or she is uninformed, follow up to make sure the interviewee is aware of the correct information. Depending on the nature of the story and the level of expertise of the source, generally don't include this incorrect information in your story.

VIDEO CHAT INTERVIEWS

How do you interview someone if you can't physically go to that person? During the COVID-19 pandemic and quarantine, journalists quickly pivoted from in-person to video chat interviews. No longer were we limited to interviews with people in our local market. We could reach out to sources across the country and the world.

This way of interviewing is here to stay. While the framing, lighting or audio may have been subpar in the early days of the pandemic because it was new to everyone, we now know how to make these interviews look and sound better. It will require you to ask your interviewee to make adjustments to the webcam and lighting before you start recording.

Framing

Here's some advice on how to frame the shot:

- Ask the interviewee to sit in front of a corner of the room where two walls come together in a V giving more depth to the shot.
- Make sure the webcam is not looking up the person's nose. Ask that the computer be put on a stack of books or a box to raise the camera to eye level. Or, if the camera is shooting down on them, ask them to raise their chair. Also keep an eye to the horizontal and vertical lines behind the interviewee. If the walls look slanted, the webcam will need to be raised.
- For variety in the screen shot, ask your interviewee to scoot a little to the left or right to mimic a rule-of-thirds broadcast shot. The video chat gallery box should be moved to the right or left of the screen for a focal point.
- If using a smartphone, your interviewee should place the phone against an object for stability. Holding the phone causes movement.
- These phone shots should always be horizontal and NOT vertical.

Lighting

We want our interviews to look good. Lighting is key. Make sure there is not a window behind the interviewee or cover the window so there is no halo-type glare

If there is a window, and the interviewee is able to move to face it, that can put a flattering light on the person's face.

If you don't have the benefit of a window, an overhead light is likely not the answer. It can cast unflattering shadows or a strange halo on the top of the head. Instead, ask your interviewee to bring over a desk lamp or LED light placed slightly above and to the side of the camera level.

Figure 6.1 Using Natural Light

Zoom Interview with Natural Light

Zoom Interview with LED (Ring) Light

Figure 6.2 Using a Ring Light

Audio

The audio in many video chat interviews can sound hollow if the person is in a room with hard surfaces and is using the built-in computer microphone. To minimize echo, ask the interviewee to move closer to the computer mic or use earbuds with a built-in mic. A carefully placed blanket below the computer screen can help muffle any echo.

It's a good idea to record two separate audio files for you and your interviewee. Check your video chat audio settings.

B-Roll

A variety of shots help add dimension. Even if you are interviewing someone through video chat and recording that interview through your computer, get another angle of the interview. Set up a camera behind you showing the person on your computer screen. If you are working with a photographer, he or she can get a few angles of that computer screen interview to use as **cutaways**.

> **Mentor Moment: Boyd Huppert, Reporter, KARE11, Minneapolis**
>
> "We're doing multiple camera Zoom interviews with three cameras. One is the Zoom camera. That's the primary shot. The second is on me getting my reaction or question. And then the third camera, the photographer is doing tights or wides. Maybe we're doing a Zoom with two people, and he's doing a tight on one or the other, depending on who's talking. Or maybe he's wide looking over my shoulder where you can see me chuckling a little bit, and we can cut to that shot. All of those things help viewers get to know you a little bit more as well as the person I'm interviewing in the Zoom call."

Figure 6.3 Video Chat Cutaways

Huppert gets creative with B-roll, too. He'll ask people to go get things and show them to him on the web cam. Or, he'll ask them to play the role of photographer with their own cell phone. Huppert did a Zoom story about a robot in a nursing home during COVID. Family members could go online, wake up the robot, which would roll into Grandma's room so the family could talk to her over the robot's video screen.

Because of COVID restrictions, Huppert couldn't physically go into the nursing home. But, he needed B-roll of the robot. So, he found a staff member, became Facebook friends with her, and used the video-calling feature in Messenger:

> I told her to hold the phone horizontally, and the photographer shot the video off the screen as I walked her through what we needed. I would say, 'OK, can you go in and get a really nice, tight shot of the bowtie?' Because they put a little bowtie on the robot. 'OK, now go as far back in the room, and lean against the wall, and hold your breath so you can hold the camera really still and get a **wide shot**.'

See the following QR code.

All of these ideas take prep time. Make sure to have a discussion ahead of time with your interviewee to help that person understand and prepare. Remember to ask for permission to record, and always check your recording before you say goodbye to make sure you captured the audio and video.

REMINDERS FOR INTERVIEWING
- Research your topic.
- Ask for permission to record.
- Always get the correct spelling of a person's name and title.
- Listen and build your next question off the interviewee's responses.
- Ask open-ended questions.

- Remember the "non-question question."
- Be assertive but not abrasive.

QUESTIONS

1. What's the difference between interviewing real people versus officials?
2. How do you best prepare for an interview?
3. What are ways to stay in control of an interview?
4. Why are open-ended questions better to ask?
5. What's a non-question question?

TRY THIS

1. Research and set up an interview.
2. Record a three-minute interview with planned intro and close, no edits to show flow, control of questions, and active listening.

NOTES

1 Sidlow, F. and Pierce, T. (2016). *Are broadcast journalism graduates job ready? A survey of skills desired by TV news directors.* Presented at the Broadcast Education Association Super Regional Conference, Columbia, South Carolina, October 13.
2 Tompkins, Al (2018). *Aim for the Heart*, 3rd. Ed. CQ Press.
3 During the COVID-19 pandemic in 2020 and 2021, masks and social distancing of at least six feet were required when outside your home to mitigate the spread of the highly contagious coronavirus.
4 Fourth Estate refers to the news media having a watchdog role—overseeing the first three estates or branches of government—legislative, executive and judicial. The term originated in England, where the three other estates were the king, clergy and commoners (from Gill, Kathy (2020). What is the Fourth Estate? ThoughtCo., January 16, Retrieved from www.thoughtco.com/what-is-the-fourth-estate-3368058).
5 Tompkins, Al (2007). Monday Edition: Bob Dotson's Essential Storytelling Tools, Poynter. Retrieved from www.poynter.org/reporting-editing/2007/monday-edition-bob-dotsons-essential-storytelling-tools/
6 Tavernise, S. and Napolitano, J. (2004). The Struggle for Iraq: Families; Grief, Mostly in Private, for 4 Lives Brutally Ended, *The New York Times*, April 2, Retrieved from www.nytimes.com/2004/04/02/us/struggle-for-iraq-families-grief-mostly-private-for-4-lives-brutally-ended.html

Telling the Story
Part 2

Seven

The VO

In This Chapter	
The Lead	93
Writing to Your Video	95
Reader	99
Graphics	99
Timing Your Video	103
Reminders for Writing the VO	104
Questions	104
Try This	104

Many of the stories you write as a reporter or producer will be read live during the newscast by an anchor. The **VO** or voiceover is a brief news story, typically 20 to 30 seconds, read live by the news anchor, who "voices over" the video. Producers may ask you to write the same story as a VO for one newscast, a **VOSOT** for another newscast and a package (PKG) for a third newscast. Because a VO is short, brevity and clarity are critical.

THE LEAD

A VO script consists of a lead—an introductory sentence or two to grab the viewer's attention—followed by the body of the story in a few short sentences.

The corresponding video consists of pictures and sound that visually complement the words in the script read live by the news anchor while the video is playing.

"Given that the average human attention span is, according to a study by Microsoft, a whopping eight seconds, you don't have a lot of time to capture someone's attention," says San Francisco news anchor Dion Lim. "Once you have that, the challenges don't stop there.

DOI: 10.4324/9781003137016-7

It's about keeping your audience focused on what you're saying so they're not checking their Twitter feed and totally tuning out what you're saying."[1]

Hence, the need to write a brief and clear script.

Do not bog down the lead with a lot of facts. Pick one or two that will be attention grabbing. Use active now writing in the lead but not forced present tense. Fill the rest of the story with the facts.

NO: {ANCHOR ON CAM}

A CAR SLAMS INTO PEEVES BISTRO ON MISSION MALL TONIGHT INJURING FOUR PEOPLE AND DAMAGING THE HISTORIC DOWNTOWN BUILDING THAT HAD JUST REOPENED AFTER A REMODEL.

{TAKE VO}

YES: {ANCHOR ON CAM}

A DOWNTOWN BAR IS A MESS.

A CAR SLAMMED INTO PEEVES BISTRO TONIGHT HURTING FOUR PEOPLE.

{TAKE VO}

YES: {ANCHOR ON CAM}

THE INTERNET IS DOWN IN SOUTHEAST CLOVIS THIS MORNING. THAT MEANS NO ON-LINE SCHOOL AND NO WORKING FROM HOME.

{TAKE VO}

YES: {ANCHOR ON CAM}

YOU COULD BE DEBT FREE BY THE END OF THE MONTH.

THE PRESIDENT IS WORKING TO ERASE YOUR STUDENT LOANS.

{TAKE VO}

What do you notice about these lead examples? The first NO example is a great newspaper lead, but it's too long and has too many facts for a broadcast lead. Also, "a car slams into" is forced present tense—something you want to avoid. The YES rewrite has fewer facts and an attention-grabbing lead: "A downtown bar is a mess." The next sentence is written in active voice: "A car slammed…"

Example number three immediately gets your attention. The rest of the story will fill in the facts and be written to the corresponding video.

The fourth example is a "you" lead. This is a style that isn't typical in newspapers but is common in broadcast news. It is as though the anchor is speaking directly to one viewer. Again, this is an attention-grabbing lead.

WRITING TO YOUR VIDEO

The video that accompanies the story should relate to the words that the anchor is reading live. How the story is written drives the editing of the video.

In the example of a 25-second VO (see Figure 7.1), you'll notice that the story is written in two columns. The right column is the **copy** to be read live by the news anchor. It is the same copy that will appear in the teleprompter.

The left column has instructions for the video editor, graphics operator and the newscast director. Editing instructions are in brackets on the left. These are video clips that correlate with the words. If you use newsroom operating software, your script will automatically be created in two columns.

[1-SHOT ANCHOR]	{1-SHOT ANCHOR}
	A LONG BEACH STATE STUDENT IS AMONG THOSE KILLED IN THIS WEEK'S TERROR ATTACKS IN PARIS.
{VO}	{VO}
[CG: Paris, France]	THE TERROR GROUP ISIS IS CLAIMING
[show three damaged buildings]	RESPONSIBILITY FOR THE ATTACKS AT SIX DIFFERENT LOCATIONS IN PARIS.
[ambulance at burned apartment building]	THE COORDINATED SUICIDE BOMBINGS AND SHOOTINGS KILLED 129 PEOPLE.
[picture of Nohemi at beach]	23-YEAR-OLD LONG BEACH STATE DESIGN STUDENT NOHEMI (no-EMM-ee)
[picture of burned restaurant]	GONZALEZ WAS AT A RESTAURANT WITH A FRIEND WHEN SHE WAS SHOT AND KILLED
[picture of Nohemi at Notre dame]	GONZALEZ WAS IN PARIS STUDYING AT THE STRATE COLLEGE OF DESIGN.
[candles and flower memorial]	A VIGIL WILL BE HELD SUNDAY TO REMEMBER AND HONOR HER LIFE.

Figure 7.1 Writing to Video

When the copy says, "The terror group ISIS is claiming responsibility for the attacks at six different locations in Paris," the editing instructions call for video of three damaged buildings—pictures that relate to the words. Video of tourists enjoying coffee and pastry in a Paris cafe would not be appropriate because that's not what the words are saying.

You may notice the same video repeats on some stories that were updated over the course of a few days or weeks. This is a trap that many newsrooms fall into when they've stopped getting fresh video for a story that demands continuing coverage. Video that's used for the sake of having some video but offers little to no connection to the story copy is known as **wallpaper video**. Some newsroom managers forbid the use of wallpaper video.

Not all video must be fresh. Some stories work just fine with file video as long as it clearly applies to the words of the story. Here are a few examples of file video being used correctly and a few fails:

- You're doing a story about gas prices and want to show people pumping gas. No problem, but what season is it right now? If it's winter and your video shows people wearing shorts and flip flops pumping gas, that's a fail. The people and surroundings of the video must match the season in which the story runs.
- You're doing a story about home sales and you want to show video of homes. No problem *unless* the file video is homes made out of red brick and pillars, a colonial-style home, when you are broadcasting from the desert southwest. If the architecture clearly does not apply to your region, that's a fail.
- Finally, in reference to a story about children and sexually transmitted disease or mental health issues, running any video of children in the classroom will *not* work if we can see their faces. That's an epic fail because it's linking those specific children to that topic. You could use blurred video of children in a classroom but because it's blurred, it is distracting to use longer than a few seconds at a time.

Know Your Shots

The key to writing to video begins with looking at the video before you sit down to write. You can't write a story without knowing what the video is.

Here's an example of a story about a home burglary:

A homeowner drove up to her house during a break-in.

The police department sent the newsroom a press release that included the what, where and when, along with home surveillance video showing the bungling intruders and the homeowner confronting them.

In stories like this, you take the viewer along for the play-by-play, writing to the specific video the audience is watching.

Scan the following QR code to view the raw surveillance video. The VO script follows in Figure 7.2.

Once you have logged the shots you plan to reference, write the script. Then, time the words in the script and edit the pictures to match the time. The best way to do that is to read the script while editing to make sure each shot comes up at the time each phrase is read. If the video comes in later or earlier than the words, either re-edit the video or change the words to match the video. It's distracting to the viewer when the video doesn't correspond with what the anchor is reading live.

Background Sound

You may not notice the background sound when you listen to a VO on TV. That's as it should be. You want natural sound running in the background, but it should not be distracting or overbearing.

In the Paris bombing story, the viewer should hear a low level of traffic, cars and the sound of people cleaning up the streets. Without these sounds, the story loses its impact. The natural sound of the environment connects the viewer to the story.

It's even more important to have background sound in a VO when the absence would confuse the viewer. For example, if you were writing a VO about a music festival with video of a band performing,

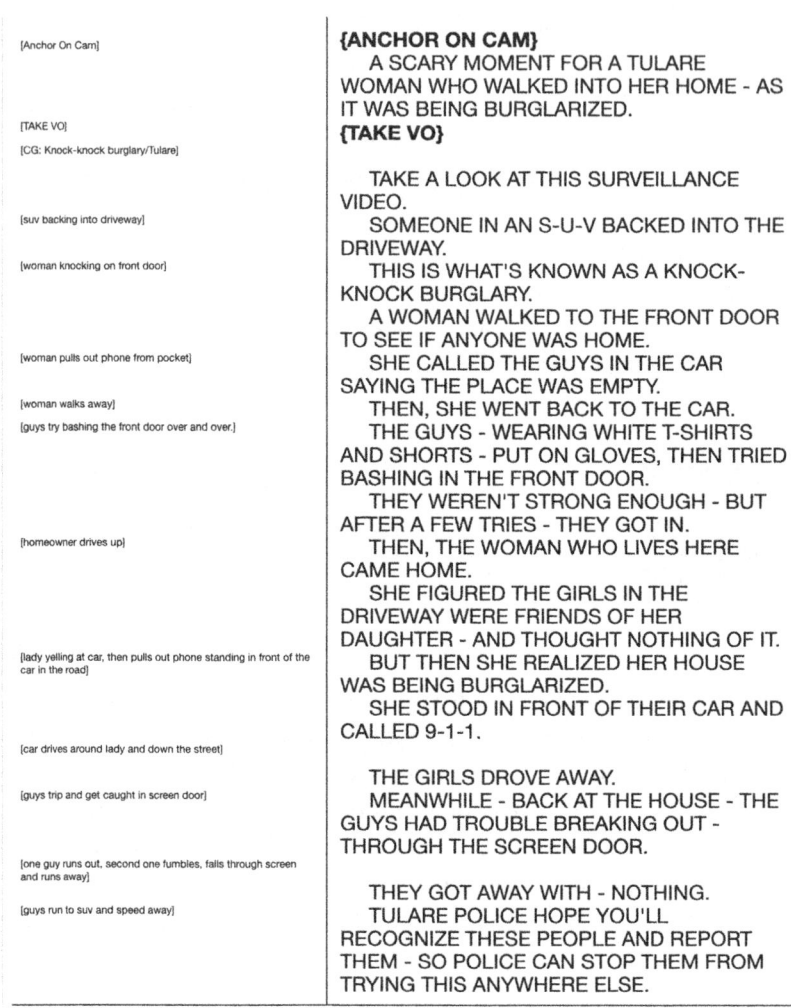

Figure 7.2 Writing to Video

but you did not have the sound of music running in the background, that would be distracting.

The same goes for video of an ambulance speeding down a city street. You can see the lights flashing, but if you don't hear the sound, it's as though a mistake has been made. Because it has. The sound was left off.

If you're doing a story about cat adoption, your video might show a cat eating kibble in its new home. The sound of the crunch pulls in the viewer. It's a sound many pet owners are familiar with. It helps the viewer connect with the story.

The next time you watch a PGA golf tournament, look around for the camera and audio crews. Someone's sole job is to hold the big, fuzzy parabolic microphone on the fairway to get the sound of the golf club hitting the ball.

During The Players Championship at Sawgrass in Florida, for example, microphones are placed at the water hazard on the par-3 17th. That's the diabolical island green where the wind blows and the balls easily roll off the firm green into the water. Hearing the plop of the golf ball is a powerful sound. If the PGA invests money for microphones like this, it's clear that natural sound matters.

READER

A story that runs without video is called a **reader**. That means the anchor reads the story live without any video. It is also called "On Cam" in the newscast rundown.

When there is no video, and the choice is to run a reader, it must be quick. Having a news anchor's face on camera for a long period of time slows down the show because of a lack of visual variety.

Props

If a news anchor can tell the story with props, then by all means bring them out. Of course, the prop must be applicable and legitimate.

For example, when an anchor read a story about an upcoming election, she held up the voter information guide that every registered voter receives in the mail. She showed the front cover so people could connect with the story and realize they had that resource at home in their mail pile.

The anchor then held up the mail-in ballot for people to know what that looked like. As long as props are clear and easy to see, they are good to use. The producer and director must know ahead of time that props will be used, so that the camera operator can be sure to frame it well.

GRAPHICS

There are a lot of different types of graphics that can be used to help tell a story when you do not have video, or have limited video. These add dimension and texture to the story and to the newscast.

Figure 7.3 Over-The-Shoulder Graphic

When clear, they can also add clarity and perspective. Here are a few examples:

OTS

Over-The-Shoulder (**OTS**) is a graphic that is seen over the anchor's shoulder. It is a picture or design with a few words describing the topic of the story. It could be a syringe for a story on the opioid crisis, an image of the coronavirus, a person wearing a face mask, a bus for a back-to-school story, or a gun for a story about gang violence or a gun buy-back program. Whoever is making the gun OTS, *please* make sure the graphic has the barrel of the gun facing *away* from the anchor's head. Yep, that was an uncomfortable, funny, terrible, innocent mistake.

Full Screen

This is a graphic that takes up the full screen of the TV. Every station has a specific graphics package making all of the graphics uniform.

If you watch TV news, and we certainly hope you are, you'll notice all NBC owned and operated stations look similar. All Sinclair owned stations have similar graphics. So do Meredith, Hearst, Univision, Scripps, etc.

A full-screen graphic has a header—that top bar with writing that clearly says the topic of the story. Then, either bullet points or a few words describe that topic in some way.

Figure 7.4 Full Screen Graphic

Anyone in the newsroom who makes a graphic must follow the station's style. The same holds true for using graphics in your digital stories. Just suffice it to say, you may not go rogue designing your own graphics. You must follow your station's look and branding.

A commonly used full-screen graphic is a quote. Many newsrooms have a specific style for quotes. For instance, if you want to run a specific quote from a high-ranking politician's public Twitter account, there is a specific graphic for that, including the blue bird insignia of Twitter and the font and color of the words.

If the quote is from a written work, the graphic may be created in a way to look as if it was ripped from or highlighted in the book, binder or file.

Some full-screen graphics are charts or graphs. Each station has its own style for those, too.

Map

Maps are helpful in telling stories. They can help show where a crash is on the freeway and where traffic is shut down or where detours are. They can show perspective and location for places that are not commonly known. They can be used to show where breaking news is happening.

In Figure 7.5, student anchor Gina Avalos is using a map to show the air quality in different Central California counties.

Figure 7.5 Map Graphic

You can also create maps to illustrate the locations of data. For example, if you were doing a story on earthquakes over the past year, you could enter that data into a Google spreadsheet and export it into a Google map. The map would then show all of the earthquakes in that area over that one-year period.

Google offers a tutorial to show you exactly how to create this type of map. Their maps are free to use for digital or broadcast as long as it's clear that you are using a Google Map. Google helps by including the credit line in the generated map.

Locator or Person's Name

The CG is the most common graphic of all. It's used in every single story. It stands for character generator—a device that produces text over video. A locator CG, as shown in Figure 7.6, is inserted the moment the VO is taken, giving the location of the video or in this case the live shot.

Every station writes CGs a little differently. Some begin with the city on the top line and the specific street on the bottom:

SAN RAFAEL
San Pedro Road

Figure 7.6 Locator Graphic

Some begin with the story title on top and location on the bottom:

WINDSURFING FESTIVAL
   San Pedro Rd., San Rafael

You must know your station's branding and style. All locators should be written in the same style.

TIMING YOUR VIDEO

One final thought about writing and editing a VO. While the script should time out to read about 25 seconds (:25), you should edit 40 seconds (:40) of video. Yes, that means that 25 seconds of video will completely match the copy of the script as read live by the anchor, and the following 15 seconds of video will likely never be seen by the viewer because there is no more script to read.

Why have this extra video? It's backup. Just in case. The technical term is **pad**. We don't ever want the video to end (also known as going to black) before the anchor finishes reading. A litany of things can happen. Maybe the anchor ad-libs or takes longer to read the script than originally planned. The anchor might stumble and has to start over. Or, a button on the switcher could stick causing the technical director to stay on the video too long.

Having pad for these just-in-case situations is helpful to avoid showing mistakes on the air.

Often, beginning journalists do not put enough, or any, pad on their stories. Let that not be you. Going to black on the air is a *huge* mistake that is easily and simply avoided by adding pad to your video.

REMINDERS FOR WRITING THE VO

- The story lead must be compelling, energetic and interesting.
- The VO script must be written to match the video.
- Wallpaper video is not useful if it doesn't match the script.
- Reader stories are good. Keep them brief.
- Props can work as long as they apply to the story and are used efficiently.
- Graphics are useful in telling stories.
- A VO script may run only :25, but add an additional :15 of pad.

QUESTIONS

1. What is a reader?
2. Name three problems that can happen when wallpaper video is used.
3. What is an OTS?
4. Name three different types of graphics and how they are used.
5. How long should your VO video run and why?

TRY THIS

1. Watch a current local newscast (or as many as it takes) to see two VOs. Answer these questions:
   a. What was the topic of each story?
   b. Describe the video.
   c. Did the video match the script?
   d. Was wallpaper video used?
   e. Using your cell phone camera, shoot a news story and write a VO.

NOTE

1 Lim, Dion (2019). *Make Your Moment: The Savvy Woman's Communication Playbook for Getting the Success You Want*, McGraw-Hill, p. 124, print.

The VOSOT

Eight

In This Chapter

Who are the Best Interviews?	106
What is a VOSOT?	106
How to Write a VOSOT	107
The Soundbite	108
Finishing the VOSOT	112
Important VOSOT Scripting	113
Ethical Writing and Editing	114
Reminders for Writing a VOSOT	115
Questions	115
Try This	115

The newsroom scanners blared with the call of an apartment fire. A neighbor saw flames and called 911. Ryan Hudgins, a morning photographer at KMPH-TV in Fresno, rolled up to the breaking news story to shoot something fresh for the morning newscast.

It was a fire. He'd been to his share. This seemed like any other fire. A few fire trucks, water on the ground seeping from the hoses and hydrants, people in their pajamas watching from the sidewalk in disbelief.

As Hudgins looked around, he saw and smelled something strange. He walked up to a neighbor who was standing on his porch watching the crews across the complex parking lot. This neighbor, Robert Wright, was barbecuing.

Yep, it was 3 a.m., and the guy was tending to a rack of ribs on the barbecue. Hudgins giggled, introduced himself and asked Wright to explain what he saw that morning.

Wright shared his story on camera, turning a regular apartment fire story into a character-driven story that is still talked about today.

DOI: 10.4324/9781003137016-8

"I was just barbecuing. I just saw a fire come out of the window. Window busted out," Wright says. "Only thing I think first is, man, make sure them ribs are right. Ran in and got my family. Brought everyone out safely. I carried everyone out myself."

"You got your kids out first? Or older people out?" Hudgins asked.

"Yeah, I got my kids first," Wright said.

> And then I thought about my ribs. I didn't want my ribs to burn because I take pride in what I do. It was like three o'clock in the morning. I was hungry, man. I was like, put them ribs on. Some hot links and stuff. I got it going, but I looked over and the fire was bursting, and I was thinking, this is crazy, man. Real crazy.¹

The only way this story turned into something memorable is because Hudgins looked around at his surroundings. He saw and smelled something different, asked for an interview and out came a character-driven story.

Scan the following code to see Hudgins' interview.

WHO ARE THE BEST INTERVIEWS?

Your goal is to conduct character-driven interviews.

Hudgins also got an interview with a battalion chief who gave the, sorry, but true, boring facts of when the first call came in, how many fire engines were called out, where crews first attacked the fire, how many apartments burned and how long the crews would be cleaning up the mess. This is information that can be paraphrased in a sentence or two in the script. Wright's interview took the story to a whole new level.

WHAT IS A VOSOT?

A VOSOT is a **V**oice **O**ver with **S**ound **O**n **T**ape. Some stations use the term VO/bite because "tape" is no longer used.

The sound brings a person's perspective. It brings emotion and color. That's the goal for SOTs, also called soundbites or bites.

> **Mentor Moment: Tracie Potts, Washington Correspondent, NBC News, Washington DC**
>
> "I never understood people who would write stories then drop in the sound bites. I do exactly the opposite every day. The interviews, plus facts to support, drive how I tell my stories."

HOW TO WRITE A VOSOT

Every VOSOT begins with a lead sentence, just like a VO script. That's the **intro** sentence that pulls in the viewer. As we discussed in the previous chapter, this lead has one or two facts written in an active, conversational style. Remember, we want the lead to be compelling and pull in the viewer.

After the lead comes the VO. That means the anchor keeps reading the script while video rolls. The words that the anchor reads match the video or explain the video the viewer is watching. In the next few sentences come a few more facts matching the pictures.

Then, it's time for the soundbite. In this fire story with Robert "Rib Rob" Wright (yes, that's what he calls himself), we'd say something to introduce him like we were at a party.

"Hi Joe, I want to introduce you to Rib Rob. He just saved his family and neighbors from an apartment fire."

That's how it would sound at a party. In a VOSOT script, it might go something like this: "A neighbor saw the fire and jumped into action." That's the introduction to the soundbite, also known as writing into the soundbite.

The best way to write into a SOT is to give some relevance to what the person is about to say without saying *exactly* what will be said. When the anchor says the same thing as the soundbite, that's called **parroting**. Think of a parrot that repeats back what it just heard. Instead, we want to be creative and add more to the story.

> **NO:** A NEIGHBOR SAW THE FIRE AND RAN AND GOT HIS KIDS FIRST.
> "I got my kids first."
> **YES:** A NEIGHBOR SAW THE FIRE AND JUMPED INTO ACTION.
> "I got my kids first."

Do you see the difference? The anchor VO in the first example parrots the soundbite: GOT HIS KIDS FIRST parrots, "I got my kids first." In the second example, JUMPED INTO ACTION is different than "I got my kids first."

THE SOUNDBITE

> **Mentor Moment: Kevin Olivas, News Recruiter, Sinclair Broadcast Group**
>
> "Human beings are three-dimensional creatures. If I not only see the story but hear it as well, then it feels like you are taking me with you. I am more likely to care about it. Let your sound bites dominate the story. Remember, stories are about giving voice to those who otherwise are not being heard. It cannot be sound just for the sake of sound. They have to be saying things that are compelling that make me care about the story."

Many SOTs run between eight and 15 seconds. In TV scripting, that looks like this: :08–:15. Yes, soundbites can run shorter or longer, but there are a few things you must remember. Many producers will assume that if someone is writing a VOSOT, the story will time out to about 45 seconds. If the soundbite runs long, making the story longer, you must tell your producer.

Also, if the soundbite runs shorter than six seconds, there isn't enough time for the director to pull up the CG of the person's name and title.

Shorter soundbites work fine in longer-form stories, called packages, which we'll get to in Chapter 9. But for a regular VOSOT, the soundbite needs to run longer than six seconds so the CG can come up cleanly and preferably no longer than 15 seconds so the viewer doesn't lose interest.

Again, soundbites should be interesting, colorful or memorable and add perspective, personality, humanity, opinion or emotion to the story. Put the factual information from an interview in the anchor VO, not the soundbite.

> **Mentor Moment: Alicia Acuna, Correspondent, FOX News, Denver**
>
> "This story's not about you. You're telling somebody else's story. Whatever the information, you're not the most important piece here. You are here to tell their story. So, don't be distracting. Pick the best sound, build your story around it."

A lot of newsrooms do not allow officials as SOTs because that factual information can be paraphrased in the script. "Rib Rob" clearly adds interesting personality and even emotion.

> **Mentor Moment: Wayne Freedman, Reporter, KGO, San Francisco**
>
> "I heard one of the best examples of a subjective sound bite from Professor Max Utsler when he taught journalism at the University of Missouri. He told the story of a state trooper who gave interviews at the scene of a fatal hit-and-run accident. To most of the reporters, the officer spoke like a typical cop. But one woman pursued a subjective line of questioning:
>
> 'You look upset. Can you step outside your uniform for a moment and tell us what bothers you most about this accident?' 'In fifteen years on the job, this is the worst I've ever seen.' "Why?' she pushed. 'The little boy's shoe,' said the cop. 'I found it across the highway. That speeding car knocked him right out of his shoe. I'll see it for the rest of my life.'
>
> It was an emotional sound bite, one that amplified the facts. How, you might wonder, did that reporter break through the officer's thick skin and get him to talk from the heart? Simple. Her question addressed his humanity."[2]

> "I was a crew chief on a B29 bomber. The ground crew takes care of the plane. **For a while there was a mission every day over Tokyo. Toward the end, there were as many as they could fly, to burn down Tokyo using fire bombs.**"

[TAKE VO] [CG: WWII Memorial, Washington DC]	{TAKE VO} JAY BUDGE IS HERE WITH HIS DAUGHTER KAREN. THEY DESCRIBE THIS AS 'HIS' MEMORIAL. AS THEY SIT AND STARE AT THE WORDS ETCHED INTO THE GRANITE, DESCRIBING THE BATTLES IN THE PACIFIC, THEY SEE HIS - TINIAN - JULY 1944. THE MEMORIES FLOOD BACK FOR THE B29 BOMBER CREW CHIEF.
[TAKE SOT] [CG: Jay Budge, WWII Veteran] [IN: For a while] [OUT: fire bombs] [TRT: 10]	{TAKE SOT} ("For a while there was a mission every day over Tokyo. Toward the end, there were as many as they could fly, to burn down Tokyo using fire bombs.")

Figure 8.1 Writing into a Soundbite

This kind of soundbite from officials, as Freedman explained, is OK to use because it adds so much emotion and compelling information. It offers humanity.

Writing Into a Soundbite

Remember, the line we use to write into the soundbite should give a clue as to what will be heard next. The following examples on writing into a soundbite come from a few interviews with World War II veterans. First you will see the reporter log of that interview followed by the broadcast script (Figure 8.1).

The bolded part of this log will ultimately be the SOT in the broadcast script. The rest will be paraphrased in the body of the script.

On the Honor Flight to visit the U.S. monuments built in Washington D.C., each veteran is matched with a guardian.

In this next example (Figure 8.2), the reporter interviewed a guardian. Again, the bolded part of the log becomes the SOT in the broadcast script. The rest is paraphrased in the body of the script.

> "Honor Flight to me is about taking care of the people who really took care of us. **We wouldn't be here today if it wasn't for what these guys have done for us here."**

[TAKE VO]
[CG: WWII Memorial, Washington DC]

{TAKE VO}
    EACH GUARDIAN PAYS HIS OR HER WAY FOR THIS TRIP.
    THEY ALL SAY IT'S A PRIVILEGE TO HELP.

[TAKE SOT]
[CG:Al Perry, Honor Flight]
[IN: We wouldn't be]
[OUT: for us here."]
[TRT: 8]

{TAKE SOT}
("We wouldn't be here today if it wasn't for what these guys have done for us here.")

Figure 8.2 Writing into a Soundbite

The next example (Figure 8.3) is a veteran who remembered a traumatic experience during the Korean War. Once again, the bolded part of the log is the SOT. The rest is paraphrased.

> "I'm an Army man. Back then, I was a platoon sergeant. I helped the platoon leader and kept an eye on the men. I was also the lookout on the 38th parallel. I remember… it was **around 11 o'clock. I saw something in front of me. I realized it was a North Korean. He threw a hand grenade. I shot. I was lucky enough the grenade didn't go off.**"

[TAKE VO]
[CG: Korean War Memorial, Washington DC]

{TAKE VO}
    SAM ESRAELIAN SERVED IN THE ARMY AS A PLATOON SERGEANT AND LOOK-OUT ON THE 38TH PARALLEL IN KOREA.

[TAKE SOT]
[CG:Sam Esraelian, Korean War Veteran]
[IN: Around 11]
[OUT: didn't go off."]
[TRT: 12]

{TAKE SOT}
("around 11 o'clock. I saw something infront of me. I realized it was a North Korean. He threw a hand grenade. I shot. I was lucky enough the grenade didn't go off.")

Figure 8.3 Writing into a Soundbite

The same paraphrasing of an interview can be done after a SOT for continued flow in the trailing VO.

FINISHING THE VOSOT

After the soundbite comes a sentence or two that closes up the story—a final few comments to help further explain the facts of the story, the SOT that just aired and the "what's next?" part of the story.

Remember, everything in the script must correspond to the video. In this business, we always write to our video.

Figure 8.4 shows the complete VOSOT script for that earlier apartment fire.

[ANCHOR ON CAM]	{ANCHOR ON CAM} A MOTHER AND HER SIX-YEAR-OLD SON ARE RECOVERING IN THE HOSPITAL AFTER A FIRE RIPPED THROUGH THEIR FRESNO APARTMENT THIS MORNING.
[TAKE VO] [CG: CEDAR & BULLARD/ NE FRESNO]	{TAKE VO} IT HAPPENED JUST BEFORE THREE ON CEDAR SOUTH OF BULLARD AVENUE. FRESNO FIREFIGHTERS SAY THE MOTHER AND SON ESCAPED THROUGH A BACK WINDOW BUT WERE TAKEN TO THE HOSPITAL AFTER BEING OVERCOME BY SMOKE. A NEIGHBOR SAW THE FIRE AND JUMPED INTO ACTION.
[TAKE SOT] [CG: ROBERT WRIGHT, NEIGHBOR] [INCUE: I GOT MY KIDS] [OUTCUE: THIS IS CRAZY] [TRT: 14]	{TAKE SOT} ("I got my kids first and then I thought about my ribs. I didn't want my ribs to burn because I take pride in what I do. It was like three o'clock in the morning. I was hungry, man. I was like, put them ribs on. Some hot links and stuff. I got it going, but I looked over and the fire was bursting and I was thinking, 'This is crazy, man. Real crazy.'")
[MORE VO]	{MORE VO} THE RED CROSS IS HELPING THE WRIGHT FAMILY AND OTHERS WHOSE APARTMENTS WERE DAMAGED. THE MOTHER AND SON ARE EXPECTED TO FULLY RECOVER. THE FIRE DESTROYED SIX APARTMENTS.

Figure 8.4 Complete VOSOT Script

IMPORTANT VOSOT SCRIPTING

One thing you'll notice that differentiates a VO script from a VOSOT is the [TAKE SOT] cue. It lets the director and anchor know when the interview comes up, so the anchor's microphone will be turned off and not heard while the interviewee's voice is heard.

You'll also see that the entire soundbite is written out verbatim. That's important for a few reasons. It helps the newsroom know the flow and focus of the story. It allows the managing editor or executive producer to re-read the entire script to approve it before it's edited. It also lets other producers, reporters and editors know what sound the station has so they can choose to use all or a piece of that SOT later in other newscasts. Finally, many stations' closed captioning is generated from the scripts. If the verbatim is left off, the hearing-impaired will not experience the soundbite.

In writing the verbatim of each SOT you must include the **incue**, which is the first few words of the SOT. The **outcue** must also be included so the director can cue the anchor's microphone to read the trailing VO of the script after the SOT is finished.

There is also a **TRT** or duration on the left side of the script. TRT stands for **T**otal **R**unning **T**ime, signifying how long the SOT runs. In this case, it's 14 seconds.

Fourteen seconds isn't very long. The man said a lot more than that. The reporter chose a clean, character-driven 14 seconds. But we love what Rib Rob said and don't want to miss any of it. So, instead, we could pick a different soundbite and write another version.

We cut out the "kids" part of his soundbite to help with the flow. We had the anchor say it instead, but we didn't change the interviewee's intent or character. This is one of the best and easiest ways to choose a soundbite and write into or out of it, by taking part of what someone said in the interview and adding that to the script leading into or out of the soundbite.

This is a perfect opportunity for the digital side of this story, too. Use part of a soundbite from Wright, include some info in a tweet and say more will come in the newscast.

A similar post could be done on Facebook or in a Facebook live. If you have a few hours before the newscast, you could pick another SOT and tweet something about the story, teasing to the newscast.

[TAKE VO]
[CG: Cedar & Bullard/NE Fresno]
 	
[Take SOT]
[CG: Robert Wright, Neighbor]
[IN: I thought about my ribs]
[OUT: what I do.]
[TRT: 08]
	(TAKE VO)
	    A NEIGHBOR SAW THE FIRE AND JUMPED INTO ACTION.
	    HE GOT HIS CHILDREN OUT OF THE SMOKY APARTMENT AND THEN WHEN EVERYONE WAS SAFE, HE WENT BACK FOR ONE MORE THING.
	{TAKE SOT}
	(I thought about my ribs. I didn't want my ribs to burn because I take pride in what I do)

Figure 8.5 Paraphrasing into an SOT

Then, at news time, post the link to the whole web story. In that web story all of the social posts should be **embedded**. And, the entire unedited interview with Wright could be included because only parts were used on-air.

You may have noticed the CG on the left side of the script (in Figure 8.5). In the VO, the CG gave the location of the story. The CG for the SOT gives the person's name and title: Rob Wright, neighbor. You could instead write a descriptive title such as Rob Wright, Saved Neighbors or Rob Wright, Cooking Ribs. It all depends on your station's style.

ETHICAL WRITING AND EDITING

If your interviewee says "um" a lot, you cannot edit the "ums" out. If your interviewee says something interesting for two seconds and then later, something else for 12 seconds, you cannot butt together the two clips as one soundbite. Why? First, our job is to seek the truth and report it. Changing words around so they sound better is not truthful. Second, it would create a **jump cut**. That jump cut gives the viewer the impression that you just changed the intent and meaning of the soundbite through editing.

The RTDNA Code of Ethics says, "Professional electronic journalists should not manipulate images or sounds in any way that is misleading."[3]

You must not editorialize or change the meaning of what someone says. You must use the true, unedited portion of the interview. That is why you must listen carefully during an interview. If you hear a lot of "ums," ask the question again to get a clearer response.

If you still get a lot of "ums," there are a couple of things you can do:

- Use B-roll to cover the edit so you don't see the jump cut, as long as you are not changing the intent and meaning of the soundbite.
- Paraphrase into the soundbite, using a shorter, cleaner version.

You must be clear, honest and transparent and not change what the interviewee is saying.

REMINDERS FOR WRITING A VOSOT
- Look for interesting characters for your interviews.
- Use official information in the body of the story, not as an SOT.
- Remember to write the entire SOT verbatim and include INCUE, OUTCUE and TRT.
- Always include an appropriate title for the person who is your SOT.
- Paraphrase part of a SOT as a way to write into or out of it.
- Always write to the video. The pictures drive the writing and the writing drives the editing.

QUESTIONS
1. What does SOT stand for and why is it used?
2. What is an OUTCUE and why is it important?
3. What's the best way to write into a SOT?
4. How long should SOTs run?

TRY THIS
1. Watch a newscast (or as many as it takes) to see two VOSOTs. Answer these questions:
    a. What was the topic of each story?
    b. Did the video match the script?
    c. Did the script write into the SOT?
    d. How was the SOT compelling, emotional or interesting?
    e. Did the trailing video after the SOT make sense, match the script and forward the story?
2. Shoot a story and interview and write your own VOSOT.

NOTES

1 Hudgins, Ryan. "Man Saves Family from Fire." KMPH FOX26. September 2015.
2 Freedman, W. (2011). It Takes More Than Good Looks to Succeed at Television News Reporting, A Wealth of Wisdom, LLC, p. 55, ebook.
3 www.rtdna.org/content/guidelines_for_ethical_video_and_audio_editing

The Package (PKG)

Nine

In This Chapter	
Journalist's Toolbox and "Go" Bag	118
Equipment	120
Time Management	121
Package Basics	125
Package Workflow	127
Shoot	128
Log	135
Write	140
Voice Track	148
Edit	150
Writing the Web Story	150
Reminders for Writing a PKG	152
Questions	153
Try This	153

This is the chapter where you learn how to make a name for yourself as a storyteller. A package (PKG) is one where you, the reporter, will be seen and heard. For many beginning reporters, it's also the story format you truly control as you shoot and edit it as well. We call that kind of reporter a multimedia journalist (**MMJ**). MMJs are the jacks-of-all-trade in the newsroom. To keep it simple, we will refer to them as MMJs, but know that many stations use a variety of titles and acronyms for this job description including multiskilled journalist (MSJ), one-man band (OMB), video journalist (VJ) and solo video journalist.

MMJs enterprise stories, shoot, write, report and edit their video, do live shots, write web and digital stories, and post on social media. They are the ultimate multitaskers. Many MMJs say they would rather shoot and edit their own stories. They like the creative control, and

DOI: 10.4324/9781003137016-9

they know where to find everything because they shot it. Preparation and planning are key skills for this job.

"Simply managing your time is the first step," says San Diego MMJ Joe Little. "You can meet these deadlines very easily if you're disciplined, focused, and you don't waste a lot of time."

Little has made a name for himself as one of the most versatile, intrepid and prolific MMJs in the nation. He relishes working alone and is prepared for just about anything the job throws at him.

JOURNALIST'S TOOLBOX AND "GO" BAG

> **Mentor Moment: Joe Little, MMJ/Director of Storytelling, KNSD, San Diego**
>
> "My entire vehicle is my office. I know some younger reporters probably have to share vehicles. If that's the case, keep things in a box so you can quickly move the box in and out of the vehicle when your shift begins and ends."

In addition to his station supplied camera, tripod and wireless lavalier mic, Little carries a plethora of items that have saved him from disaster time after time.

Most MMJs and reporters carry a "go" bag at all times. The go-bag, also known as a kitbag or crash bag, is kept in the trunk of the car or under the desk in that box that Little mentioned.

He may carry more than most "one-man bands." Little carries three go-bags. One has fire gear and a change of clothes. A smaller bag holds his GoPros, extra batteries, headphones and three additional lavalier microphones. A third bag has his laptop with editing software.

Little also carries a light kit and stands, which he uses for lighting but also to frame and focus his stand-ups, which he shoots himself.

He has multiple backup batteries for his camera and wireless lavs, and he keeps a battery and extra SD cards in a bag attached to his tripod. He is always prepared.

He has a supply of duct tape, gaffers' tape, extra **XLR** cables and magnetic lights. His two GoPros with all of the attachments allow him to shoot from outside a moving car, under water or from inside a fuel line. That's how he shoots those creative solo stand-ups that he's famous for.

> **Mentor Moment: Joe Little, MMJ/Director of Storytelling**
>
> "One of my favorite tools is a device called a steady bag. It is a black bean bag with a shoulder strap that I can throw on any uneven surface and then slot my camera into it and just eyeball it as a tripod. It is the most glorious tool, especially for those low angle shots. I can throw it on my shoulder, throw it on the ground and put my camera on it and instantly have a steady shot."

Other MMJs and reporters carry extra notepads and pens, a selfie-stick, a mini tripod, external hard drives, portable battery packs, extension cords and surge protectors. And don't forget makeup, hairbrush, toiletries, mirror, extra socks, snacks and water.

More recently, because of the COVID-19 pandemic and the Black Lives Matter protests, reporters have added face masks, rubber gloves, hand sanitizer and even gas masks and body armor.

> **Mentor Moment: Chad Hypes, News Director, KTVL, Medford**
>
> "We will see a lot of changes in the coming years because of COVID-19. The traditional newsroom will never be the same. We have reporters, producers and the digital team working from home full-time. Reporters may keep their gear with them and be more mobile in the coming years now that everyone has **LiveU** or TVU technology to go live within minutes. Many in-person meetings are happening virtually now because of COVID. This saves time—the most valuable resource in a small newsroom. Being able to react quickly and send video, pictures and info back in real-time has always been important, but we have all gotten better at this over the past nine months."

There's another part to this toolbox that is equally, if not more, important. It's your list of sources and resources. The Society of Professional Journalists (SPJ) hosts a website called The Journalist's Toolbox, edited by University of Illinois professor Mike Reilly. It has

20,000 resources for journalists. It is updated twice a week, and it's free. It is a valuable asset for all journalists but especially for those just starting out. The Journalist's Toolbox contains tips for covering everything from fires and protests to getting a drone certified or learning to code. And it has a section specifically for students.[1]

EQUIPMENT

Until recently, most TV news photographers and MMJs used large, professional video cameras to shoot news stories. MOJO, mobile journalism, was practiced by only a few MMJs.

The COVID-19 pandemic changed that. Physical distancing practices allowed reporters and MMJs to experiment with mobile technology, and news stations discovered it was difficult to distinguish video shot on smartphones from video shot on professional cameras. Limiting the use of big cameras with station logos at protests and other potentially dangerous situations also allows MMJs to blend in with the crowd and makes them less of a target.

That's not to say professional video cameras are going the way of the dinosaur. If you are planning a career as a photojournalist or MMJ, you'd better learn how to use one. But there are many other options out there, from smartphone cameras and DSLRs to small point-and-shoots, and even virtual reality cameras and drones.

> **Mentor Moment: Carmaine Means, Photographer and Drone Pilot, CNN, Chicago**
>
> "You have to know why you're working with what you're working with and why it's needed. You have to know your tools. The number one thing about lighting and using the camera is why are you doing what you're doing? The photography is intentional."

Whichever camera you use, you will need important accessories to ensure you get quality video. At the minimum, you will need a good microphone (preferably a wireless lavalier), a tripod and a light kit.

Not all stations provide all of those accessories. Resourceful photographers and MMJs purchase their own wireless lavaliers and light kits, which can mean the difference between a good story and a great story. Years ago, the cost of such items was prohibitive, but nowadays a decent light kit can run $100 and you can get a respectable wireless lav for about the same price.

Many photographers use a checklist to make sure they have everything they need including their camera.

> **Author Note—Faith Sidlow**
>
> "This is no joke. One of the photographers at our station drove more than two hours to an assignment. When he got to the scene of the news story, he realized he forgot his camera. This was before cellphones. Now, you can pull out your phone and save the story. That wasn't the case then. I still need to consult a list to make sure I have everything. Not long ago, I went to a shoot without an SD card. Fortunately, I was able to borrow one."

TIME MANAGEMENT

Time management can make or break an MMJ's day. In order to be successful and make deadlines, you need to know how long it will take you to perform each task. This is about focus. Focus will help you plan your interviews and get the best characters to make your story relevant to viewers. Focus will help you get the shots and sound you need without wasting time. It will help you edit your story quickly and efficiently.

Your professors may have taught you about the inverted pyramid. It requires you to tell the whole story in the beginning, with the who, what, when, where and why.

In video storytelling, we want you to think about a diamond shape when planning, shooting and editing your stories.

The top of the diamond (as shown in Figure 9.1) is that personal or central character we talked about in Chapter 2, when you pitched your story.

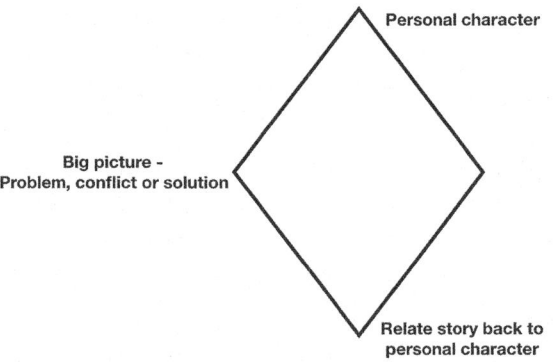

Figure 9.1 Storytelling Diamond

The wide part of the diamond is the big picture—how your character's experience relates to the real world, a problem, conflict or solution. The bottom of the diamond returns the story to that main character.

By using visuals like a diamond, you can visualize the focus of your story, which helps you avoid wasting time on elements that aren't relevant.

Little uses a similar model. He calls it the Pregnant I (see Figure 9.2).

Many experienced MMJs, reporters and photojournalists **backtime** their day. Producers and anchors do, too. In fact, this is a great habit to develop for any job.

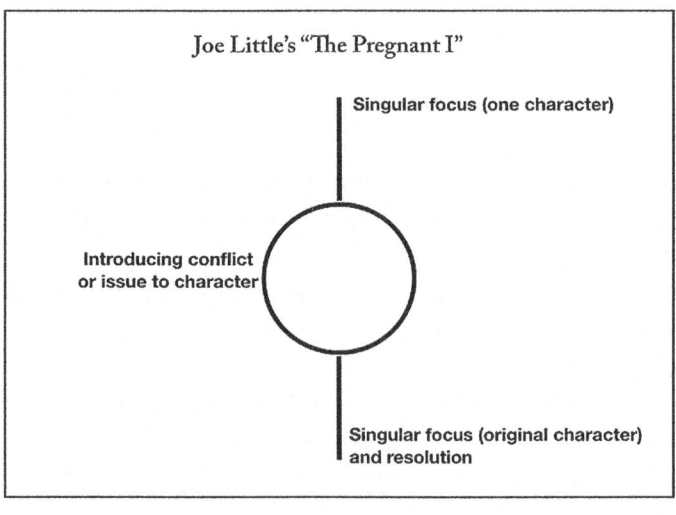

Figure 9.2 Storytelling Pregnant I

> **Mentor Moment: Joe Little, MMJ/Director of Storytelling**
>
> "The 'pregnant I' is the solution to everything in my life that is difficult. It is how I shoot every story. It's how I write every story. It's how I edit every single story. It's how I know you can give me any subject right now, and I can tell you how it's going to look in eight hours based on the pregnant I. I know what my goals are. I don't even know what my story assignment is for tomorrow. But whatever it is, I know what it's going to look like. Most of the time. Of course, there's always variables and things change and rules are meant to be broken. You can't break the rule unless you understand the rule. And the rule for shooting quickly as an MMJ, as a traditional crew, as a Dateline 15-person crew—a better story is the pregnant I."

Little says it starts by compiling a list of all of the tasks you must complete during your workday. How long does it take you to shoot a story? Log a story? Write a story? And edit a story?

If you're reading this chapter for a journalism or multimedia class, your day is most likely different from the hectic day of a professional MMJ. You may get assigned a package one or two weeks before the deadline. An MMJ may get an assignment four hours or less before a deadline. In either situation, backtiming is important.

"You cannot go into a day with your head on fire," Little says. "You can't just roll with the punches."

When Little backtimes his day, he starts by creating a table and listing all of the tasks he must complete that day. Little's table is direct and to the point:

Backtiming Your Day	
4 p.m.	Deadline
3 p.m.	Start editing
2 p.m.	Start writing
1:30 p.m.	Finish shooting story
9:30 a.m.	Start on story
9 a.m.	Production meeting starts

"By giving myself these little mini deadlines to keep hold of, I know I'm always going to be fine. There's no panic. Because when panic sets in, you start making bad decisions," he says.

Little has been at this so long, he knows exactly what he has to do between 9:30 a.m. and 3 p.m., how long it will take him for each element, and he has a backup plan for when Murphy's Law kicks in.

> Murphy's Law is an old adage that says, "Anything that can go wrong, will go wrong." It has been attributed to a number of sources including 1950s newspaper cartoons and a bungling mechanic named Murphy.

Many of us have been burned because we underestimated the amount of time we needed to do a story. There's nothing producers dislike more than a reporter who misses slot, otherwise known by directors, producers and news directors as, "You screwed up my newscast."

Journalism professor Greg Vandegrift keeps a pair of heavy, one-inch bolts on his desk at the University of St. Thomas in St. Paul, Minnesota.

"I pass them around in my reporting classes because they're a symbol of a deadline I missed early in my career," says Vandegrift, who worked as a reporter for KARE11 in Minneapolis before becoming a professor. He still freelances for the station.

Vandegrift recounts the story from his second TV job in a medium market in Illinois in 1986. A semi-truck carrying a "gigantic electrical transformer" hit a dip in the road, and when it came up, the transformer slammed into the bottom of an overpass. The force of the impact bent the bridge's I-beam.

"You can imagine the sound. Bam!" Vandegrift shouts.

Vandegrift says he picked up three of the bolts that had been sheared off by the force of the impact thinking he had the greatest story. But he said he was so young that he let his enthusiasm take over.

"I didn't adjust for the deadline, and I missed it by about 15 minutes. It was catastrophic. I felt horrible. It was all my fault. I tried to do too much with what I had at the time," he says.

Now, Vandegrift's motto is "deadlines matter."

Staying committed to deadlines is important in this career. The fun is to work with them and not let them overwhelm you. It's critical when it comes to writing a package. That's where most inexperienced reporters run into trouble.

PACKAGE BASICS

The news anchor reads the VOs and VOSOTs live on the air. The PKG is a pre-produced, self-contained story composed of several elements including video (B-roll), the reporter's voice track, natural sound (**NATS**), interview soundbites, a stand-up and, sometimes, graphics. The anchor introduces the reporter package, but the rest of the story is voiced by the reporter. The anchor may also say something after the package airs, which is known as an anchor tag.

> **Mentor Moment: Tracie Potts, Washington Correspondent, NBC News, Washington DC**
>
> "My stories average 1:15. That's 75 seconds to give someone a good overview of what can sometimes be a complex story. Mastering how to write for broadcast takes years of practice. With limited time, deciding what to leave out—without impacting the context of the story—can be as important as deciding what to say."

While it may take you only a few minutes to write a reader or VO, a PKG could take an experienced reporter one to two hours to log and write depending on the complexity of the content and the number of elements. Having a strong story focus helps with that timing and efficiency because it keeps you focused on the main topic of the story.

Most PKGs should have interviews from at least two subjects, preferably three, and include diverse voices and viewpoints.

That can be achieved a number of ways depending on the focus of your story. Interview people from diverse socio-economic backgrounds, but take care that you are not just checking off boxes or stereotyping. Look for people who can add to the story and offer a different voice or perspective.

> **Mentor Moment: Luis Felipe Godinez, News Director, Univision, Sacramento**
>
> "There's a lot of racism within the Latino community. So, I try to portray that. You probably wouldn't see that at an English station. Here, the Latino also goes through racism and we explain that and portray those stories."

WFAA's Jobin Panicker cautions reporters to resist the temptation to cover all stories with the same formula. He says it's good to have a focus, but don't let that focus determine your story *before* you go cover it.

He points to a story he did about a bunch of birds that invaded a neighborhood. Panicker's plan was to show how horrible it was to live in that neighborhood. But when he got there, he found out that wasn't the story. He had to change his focus.

"There were balloons everywhere," Panicker says. "And we were like, man, it looks like a party. And then we hear a soundbite where a woman says, 'Yeah, it's like a party out here. Except, it's for the birds.' And so, our focus shifted immediately."

Scan the following code to see how Panicker covered the story.

Using Natural Sound (NATS)

You will notice Panicker used a lot of natural sound. Every few words were punctuated by NATS. Packages are perfect pieces to use natural sound "pops." These nat breaks are quick, running a second or two, but they bring the viewer into the emotion or sense of the story.

> **Mentor Moment: Cyndee Hebert, Managing Editor of News Content, WTHR13, Indianapolis**
>
> "A laugh, a pause, a sigh. It doesn't have to be a word. To me some of the things that really catch your breath is when the reporter, photographer or editor will leave a second of quiet or the trailing sound of a laugh. That's what makes the piece. What people will remember."

Natural sound moments help transition between interviews, locations or time.

> **Mentor Moment: Greg Vandegrift, University of St. Thomas Professor and Freelance Reporter, KARE 11, Minneapolis**
>
> "Video stories are like a tapestry. You are moving from one piece of sound to a sound bite to another nat and maybe to another soundbite. I'm looking for continuity. And I'm looking at what moves from that to there thinking about the video that's going to cover that section. And, and if you don't know those things, how can you write to any of it?"

PACKAGE WORKFLOW

While no story is written the same way, the workflow is the same because it helps you stay focused, write to your video and be time efficient.

SLWVE: Shoot, Log, Write, Voice Track, Edit

SLWVE is an acronym we borrowed from Vandegrift. He calls it SLWE (SLOO-ee)–shoot, log, write, edit. We tweaked it a little and added "voice track" to make it SLOO-vee. SLWVE helps you remember the order of the steps to write a quality TV news package on a deadline.

Shoot, log, write, voice track, edit.

This is your mantra. It helps you maintain your story focus. It helps you work efficiently and meet your deadline. It keeps you keep on track. It only works if you do it in this order: Shoot, log, write, voice track, edit.

We will talk about the technical side, shooting and editing, in the next chapter. Right now, we want to concentrate on the editorial side of putting a package together. You need to be of the mindset of creating a package with words, pictures and sound, whether you shot them or a videographer did.

Vandegrift works with a photographer, who shoots and also edits his packages. They work together as a team. MMJs do everything themselves. Either way, the workflow is the same.

SHOOT

Your video and audio are two of the most important elements of your package. Reporters should communicate with the photographer throughout your shoot—after getting the story assignment, on the way to the shoot, during the shoot, driving from one location to the next, and on the way back to the station. MMJs should have this conversation with themselves, planning and visualizing instead of listening to a podcast or talking on the phone on the drive to the assignment.

Think about the sound you want to get, your interview locations, and the stand-up. When you get back to the station, the coffee shop or the location where you will log and write your story, you need to talk about the shots and sound you did get and how they will play out in your story. What video and sound will you use to start your story and how will you end it? If you are working with a photographer, being able to bounce ideas off of each other is a bonus.

> **Mentor Moment: Da Lin, MMJ, KPIX, San Francisco**
>
> "I'm a one-man band reporter. I shoot about 95% of my stories and I edit 100% of my stories. A live truck operator typically meets me an hour before the show to shoot my live reports. It takes time to be a good photographer and a lot of practice. So, I'll keep it simple. Remember to always get close, medium, and wide shots. And try to always use a tripod. These are simple things that people often neglect to do. Start from there and everything will come later."

We can't emphasize enough the importance of a tripod and the importance of steady video. Even if you think you are steady, you must use a tripod. There's nothing more distracting than shaky video in a story. Also important to consider, MMJ candidates have missed out on job opportunities because it was clear they didn't use a tripod in the stories on their demo reel.

The Stand-Up

We do stand-ups in packages to further the story, demonstrate something, transition to a different location or time, give perspective, fill in missing video and show reporter engagement.

You should be thinking about this element from the moment you come up with your story idea. When you pitch your story, you should be thinking about your stand-up.

> **Mentor Moment: Joe Little, MMJ/Director of Storytelling**
>
> "When you get your assignment, start planning your stand-up. Start thinking about those on-air opportunities. Plan ahead. Put away your notes and your cell phone. You're having a conversation with one person at home. You're talking to one person through the lens. We're communicators. We're storytellers. There's nothing more robotic than a reporter standing there doing nothing guarding the front door of a building or guarding the lawn after something happened."

As with all shooting locations, when you're deciding where to shoot a stand-up, look behind you. Make sure there aren't any distracting features, but also notice what you have available to talk about. If you talk about what is going on behind you, a script isn't necessary. You'll be doing a play-by-play of what is happening during your stand-up.

"Live in the moment. If something is happening that would make a good stand-up, grab the opportunity and do a stand-up," Little says.

You may want to illustrate the size of a big pipe being used for irrigation in a road project or show how expansive a room is. It's hard to show that big, wide expanse with video until you get in the shot to show the size difference.

Figure 9.3 Stand-Up with Graphics

A stand-up is also an opportunity to explain something that has no corresponding video. You can use graphics to show that information, as the student reporter did in Figure 9.3 in a stand-up about apartment hunting for a new job. When she shot this part of her stand-up sequence, she intentionally left room on the left side of the screen to add pop-on graphics in post-production.

> **Mentor Moment: Joe Little, MMJ/Director of Storytelling**
>
> "It is as simple as pointing out where you are all the way to actually demonstrating something: This is how you use Zoom; this is how you use a vacuum cleaner; this is how you tie your shoes. I've pre-programmed pictures into the gallery on an iPad and have used it as a handheld over the shoulder graphic. I'll hold it up and say, 'Here's the bad guy.' Then I'll swipe left. 'Here's the prosecutor.' Swipe left. 'Now, here's the defense attorney who says the bad guy didn't do it.' I was demonstrative. I was pointing things out. I was showing the viewer something. I was giving them something to focus on other than me. If you find yourself standing there staring at the camera and doing nothing else but talking to the camera, you are failing as a reporter. Whether you're live or recorded, that's wasted television time."

Figure 9.4 Demonstration Stand-Up

If you are explaining an amount, use a visual. For example, in Figure 9.4 the student reporter used a pie to illustrate the number of available parking spaces on campus versus the number of students who needed them.

There are three main types of stand-ups: a **bridge**, a close, and a **look-live** or **as-live**.

Stand-Up Bridges

The stand-up bridge is the most common. Generally, it runs between eight and 15 seconds (similar to an SOT) and usually appears in the middle of the story, transitioning from one idea, place or time to another. This is an opportunity to demonstrate or point out something. It can help you tie together two different soundbites or two different thoughts or sides of a story. It's a good way to explain something that has no corresponding video.

> **Mentor Moment: Wayne Freedman, KGO, San Francisco**
>
> "It's good practice to do a stand-up bridge in the first half of a story. Why? The later you appear in a piece, the greater your risk of intruding, although this isn't a hard and fast rule. When I put a bridge in the second half of a story, it often reveals a twist."[2]

Don't do a random stand-up as an afterthought. You might shoot a few versions of your stand-up, and choose the one that works best for your story. Be intentional. Think about how that stand-up bridge will fit in your story. Picture the sentence or soundbite that will lead into or out of the stand-up and make sure it will flow smoothly between the two.

> **Mentor Moment: Boyd Huppert, Reporter, KARE11, Minneapolis**
>
> "The best tip that I ever got for stand ups came from photographer Jonathan Malat when he asked me, 'What are you going to say in the line before your stand-up?' And I said, 'I don't know.' And he said, 'Well, shouldn't you?' And I said, 'Yeah, I suppose.' And it changed the way I do stand-ups. So now I write a line in my notebook. And then I write the stand up. And then I write the line after the stand-up. Because sometimes you go out and do a stand-up, and then you come back and it doesn't fit. And then you have to try and make it fit, but it's awkward. Or, you leave it out because it didn't work. But if you write in your notebook the line before your stand up and the line after your stand up, you'll write your stand up differently."

Here's an example of how Huppert wrote into and out of his stand-up for one story about a gifted five-year-old girl:

> *VO before the stand-up:*
>   LEXI DIETZ HAS MET MORE CHALLENGES IN HER FIRST FIVE YEARS THAN A SIXTH YEAR HARVARD Ph.D.
> *Huppert Stand-up (Transition from house to the classroom):*
>   **But the thing about challenges is they just keep coming.**
> *Teacher SOT after stand-up:*
>   "You need to come over here and start it."

Scan the following QR code to watch the Lexi Dietz story and Huppert's stand-up.

Stand-Up Close

In a stand-up close, the reporter ends the story with a concluding sentence—a final piece of perspective or information in the stand-up and then says, "At this location, Bob Wilson, name of news station."

As-Live or Look-Live Open and Close

In the as-live, the reporter does a stand-up open and stand-up close, similar to what might be said in a live shot. It's like a bookend for the PKG beginning and ending it. You must be transparent, though, when doing an as-live, and don't attempt to come off as though you actually are live. That's deceptive.

It's called as-live because it's done as if it's live with no edits. The reporter talks directly to the audience showing something to help the audience feel as if they are there.

Solo Stand-Ups

How do you shoot a stand-up if you're the person shooting and doing the stand-up at the same time?

Joe Little has a trick for that as shown in Figure 9.5, moving clockwise from the top left.

Little uses a light stand to gauge how to frame his shot. He places it in the spot where he plans to do the stand-up and extends it to 6'4" (his height). Then he zooms in to get the focus and, using

Figure 9.5 Stand-Up Framing Trick

the rule of thirds, frames the light stand to give himself the appropriate **headroom**, making sure his feet aren't cut off. He marks a line where he will need to stand to do the stand-up and removes the light stand.

Little is known for his energetic and interactive solo stand-ups. Each year, he posts a reel of his stand-ups on YouTube so others can learn some of his tricks. Scan the following QR code to see some examples.

> **Mentor Moment: Da Lin, MMJ**
>
> "As a one-man band reporter, it's hard to create movement in my stand-ups. So, I use a lot of sequences to convey movement and pace my stories."

By **sequences,** Lin means taking a series of shots of the same object or topic from varying angles and focal lengths.

KNDU news producer Brittney Steele used this technique when she was a student journalist. In her stand-up about a new drinking water system, Steele started on a wide shot talking about waste created when people throw out plastic bottles. She cut to a **closeup** of a plastic bottle going into the trash followed by a **medium shot** of her using the new water fountain to fill up a reusable bottle. She ended the sequence with a super tight shot of the reusable bottle and the water fountain. Even though she shot the entire stand-up herself, she was able to make it interactive because of the sequences.

The key to remember is this: Stand-ups can get you that job in the real world. If you have a variety of stand-ups in different locations showing different things and offering an interactive perspective, you can add those to your reporting reel. It could help entice a news director to want to watch more of your work. So, do stand-ups.

Figure 9.6 Stand-Up Sequence

LOG

> **Mentor Moment: Greg Vandegrift, Freelance Reporter**
>
> "I believe religiously in logging. You can have a great shoot and miss the story without logging. You can have a so-so shoot and save it with good logging."

Before you start **logging**, you need to get organized. At many news stations, photographers or MMJs will immediately ingest the video in the system and access it from a computer at a newsroom desk. But, as a student, you will more likely be ingesting or uploading your own files, either on your computer or on an external hard drive.

It is best to use an external hard drive to keep all of your files together. This is how you should organize it. Make a new project folder, and give it the same name as your story slug. For example, if you're doing a feature story on woodturning, you might name the project "Woodturning."

Now create additional folders inside your "Woodturning" project folder. A good workflow includes the following folders: Audio. Video. Still images. Documents (see Figure 9.7).

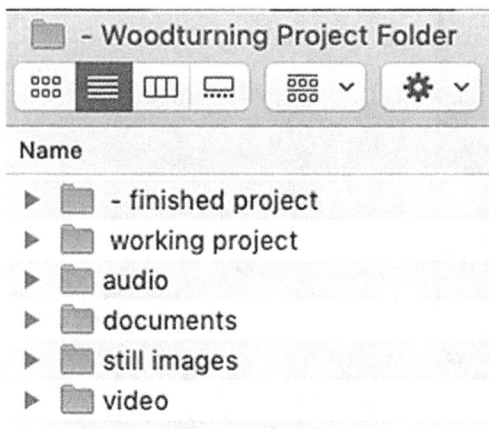

Figure 9.7 Organizing Workflow Folders

Load all of the assets that you plan to use in your story into that media folder. This is key. If you are using files from a video camera, drag the entire SD card onto your hard drive. After your files have finished uploading, remove any hard drives or flash drives to ensure your editing system is only using video from your hard drive and not the SD card. Then, drag them to the appropriate folders. Your logging notes will go in the document folder.

Logging Sound (Natural Sound)

> **Mentor Moment: Greg Vandegrift, Freelance Reporter**
>
> "The purposeful use of nat sound makes stories truly stories and takes advantage of the power of video. If you are living in the world of track, bite, track, bite, you are failing because you are not maximizing your opportunities."

Logging is the act of transcribing your interviews and creating an inventory of your B-roll or video.

Once you've shot your B-roll, interviews and stand-up, and ingested all of your assets, you must log that video. It's simple. It's not up for negotiation. You must log, and you must log before you write.

Start by creating a multi-column document. The number of columns is a personal preference.

Vandegrift considers himself a compulsive logger. "I log every word and most shots," Vandegrift says. "You don't write what the viewer can see, but your copy must complement the images."

Vandegrift says when he has time, he logs everything because it helps him visualize the story as he writes it, enabling him to weave his narration into and out of the soundbites and natural sound. He's looking for crucial elements. His first goal is to find great images—the visuals that drive the words—"springboards" for his writing.

"Second, I look for great natural sound. Sound reveals, provides **pacing**, offers emotion, takes the viewer there. If there's a celebration, let's hear the crisp sound of the celebration. Don't just write, 'They celebrated,'" Vandegrift says.

Third, he looks for powerful soundbites.

"You know them when you hear them. If you catch yourself saying, 'Wow,' and the soundbite supports your focus, you better use it."

Vandegrift says all three elements can amount to **moments**—the foundation of good storytelling. Logging allows you to find those moments. But logging takes time. Budget at least one minute for every minute of video and at least two minutes for every minute of interview. A 20-minute video will take 20 to 40 minutes to log—one reason it's important not to overshoot. And remember your backtime schedule.

"Log what the clock allows," Vandegrift says. "If I have more time, I'm looking for every nugget I can find. If on a tight deadline, don't go fishing; pick only what you need. *The deadline matters.*"

Depending on where he is, Vandegrift will either log by hand using a legal pad and pencil, or he'll log on a computer. As he logs, he notes sections that work best with his story focus. Then, he'll go back with colored pens and highlight the best video, natural sound pops and interview soundbites that he plans to use in the story.

You can do the same thing with asterisks or the highlight feature on your computer.

Logging Video (B-roll)

In each story log, write the clip number or file name in the first column and the time code of the specific shots in the second column. Describe the sound in the third column. In the fourth column, describe what's happening in the video and note whether it is a **wide shot (WS)**, **medium shot (MS)**, **closeup (CU)** or **extreme** closeup **(XCU)**. You'll want to pay attention to **cutaway shots** that will help you with transitions, and highlight or mark those natural sound "moments" that Vandegrift mentioned.

Table 9.1 is a small section of a log for a story on a woodturning hobbyist.

Table 9.1 Story Log Example

Clip#	Timecode	Audio	Video
36	:10	NATS: Click, click, click	MS putting together lathe
	:20	NATS: tat, tat, tat	CU concentrating
	:33		XCU eyes
	1:42	Click of wheel going on	MS wheel spinning
		NATS: tat tat tat of tool on wood	CU slow push in to wood on wheel
37	:10	NATS: lathe	XCU face behind shield
	:17	NATS: whirring	CU hands enter frame with wood spinning
	:22	NATS: lathe	CU wood chips flying***
39	:05–06	I'm just a novice	CU from below looking down at lathe
	:12–:16	they taught me just enough to be dangerous***	MS picking up tool
	1:15–1:25	there's a lot of kinetic energy and if something should break loose or a piece should fly loose it's like	CU hands on tool against wood
	3:22	a bullet bouncing around in the shop	
		NATS lathe	CU foot trembling
40	:23–:33	one of the reasons I was intrigued with wood turning is to try and do something creative with my hands that is not overcome by tremors***	MS side shot
041	:05–:10	NATS wheel turning	XCU WOOD SHAVINGS ON HAND

Logging Interviews (SOTs or Soundbites)

When he can, Vandegrift logs every word of an interview. If he's in a crunch, he logs only what he needs for the story—the verbatim of a soundbite that he will use or the context of a soundbite that he will paraphrase.

Jotting notes on your notepad *during* the interview can also help. Make a note when you hear something great that you'll want to include. That can also cut down on logging time.

Log the incue and outcue time for all soundbites. The soundbite in Table 9.2 with five asterisks is ranked a 5 on a scale of 1 to 5. This would most likely be used in the story.

If a bite is good but may not work as a stand-alone SOT, log it anyway and make a note to paraphrase the contents. There are many instances when you can say something more efficiently and concisely than your interview subject. This is especially true when you interview a public official who is speaking in **legalese**. But it is also the case when the information is convoluted or confusing; there are grammatical errors that detract from the message; the person is difficult to understand; or, the audio quality is bad.

Thorough logging helps you avoid repetition or parroting. Instead, write *into* the soundbite as we talked about with VOSOTs.

When you thoroughly transcribe your interviews, you know the contents of your soundbites, and you can more easily write around them.

You do not need to log every single word your interviewee says—especially if the interview is longer than five minutes. But log everything when you hear a "Wow" soundbite.

"And if you find something cool, but it doesn't support your focus, don't use it. It will slow down the story. You can tell you don't need it if you must work too hard to fit it in the story," Vandegrift says.

Table 9.2 Logging Soundbites

Clip#	Timecode	Audio and NATS	Video
041	7:45–7:59	7:45 My voice is what earned my living for 50 years. That has been my vocation and my livelihood for almost my, well, for my entire career. 7:57*****	CU looks at cam

However, there's no reason those nuggets should be wasted. Use them in your digital story. Use them in your social posts about the story. Tell your producer and it could be used in a headline or tease for the story. There's always a place for good content.

WRITE

Now that your story has been shot, you've logged the video, transcribed the soundbites and selected your stand-up, you may start writing.

Of course, this is not the first time you've thought about what you're going to write. When you pitched your story, conducted interviews, shot your B-roll and stand-up, and logged your video, you always kept your story focus in mind. You've thought about the story's beginning, middle and end and you know what video you are going to use to start and end your story.

> **Mentor Moment: Greg Vandegrift, Freelance Reporter**
>
> "TV reporters need to get over themselves. The sooner a reporter learns that he or she is not the story the better. You cannot be a successful storyteller if it's all about you. That attitude causes reporters to overwrite, which takes away time for great moments and sound—the things that set video storytelling apart from other journalism platforms. It also robs your ability to focus on the person you are interviewing. Journalism at its core is about people."

Anchor Intro

It's a good idea to write the anchor intro first—before you write your package. It will help you improve the flow of your story, avoid repetition and make your producer happy. You may have already written your intro in the car on the way back from the story or before shooting your stand-up.

Remember, the lead should grab the viewer's attention. Write something that is happening right now, is new or is an update using active, conversational voice.

The anchor intro should begin with that attention-grabbing lead and then include what we call the reporter **toss**. That's the part where the anchor says, "As Lakshmi Gade shows us, all it takes is a lot of time and patience."

A11 - GADE WORDTURNING INTRO	
[ANCHOR]	{ANCHOR} YOU CAN GET PLENTY OF SATISFACTION CREATING A WORK OF ART WITH YOUR OWN TWO HANDS. AS LAKSHMI GADE TELLS US, ALL IT TAKES IS A LOT OF TIME AND PATIENCE.
[PKG] [CG: Stan Kramer/Hobbyist @ :20] [CG: Lakshmi Gade/ Reporting @ :36] [CG: Peggy Kramer/Stan's wife @ :45] [CG: Dr. Jenna Lee/Neurologist @ 1:15 [TRT: 1:26 + 10 seconds pad]	{PKG}

Figure 9.8 Package Intro Script

Figure 9.8 is an example of an anchor intro script.

Every intro script must be complete on the right side for the anchor and the left side for the editor and/or director. That includes indicating when the director should roll the package and when to insert the graphics, also known as CGs. Those include locators, interview names and the reporter's name for the stand-up. These CGs are usually only used once no matter how many times a location or interview is shown in the story.

The Package Script

This is your reporter script where pictures are melded with words. The best way to do that is to first know what pictures and sound you have. When you log your video and sound, your soundbites and pictures will drive the way you write your story. When you edit, your writing will drive the way you insert the pictures.

Figures 9.9 and 9.10 show part of the package script for the woodturning story. The story relates to the video log you saw earlier in this chapter. Remember, we're writing everything read by the reporter in upper case letters. Soundbites are in lower case.

Notice that the story begins with the sound of the lathe, the machine that carves the wood. The first line of narration does not say the lathe is carving the wood—the viewer can see that. Use the natural sound to tell that.

Avoid starting your package with a soundbite from an interview—unless the anchor intro clearly introduces the person who is

[PKG] [NAT SOT]	{PKG} {NAT SOT} (nats word turning)
[Editing Note: CU face Clip 36 :20] [CLIP 36 Stan] [IN: I'M JUST] [OUT: A NOVICE] [02]	THE SOUND OF METAL ON WOOD. FOR STAN KRAMER, THAT'S THE SOUND OF SALVATION. (Stan: I'm just a novice)
	IT'S A DANGEROUS HOBBY. ONE THAT REQUIRES A STEADY HAND.
[NAT SOT] [02]	{NAT SOT} (nats word turning)
[CLIP 36 Stan] [IN: There's a lot] [OUT: in the shop] [10]	(Stan: "there's a lot of kinetic energy and if something should break loose or a piece should fly loose it's like a bullet bouncing around in the shop.")
[Editing Note: CU LATHE Clip 40 / :20]	KRAMER LIKES THE CONTROL HE GETS WORKING THE LATHE {NAT SOT} (nats word turning)
[Editing Note: CU LATHE FOOT TREMBLING CLIP 44 / 7:00]	IT MAKES UP FOR HIS INABILITY TO CONTROL OTHER THINGS.
[NAT SOT Stan] [02]	(Stan: we're going to make a thing kind of like this)
[CLIP 40 Stan] [IN:ONE OF THE REASONS] [OUT: OVERCOME BY TREMORS] [10]	(Stan :23 one of the reasons I was intrigued with wood turning is to try and do something creative with my hands that is not overcome by tremors :33)

Figure 9.9 Package Script Example—Woodturning Story

speaking. Most anchor intros introduce the reporter who is narrating the package. If the intro said, "Lakshmi Gade tells us all it takes is a lot of time and patience," we're expecting to hear Gade's voice, not the voice of someone else.

In other words, when the anchor introduces the reporter, the reporter's voice should be the first thing heard after a natural sound pop or natural soundbite. If the reporter is introducing her own package from the studio or a live shot, then starting with an interview soundbite could make sense.

	THE TREMORS STARTED ABOUT TWO YEARS AGO. SHORTLY AFTER KRAMER NOTICED A CHANGE IN HIS VOICE.
[CLIP 41 Stan] [IN: 7:45 MY VOICE IS WHAT EARNED] [OUT: OVERCOME BY TREMORS 7:57] [12]	(Stan: My voice is what earned my living for 50 years. That has been my vocation and my livelihood for almost well for my entire career. 7:57)
[CLIP 45 Stand-up] [IN: 1:32 AFTER YEARS OF [OUT: WHAT HE FEARED. 1:41] [09]	(Lakshmi Gade- After years of searching for answers, the diagnosis was what he feared.)
[CLIP 42] [IN: 2:47 PARKINSON'S DISEASE. IT'S [OUT: ELSE THIS TIME. 7:58] [11]	("2:47 Parkinson's Disease. It's not the worst thing in the world but it is the kind of thing that always happens to somebody else, and I'm the somebody else this time.) (nats word turning)
[NAT SOT] [02]	NOW HE CREATES WORKS OF ART FROM WOOD. (nats word turning) IT REQUIRES, STRENGTH, SKILL AND A STEADY HAND.
[NAT SOT] [02]	
[NAT SOT] [02]	(nats word turning) WOOD TURNING GIVES HIM CONTROL, EVEN WHEN PARKINSON'S TAKES IT AWAY. IN CENTERVILLE, LAKSHMI GADE, TEN NEWS.

Figure 9.10 Package Script Example—Woodturning Story

The "Handshake Shot"

> **Mentor Moment: Boyd Huppert, Reporter**
>
> "The handshake shot is introducing someone in a story the way you would meet them in person. It's extending a hand, getting close, looking them in the eye, drawing conclusions."

KARE11's Boyd Huppert coined the term, "Handshake shot." It's a technique he uses in nearly all of his stories:

> There have been studies done on forming impressions. Within a couple of seconds of meeting someone, we form an impression of them. And most of the time we're right. That's what the handshake shot is. I want to introduce that person in a context that will propel you into the story.

Huppert says if your character is in a hurry or if it's a hectic day, then you introduce them when they're in a moment that will help the viewer understand they're really busy. If they're gregarious, then you introduce that person being gregarious.

"I don't necessarily need you to like the person," Huppert says. "I want you to be interested in the person on the first meeting. That to me is a good handshake shot. Get close, extend a hand, look them in the eye, have some understanding almost immediately of what they're about."

Note: Huppert doesn't mean you should actually shake the person's hand. The term "handshake shot" is a metaphor. Just get a good closeup shot of your subject's face as she or he is doing something. After that first line of narration, or even during that first line of narration, introduce your main character.

Scan the following QR code to hear Huppert explain the handshake shot.

In the woodturning story, the first line of narration introduces Stan Kramer, and we see the handshake shot. It's a closeup of Kramer's face as he's working the lathe. And we hear a colorful soundbite that tells you a little about who he is: "I'm just a novice."

The next reporter track sets up the possibility that there might be something wrong: "IT'S A DANGEROUS HOBBY. ONE THAT REQUIRES A STEADY HAND." Kramer reinforces that statement by saying, "one slip, and it's like a bullet bouncing around the shop."

The reporter's voice track explains that Kramer does this hobby to give him control: "IT MAKES UP FOR HIS INABILITY TO CONTROL OTHER THINGS."

A quick natural sound break, "We're going to make a thing kind of like this," as the camera cuts away to a photo on the wall of an urn he's making and then an emotional reveal. Kramer does woodturning because he is living with something that causes tremors.

The story transitions to the past when Kramer noticed a change in his voice. This leads to the conflict in the story. Kramer has Parkinson's Disease.

Figures 9.9 and 9.10 show a condensed version of the original script. Other supporting characters are in the full story. Notice the bridge stand-up in the middle of Figure 9.10: "After years of searching for answers, the diagnosis was what he feared." This stand-up helped the story transition from the past to the present.

The story ends with a concluding sentence: "Woodturning gives him control, even when Parkinson's takes it away," and then the tag-out, "In Centerville, Lakshmi Gade, Ten News." The tag-out identifies the reporter, the station and the location where the story originates. It's similar to a **byline** in a newspaper or web story.

Letting Sound Lead Your Writing

Let's look at some other examples of package scripts using soundbites to tell a memorable story.

Although the general rule is eight- to 15-second soundbites, Vandegrift has used longer and shorter SOTs in his packages.

For example, in a story about a license plate collector, Vandegrift sets up the theme of the story with an incomplete sentence to lead into a one-second soundbite from the central character, Doug.

Vandegrift says: "YOU HEARD RIGHT. MORE THAN 300-THOUSAND LICENSE PLATES IN WHAT COULD BE CALLED ..." Doug completes the sentence by saying, "library of license plates." This technique, writing an incomplete sentence and then completing it with a soundbite, is effective if used properly. It should not be overused because then it becomes a cliché.

That quick soundbite is followed by the **nat sound (NATS)** of the clinking of license plates and Vandegrift's voice track completing the thought: "And Doug's the librarian."[3]

Vandegrift reinforces the theme with a one-second NATS pop of Doug pausing and saying, "Hmmm," as he searches the library storage shed for a specific license plate.

How did Vandegrift find those soundbites? He discovered them when he logged the video. It's a moment when, if you're not logging closely, you'll miss it.

[NAT SOT @ 4:21] [02]	YOU HEARD RIGHT. MORE THAN 300-THOUSAND LICENSE PLATES IN WHAT COULD BE CALLED... **{NAT SOT}** (Doug: Library of license plates) **{NAT SOT}**
[NAT SOT @ 8:36] [02]	(clinking of plates @ 5:32) AND DOUG'S THE LIBRARIAN. **{NAT SOT}**
[NAT SOT] [02]	(Hmmm.) WITH A CENTURY'S WORTH OF METAL HISTORY PAGES.
[Notes: 9:45] [SOT: Doug] [CG: Doug/License Plate Librarian] [IN: There's a Maine @ 10:15] [OUT: out of brass 10:23] [08]	("There's a Maine plate from 1948; it's made out of brass.")

Figure 9.11 Package Script Example—License Plate Story

Natural sound can be punctuation—an exclamation mark basically saying, 'You're darn right. He's the librarian; he knows where these things are.'"

Scan the following QR code to see the story.

Similarly, Vandegrift used a series of soundbites and natural sound that ran a total of 30 seconds in a story about a four-time high school state wrestling champion.

[NAT SOT] [02]	{NAT SOT} (applause)
[CU face Clip 36 / :20]	HISTORY IS WRITTEN
[NAT SOT] [18]	{NAT SOT} (applause, screaming, yelling)
[CLIP Coach] [IN: I love] [OUT: you dad] [03]	(I love you, guy. Great job.) FOUR YEARS 158 AND 0.
[CLIP Coach] [IN: it's yours] [OUT: this one] [04]	("Get to your family. You gotta enjoy this one.")
[NAT SOT: Dad] [03]	("Yahoo, yahoo, yahoo.")
[CLIP Kevin's mom] [IN: it's so great] [OUT: honey] [03]	("It's so great, honey")

Figure 9.12 Package Script Example—Wrestling Champion

"That story reinforces my philosophy about writing," Vandegrift says. "Don't say 'They celebrated.' Let's hear the celebration."

That is exactly what Vandegrift and his editor did. They let the excitement and emotional celebration run for 33 seconds.[4]

Figure 9.12 is the script from the NATS section of the wrestling story.

Scan the following QR code to watch the story about the wrestling champion.

As you're writing your story, visualize the video that will go with your words. It helps to note the shots you're planning to use for each sentence or phrase in the left column of your script.

{ANCHOR TAG FULL}
THE PARKINSON'S PROJECT IS HOLDING A SUMMIT THIS WEEKEND AT THE FIRST PRESBYTERIAN CHURCH IN CENTERVILLE.
IT'S AN OPPORTUNITY FOR PEOPLE WITH PARKINSON'S TO GET TOGETHER AND SHARE STORIES.
THEY ALSO LEARN HOW OTHERS MANAGE THE DISEASE WHILE LIVING LIFE TO ITS FULLEST.

Figure 9.13 Anchor Tag Example

Anchor Tag

The anchor tag contains a nugget of information not yet said in the story. Maybe it didn't fit with your story focus but you find it interesting as an "oh, by the way" comment that the anchor can add for an on-camera tag.

Or, it's a piece of information that forwards the story, like the one in Figure 9.13 for the woodworking story.

The anchor tag can also include a way to help the viewer get more information about a closely related topic. One idea could be a story on a procedure called deep-brain stimulation that is helping people with Parkinson's get control of their tremors. Another might be a fitness program, where people with Parkinson's work out together. You could promote a story on that topic coming up tomorrow or in the following newscast.

Make sure this anchor tag has substance to it—something that truly completes the story, expands on it or helps the viewer.

The tag can also be something that promotes the station website or something else you added in the web story. In this example, you could include interviews you didn't use in your broadcast story—or even the full, unedited interview if it was exceptionally interesting or enlightening. You could also include resources about Parkinson's Disease in that web story.

VOICE TRACK

Once you are finished writing your story and your script has been approved, you will record your voice track. Do not attempt editing without first tracking your story.

You must use a good quality microphone—a lavalier or stick mic—to record your track. If you must record your track on your phone, use a high-quality mic made for smartphones. You may need an adapter and a recording app to get quality sound from your phone.

It's best to record your track in a room with good acoustics such as an audio booth. Avoid rooms with hard, flat edges and surfaces, which create an echo. If you don't have access to an audio booth, or if you are out in the field, sit in a car or room that does not echo, and record your voice track. If there is an echo or hollow sound, use a jacket or blanket as a baffle, placing it over your head and recording device, and record that way.

You can make a DIY audio booth in your bedroom closet with clothing, pillows or blankets.

Figure 9.14 shows a couple of examples of makeshift audio booths. The one on the left is a thick blanket suspended from the corner of a room—leaving space for the reporter to stand inside. The blanket absorbs the sound. The photo on the right uses sofa pillows to create an audio booth on top of a desk.

Once you've found an acceptable location, record your track. Many stations recommend you mark each track with the number and "take" and count down from three to one. This helps to keep track of each part of the script and your takes. For example, "track one, take one; track one, take two," etc.

Makeshift Audio Booths

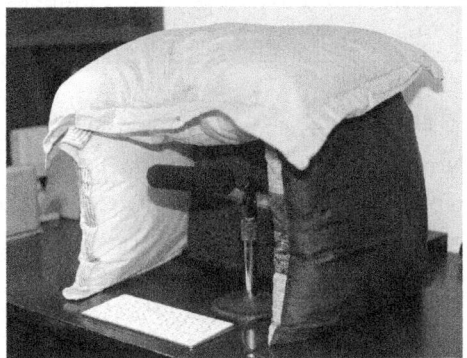

Figure 9.14 Makeshift Audio Booth

Here are some other things you must do:

- Be yourself. Don't try to sound like someone you are not.
- If you make a mistake, stop and record a second take of the sentence or paragraph where you stumbled. Do not use a voice track with stumbles or errors.
- Remember the energy of the story. The voice track must match that energy. Visualize your video. What part of the story is your track coming out of and going into?
- Don't shout, but make sure your voice is a proper, controlled level of sound, meter, tempo and energy to match the story.
- Once you finish recording, upload your voice track to the audio file of the project folder on your external hard drive. You may also record your voice track directly into your editing timeline, but you should use a good quality microphone if you plan to use this method.

Mentor Moment: Will Tran, MMJ, KRON, San Francisco

"I think what is so important and not emphasized enough by news directors and professors is the need to use YOUR VOICE in the story. If it's a fun story, sound like you're having fun. If it's a serious and sad story, sound like you care. It drives me nuts that most reporters sound exactly alike in every story they do."

EDIT

Now it's time to hand your script, voice track and video to the photographer or editor to put the story together. MMJs and most beginning reporters edit their own stories. We will discuss the technical side of editing in Chapter 10.

WRITING THE WEB STORY

While the editor is working on your story, or if you're an MMJ and you've finished editing, it is time to meet with the digital producer and update your web story.

Figures 9.15 and 9.16 give an example of a broadcast script followed by the corresponding web script.

[SOT] [NATS LEAVES RUSTLING] [02]	{SOT} (rustling sound of leaves) WITH EACH GUST OF WIND, THE COLORS OF FALL COVER THE CENTRAL STATE CAMPUS.
[SOT] [NATS I love the yellow one there] [03]	{SOT} (Fatima - "I love the yellow one there.") FALL IS FATIMA TEIXEIRA'S FAVORITE TIME OF YEAR ON CAMPUS. AND THIS IS ONE OF HER FAVORITE STUDY SPOTS.
[SOT] [CG: Fatima Teixeira, Student] [IN: just makes me smile] [OUT: it's so pretty] [09]	("just makes me smile. The cooler temps give me more energy. I now spend more time on campus because I think it's so pretty.")
[SOT] [NATS SNEEZING] [01]	{SOT} (woman sneezing) OTHERS, LIKE STUDENT KELLY BATES... AREN'T SO FOND OF THIS TIME OF YEAR. ALL OF THE STUFF GETTING BLOWN AROUND MAKES IT TOUGH IF YOU HAVE ALLERGIES.
[SOT] [CG: Kelly Bates, Student] [IN: As soon as I] [OUT: for my allergies.] [08]	("As soon as I see the first leaf change color, I grab my allergy meds and keep them with me. This is the worst time of year for my allergies.")
[SOT] [NATS FRISBEE SOUNDS] [02]	{SOT} (nats - frisbee group) BUT AS YOU WALK AROUND CAMPUS. YOU CAN FEEL THE ENERGY. PEOPLE ARE COMING OUT OF THE SUMMER HEAT SLUMP.
[SOT] [CG: Rick Pendergast, Student] [IN: It's so great] [OUT: until spring.] [15]	("It's so great to be out here and not be sweating! I get a good group to join me these days, but as soon as it gets super cold, forget it. These guys go into hibernation until spring.")
[SOT] [CG: Joc Cooper, MCJ 124] [IN:AN INFORMAL] [OUT: STD.] [18]	("An informal poll of students ranked this Ginkgo tree as the favorite tree on campus- (CUT TO)- but those who prefer red pick this maple outside Joyal. No matter which one is your favorite, you'll get to enjoy the colorful fanfare for several more weeks. At Central State, Joc Cooper reporting.")

Figure 9.15 Package Script Example—Fall Colors Story

You'll notice that they're both similar in content but different in typesetting and, in some cases, AP style.

When breaking down a broadcast script and turning it into a web story, a simple way is to copy your package script into a document and then, using AP style (or whatever your station guide is), reformat your script to follow that. Again, each newsroom has a different style for web stories.

You'll notice in the fall colors web script there are a number of links. You'll see them underlined, beginning with "Central State" and ending with "tips for taking great fall photos."

Central State students welcome fall colors but not the pollen

CENTERVILLE--The Central State campus is starting to look different these days. The colors of fall are coming.

This is Fatima Teixeira's favorite time of year on campus. She has a few favorite trees and study spots.

"The cooler temps give me more energy. I now spend more time on campus because I think it's so pretty," she said.

Others aren't so fond of this time of year because it is tough on their allergies.

"As soon as I see the first leaf change color, I grab my allergy meds and keep them with me. This is the worst time of year for my allergies," Kelly Bates said.

As you walk around campus you can feel the energy. It's like people are coming out of the summer heat slump and playing.

"It's so great to be out here and not be sweating," said Rick Pendergast, while playing Frisbee with a group of friends. "I get a good group to join me these days, but as soon as it gets super cold, forget it. These guys go into hibernation until spring."

Some say the ginkgo tree to the north of McKee Fisk is the number one best tree in the fall. Others prefer the red maple outside of Joyal Hall. The Central State grounds crew says if next weekend's temperatures do fall into the 40s as forecast, the colors should peak the following week.

You can follow the grounds crew on Twitter to find the most colorful tree on campus each day for that perfect photo opp. The campus photography department offers these tips for taking great fall photos.

Figure 9.16 Web Example—Fall Colors Story

In Chapter 12, we'll talk more about best practices for web writing and links. The goal is to offer your audience a few different locations and formats to see your story. It's on TV once at a specific time, but when you post it to the web it lives there longer. It can be watched anytime and can be shared through social media to an even broader audience.

REMINDERS FOR WRITING A PKG
- Backtime your day and plan ahead.
- Remember the SLWVE process in story building.
- Sound (natural and from interviews) are powerful parts of storytelling.
- Know what you're going to write before and after your stand-up bridge so the stand-up flows with the story.
- In stand-ups, be aware of what's behind you and talk about it.

- Demonstrate or show something in your stand-up.
- Writing into and out of a soundbite creates flow.

QUESTIONS

1. What is a handshake shot?
2. Why is logging your video and interviews important?
3. What are Greg Vandegrift's three logging goals?
4. What does SLWVE stand for and why is it important?
5. Why should you avoid starting a package with a soundbite from an interview?

TRY THIS

Watch two local newscasts. Pick two packages to study. Answer these questions:

a. How did sound, visuals and interviews help tell each story?
b. How did the reporter help you understand the character of the story?
c. Explain how the anchor lead and tag helped introduce and further the story.

NOTES

1 Journalist's Toolbox, Retrieved from www.journaliststoolbox.org/
2 Freedman, W. (2011). *It Takes More Than Good Looks to Succeed at Television News Reporting*, A Wealth of Wisdom, LLC, p. 165, ebook.
3 From Vandegrift's KARE-11 License Plates story, Retrieved from www.youtube.com/watch?v=kV3FnvdJuWM
4 From Vandegrift's KARE-11 Wrestling story, Retrieved from https://youtu.be/zA0UQVZ0zqw

Shooting and Editing Video

Ten

In This Chapter	
Shoot Like a Photojournalist	154
Lighting	162
Sound Matters	165
Shooting Interviews	168
Editing Efficiently	172
Reminders for Shooting and Editing	177
Questions	178
Try This	178

SHOOT LIKE A PHOTOJOURNALIST

Photojournalism is an art and something you should strive to learn and improve. Photojournalists shoot to edit. In other words, they shoot with intention and are mindful about the video they record. You may think you have hours of space on your 64GB SD card, but the more you shoot, the longer it will take to log, write and edit the story.

CNN news photographer and drone pilot Carmaine Means says you should know why you're shooting what you're shooting, and you're not just getting extra B-roll because you think you might need it.

"If you understand sequencing and understand where the story is going, you don't need all that extra B-roll," Means says.

The National Press Photographers Association tells its members to commit the basics to memory. Their disciples, including Joe Little, call it the NPPA mantra. They say it helps MMJs and photographers tell better stories.

> **Mentor Moment: Joe Little, MMJ/Director of Storytelling, KNSD, San Diego**
>
> "We all use a variation of that mantra. Vary your shots—wide, medium, tight. Shoot and move. Whenever you have an action, get

DOI: 10.4324/9781003137016-10

> the reaction. If someone says something, look for the response to what they say. When shooting B-roll, allow your subject to enter the frame rather than starting with the person already in the frame. And when you have overlapping action, when someone does the same thing, shoot it from several different focal lengths and angles."

If you commit that mantra to memory, it will help you shoot and edit sequences.

Sequencing

Sequences are two or more shots of the same action from varying angles, focal points and distances. Sequences help to compress time, allowing us to move through a process quickly without slowing down the story. Sequences make editing easier.

One way to remember this is with the acronym WOCHU: **W**ide shot or medium shot, **O**ver-the-shoulder, **C**loseup of face, **H**ands closeup, **U**nusual shot or side angle. This works for B-roll, but it also works well for interviews.[1]

At least half of your shots should be closeups or tight shots and extreme closeups. You want to bring your viewer into the action and those super-tight shots will give you more to work with when you edit. They also help with transitioning from one location or time to another.

Wide shots are important, too, but you won't need more than one or two. A wide shot gives perspective and helps establish where a story is taking place.

> **Mentor Moment: Wayne Freedman, Reporter KGO, San Francisco**
>
> "Generally, you shouldn't need more than 90 seconds of set-up video from any one scene. Ninety seconds should allow you to get a basic sequence with wide, medium, tight and cutaway shots. If you have more time, go for style points with a couple of extreme close-ups to use as natural sound and transitions."[2]

Framing

When composing your shots, it's important to note where your subject is in the frame, especially when shooting interviews or closeups.

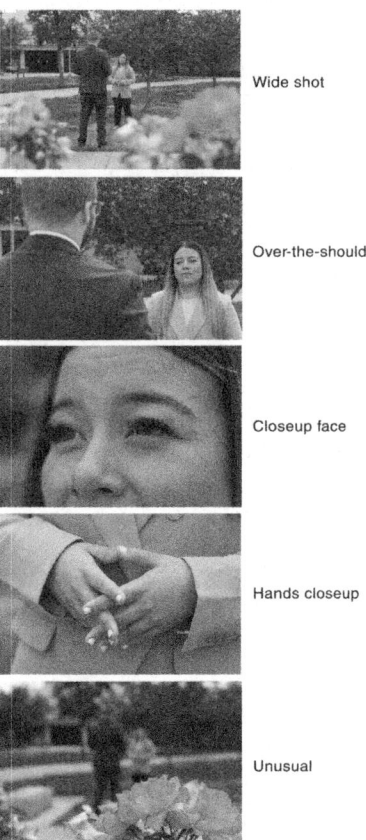

Figure 10.1 Sequencing Shots

We do this with the rule of thirds—an imaginary grid that divides the screen into thirds and helps us pinpoint where your subject should be framed. If looking to the left, your interviewee should be placed in the right third so that he or she is looking into the left two-thirds of the screen. You want to make sure your subject has "looking room" or "lead room."

The rule of thirds also helps us determine how much headroom to give your subject. You don't want too much headroom—space above the head. Fill the frame with the person's head, taking it almost to the top of the frame. If, when looking through the viewfinder, you place the subject's eyes on the intersection of the top third of the grid, that will give you the right shot.

Figure 10.2 Camera Shot Types

If your subject is moving through the frame, you should allow about two-thirds worth of lead room in front of the person so he or she is always moving with enough space.

Another option is to keep your camera still and allow the person to enter or exit the frame. Allowing the subject to enter the frame gives

Figure 10.3 Rule of Thirds

OR: Allow subject to exit frame and enter frame to compress time

Figure 10.4 Lead Room

you many more editing options and will get you out of trouble, also known as a jump cut.

Explore your angles. When shooting an interview, vary the camera angles—especially when shooting medium shots. Once you get a shot, move at least 30 degrees before taking your next shot. That's what Little means by shoot and move.

180-Degree Rule

Pay attention to the direction your subject's nose is pointing. This will help you avoid crossing the "action axis" and violating the 180-degree rule.

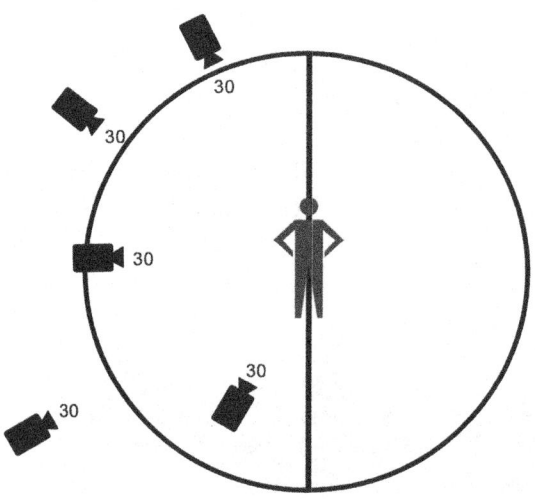

Figure 10.5 30-Degree Rule

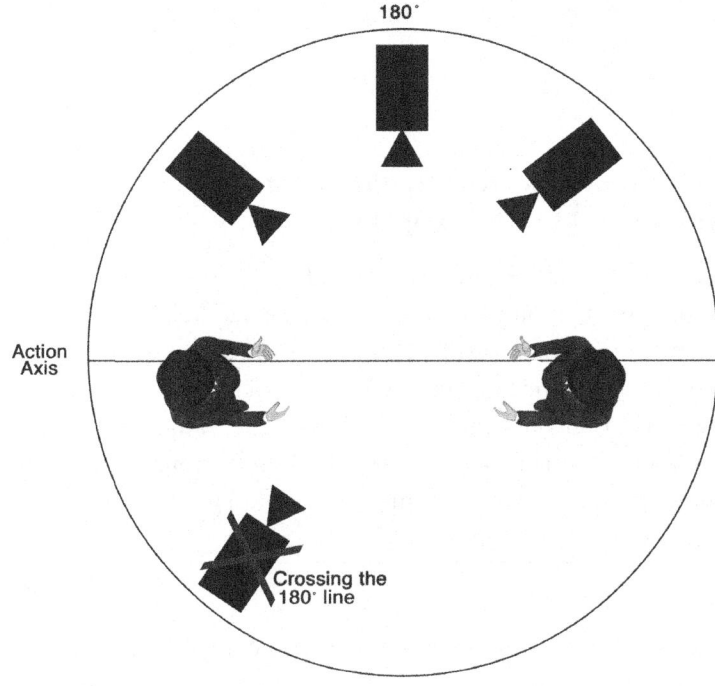

Figure 10.6 180-Degree Rule

When you shoot **cutaways** during an interview, you must stay on one side of the action axis. That 180-degree line is divided with your subjects' shoulders.

Everything on the shoulder side of that line is safe territory. But if you cross the line, you break the continuity.

That's why we say "watch the nose." Make sure that the nose is always pointing in the same direction. That will keep you on the correct side of the line. The same concept applies to shooting a moving car. If you shoot the car from one side of the street, its headlights are pointing to the right of the frame. If you shoot from the opposite side, the car will appear to be facing in the opposite direction—when it hasn't moved at all.

If you break the 180-degree rule, your action won't make any sense. However, super tight shots will allow you to cross the 180-degree line because the eye doesn't see the perspective of where the camera and your subject are positioned.

"Tight shots will save you every time," says former CBS News photographer Les Rose.

Anticipating

> **Mentor Moment: Chad Nelson, Director of Photography, KARE11, Minneapolis**
>
> "I was a baseball player growing up and everything was about formulated guesses. You have to react fast when a pitch is coming in at 90 miles an hour, but if you have a formulated guess that it's going to be a breaking ball, you are looking for that, and you can react faster. Shooting, to me, is the exact same thing. It's just making these formulated guesses and observations of things happening. You can set yourself up in the right spot to get what you need and win."

A good example of this is an observation Nelson made before shooting a story about a woman who was giving free hugs in front of a department store. On their way to the story, reporter Boyd Huppert asked Nelson how they were going to make this hug shot work. Nelson explained:

> I told him, don't worry about it, it'll be fine. I know where they're going to hug because everyone hugs the same way. That's just an observation that I've made. Some photographers will say, 'Yep, I know that. Yep, I've done that.' But a lot of them say 'Wow, I never thought about that.' It's just one more piece of knowledge that you have so you don't have to guess.

It's easier to anticipate an action when it's repetitive action. Scan the following QR code to see Nelson and Huppert's hug story.

> **Mentor Moment: Les Rose, Professor of Practice, Syracuse University, Former CBS Network News Photographer, Syracuse**
>
> "Repetition is like a photographer's best friend. A flight attendant comes down an aisle, and it's time to serve drinks. You think in advance, what shots am I going to need? You're going to need a tight shot of the finger going on the Coke can; a shot looking down; a wide shot of how many people are on the plane; and an over the shoulder shot. But what most people forget is the anticipation shots and the reaction shots. The action is popping the Coke can and pouring the drink. The reaction is 'I'm really thirsty.' And you've got to remember action reaction. It's not all about throwing the football and catching the football. That's the action. It's about the granny in the stands who's been to every game for the past 40 years. And her going crazy, represents us the viewer."

Action Reaction

The action reaction concept that Rose mentioned applies to all stories. Many beginning MMJs do a great job of shooting the action, but they forget about the reaction. It's the reaction that tells the story, but you have to look for it.

Think about sporting events and the fans' reaction to the action on the field. This is where you will capture emotion and excitement for your story. Remember the wrestling champion story in Chapter 9? What would that story have missed if the reporter didn't show 24 seconds of reaction from the athlete, his family, his friends, the coach and all of the fans? It would have been just another wrestling match.

Finally, Rose says you should remember the difference between positive action and negative action:

> You have to shoot action coming *toward* you for an opening and going *away* for a close. That's positive and negative action. This is a major deal. I've seen too many stories on skateboarders, motorcyclists, and race car drivers where the story starts with the action going away. You want positive action because the viewer's brain knows that if something is going away, it's the end of the story.

> **Mentor Moment: Chad Nelson, Director of Photography**
>
> "My best advice for shooting a TV news story would be to be quick but patient. It seems counterproductive, but be patient enough to let things happen in your lens and quick enough to react before or after that moment. Being well prepared and knowledgeable about your gear is also very important to be a good photographer. The more you understand how a camera works, the less time you need to spend messing with your camera and the more time you can spend on being patient."

Panning and Zooming—Don't Do It

You may hear the pros say, "Zoom with your feet." If you have to move closer to a subject, don't use the zoom feature on your camera. It never looks natural and it makes editing difficult. Instead, walk toward your subject, adjusting the focus as you move.

And avoid **panning**. Think about the way your eyes move when you walk into a room. Do you frantically scan the room back and forth, not taking in any details? No. When you walk into a room, you focus on one object or person at a time. You should do the same with your camera. If there's a reason to look at the entire room at once, use a wide shot. Then take closeup and extreme closeup shots of details inside the room.

It's OK to move the camera when you are following action. It's even better to allow your subject to enter the frame.

Use a Tripod (also known as "sticks")

We can't say this enough. Use a tripod. The pros call them sticks because in the old days, tripods were made out of wood. Now, sticks are much lighter and easier to carry. They may seem like an unnecessary hassle, but they will help you avoid shaky video, and that's important. If you find yourself in a rare situation where sticks aren't feasible, use a steady bag or brace yourself against a building and shoot wide. Tighter shots require a tripod.

LIGHTING

Lighting is, unfortunately, one of the last things a beginning MMJ thinks about, but it's one of the most important elements of storytelling. Carmaine Means says:

Within the last 10 years, our industry was moving toward lighting not being important. I'm here to tell you that's not true. Photographers need to truly learn lighting and how to light really well. It's nothing against MMJs, but we're responsible as a photographer. Our number one responsibility is image control—what your image looks like. And that has a lot to do with everything that you need to know about the camera and everything you need to know about lighting.

> **Mentor Moment: Carmaine Means, Photographer/ Drone Pilot**
>
> "If you're going to be a photographer or MMJ, you have to invest in yourself. And I know that's harder when you're starting out and you're in smaller markets, and you're making a certain income. It is not about what the station will and will not buy you. You can talk to some managers until you're blue in the face, and you still won't get a light. But what are you going to do? You can't continue to shoot bad video. That's your brand. How the heck can you ever put that on a demo reel and get to a larger market? They're not going to take you. You have to invest in yourself. You've got to buy your own lighting. If it gets you out of market 134 into market 40 and then from market 40 into market two, you're golden. It'll be worth it to spend $100 on some LED lights. Just go do it. I know it sucks, but that's what you've got to do."

One of the simplest and most effective lighting strategies is something Les Rose refers to as the **reporter sandwich**.

> **Mentor Moment: Les Rose, Former CBS News Photographer**
>
> "The number one thing to remember about lighting interviews is the darkest side of the face is closest to the camera. It's called the 'shadow side to the camera.' The reporter is always between the key light and the camera creating a 'reporter sandwich' and a much better look. A bit of shadow on the face closest to the camera gives the face depth. Once you know this, you will see it everywhere—in movies, 60 Minutes stories, advertising, magazines. And you will notice flat lighting (same on either side), which is OK for reporter live shots, stand-ups and cut shots."

"During the interview, the interviewee looks at the reporter," Rose says. "The **key light** and the camera are never together. They're always separated by the reporter in the middle."

Rose says it may not make sense at first because your brain is thinking you need to light the side of the face that's closest to the camera. But that would create a flat look. Just remember: The darkest side of the face should be closest to the camera.

If you don't have a light, you can get a similar effect using natural light. Make sure the light from a window is facing your interviewee and that you have placed yourself between that light and the camera. That way, you'll be able to use the light source as your key light.

Never ever place your interviewee in front of a window so that he or she is backlit because that will create a silhouette

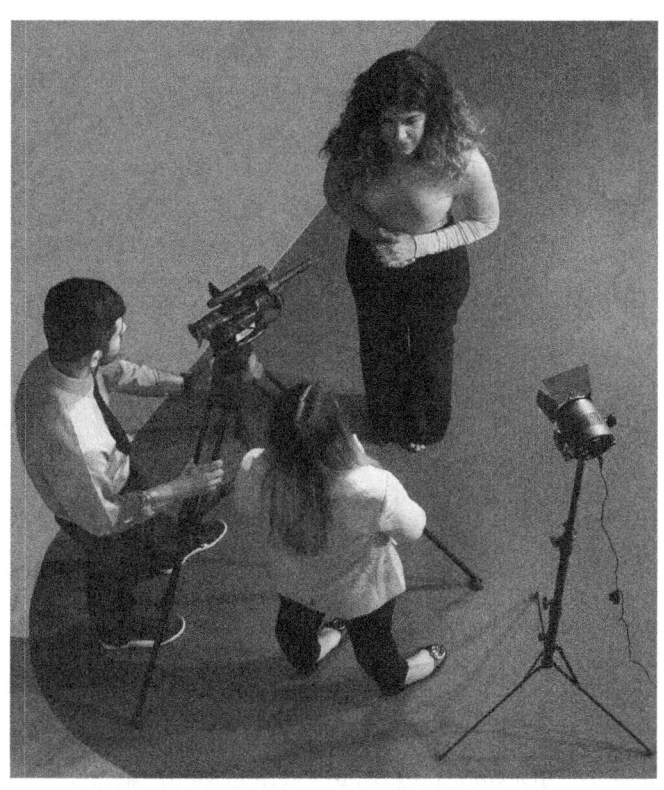

Figure 10.7 Reporter Sandwich

Figure 10.8 Example of Backlit Subject

effect—something you don't want unless you are intentionally doing an interview and don't want the person to be recognized. Instead, place your interviewee at an angle so he or she is facing the window or light.

Once you have set up the camera and lights, set your white balance. It doesn't matter what type of camera you are using, the few seconds you take to white balance will save you in the end. Simply focus the camera on a piece of white, non-reflective material, a white piece of paper works fine, and press the auto white balance (AWB) button. If you are shooting inside, once you set the white balance, you won't have to set it again. But if you are outside and the lighting changes with the time of day or clouds move over the scene, you'll need to adjust the white balance. The same goes if you move from outside to inside or vice versa.

SOUND MATTERS

Film director George Lucas said: "Sound is 50 percent of the moviegoing experience." British film director Danny Boyle gives audio even more weight saying, "Sound is up to 80 percent of a movie."

There's no question that audio plays a huge role in filmmaking, but the same is also true for news reporting and storytelling.

> **Mentor Moment: Les Rose, Former CBS News Photographer**
>
> "Natural sound is critical. Write to it precisely, not generically. Silence is the hardest thing to write to, and can be the most powerful moment in the story. It gives the viewer a moment to focus on what it is like to BE that person."[3]

And that's why sound matters. The Poynter Institute's Al Tompkins says, "Sound allows viewers to experience the story."

Powerful NATS could be the sound of a wildfire roaring, a skidding car, a child's laugh, a parent's painful cry, the splash of a satellite into the ocean, someone yelling, a building blowing up or even the sound of a dog sniffing.

> **Mentor Moment: Al Tompkins, Senior Faculty, Poynter Institute, St. Petersburg**
>
> "If I'm doing a story on the COVID sniffing dogs at the Miami Heat stadium that started sniffing people coming into the stadium, the magic of that story is going to be in hearing the dogs do their work. If I stand back 30 feet and get a picture of them with a zoom lens, I can even get close up. But until I get right next to the dog with a microphone, and you hear that dog do its work, you hear the handler talk to the dog and hear the dog make noise back to the handler, that's the connection. There's a difference between what I call point-you-there and take-you-there storytelling. Point-you-there means, well, look at that. Look at this. You're just pointing me there. But if you take me by the hand and walk me through the story, then we experience the story together. *Sound takes me there.* Sound always tells me how close to the action you were."

Microphones

Think about sports events on TV. Tennis, football, soccer, even golf. What would it be like to watch those games without sound? If anything demonstrates how important sound is in telling a story, look at the person whose job it is to walk the golf course with a huge microphone to hear the sound of the golf club hitting a small, white ball.

Other microphones are small but play an important role. The wireless lavalier mic is one example.

> **Mentor Moment: Greg Vandegrift, University of St. Thomas Professor and Freelancer KARE 11, NBC, Minneapolis**
>
> "The wireless mic is the most powerful storytelling tool because it brings the subject closer. Think about it. Take the same image, say, a distant shot that requires use of the zoom to get close. If the sound is on the shotgun mic, it's worthless. If it's on the wireless, it's like you are standing next to the person."

A wireless lav frees you and your interview subject to move around during the interview. Make sure the microphone is in place, clipped to the person's shirt or jacket and is pointed in the direction of their mouth.

When you use a wired lavalier microphone, the cord should never be seen. Hide the cable under the interviewee's clothing. Always.

> **Mentor Moment: Chad Nelson, Photographer/Editor**
>
> "The best way to capture good natural sound is to get the mic close. This could be using a wireless microphone on a person to hear them speaking clearly or moving a shotgun mic close to something making a sound. I would also say to not settle for 'empty sound.' What I mean by that is when I was young, I would put 'natural' sounds that weren't really clear because the mic wasn't close enough. Train your ear to want everything to be crystal clear, and it will create good habits."

Headphones

In addition to the wireless lavalier mic, there's one other piece of equipment that can make or break a story. Headphones. Make it a practice to wear headphones whenever you are recording sound. If you can't wear headphones (for example, when you're doing a stand-up), before you leave the location, listen back to your audio to confirm you actually recorded the sound and your microphone didn't cut out. Taking three minutes to double-check your audio can save you hours of frustration.

Before you leave your shooting location, record at least one minute of **room tone** or ambient sound. It's sound that may not be noticeable to you unless you stop and listen. It could be the hum from the computer, the whirring sound of a ceiling fan or noise from traffic outside a window. Room tone will help you during the edit process by filling in audio from a location with no sound or to enrich your voice track.

Remember to keep quiet when gathering sound. You'll have to stop talking with your interviewee or any other people at the story site. Just explain you need some natural sound without the sound of your voices talking to each other.

SHOOTING INTERVIEWS

The Poynter Institute recommends you angle the interviewee slightly away from the camera, squaring his or her shoulders toward the MMJ who is standing beside the camera, not behind it. The interviewee should be looking at you, the MMJ, not straight at the camera. People will feel more comfortable talking to you instead of the camera lens. And you'll get a more natural looking interview. Another reason why it's important to use a tripod.

But, don't stand too far away from the camera. In Figures 10.9 and 10.10, the reporter is standing several feet to the side of the camera. The interview subject is looking at the reporter, turning her head away from the camera.

To avoid getting a profile shot like this, also referred to as the "talking ear," shoot the interview subject so you can see both eyes. It may mean you need to move a few steps closer to the camera to get a better shot.

In the field, you'll want to make sure you are shooting the interview from the appropriate level.

If you are shooting from above your subject, you're forcing the person to look up to you, which gives the wrong impression and is not complimentary. If you're shooting level with your subject's eyes, you are giving the impression that the person is on the same level as you, which is a more appealing look.

Figure 10.9 Talking Ear Shot

The Background

Consider what's going on behind your interviewee. You want to avoid garbage cans and messy desks, unless the story is about garbage or messy desks. Once you know where you want to shoot your interview, look through the viewfinder and pay attention to tree branches and

Figure 10.10 Off-Camera Shot

NO YES

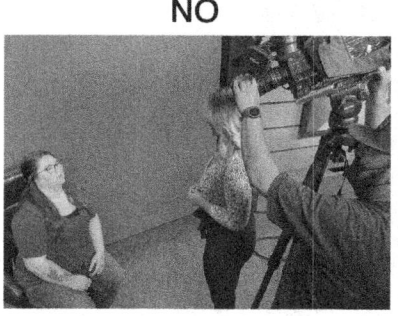 

Figure 10.11 Eye-Level Shot

poles that appear to stick out of your subject's head. If there are a lot of distractions behind your interviewee, consider a tighter shot or move.

> **Mentor Moment: Les Rose, Professor of Practice, Syracuse University**
>
> "You don't want anyone to pay attention to your lighting or your writing or any of the cinematics. You don't want them saying, 'Gosh, that was great sound,' or 'That was a cool shot.' You just want them to say, 'That was a great story,' because they're so sucked into the story that they don't notice any of that. That's why you have to avoid hand mics and live trucks in the background."

Active Interviews

> **Mentor Moment: Boyd Huppert, Reporter, KARE11, Minneapolis**
>
> "I've had phenomenal news directors at every step of my career. In Wausau, I worked for a guy named Mark Zelich, who'd been a news director for more than 30 years. He was kind of near the end of his career. He was a put-your-arm-around-you kind of guy who made sure that you were mentally healthy, too. A nurturing

> kind of news director, the perfect person for a first job. He loved active interviews. It's something I remember to this day. He called it 'grooming the cow.' He would say, 'Boyd, when you go interview the farmer, do the interview while he's grooming the cow. Don't interview the farmer and then get a shot of the cow. Do the interview while he's grooming the cow.' Farmers don't really groom their cows. But it still sticks with me."

Huppert is famous for his active interviews. Rarely will you see an interviewee sitting in a chair, unless that chair is part of the story. Grooming the cow applies to most stories. Whether it's fuel prices at a gas station, children in a kindergarten classroom or a physician in the emergency room, the best interviews are those that take place while your subject is doing something. It may take a little more work and planning, but the results make it worth it.

Remember the visual elements of an interview. You may have the best soundbites and content, but if your interview isn't shot properly with good audio and lighting, you are doing a disservice to your story.

During your interview, listen carefully and make note of the responses. Then, grab shots of the items or topics your interviewee mentioned to use in editing to avoid the dreaded "talking head." Get those additional shots after the interview, not during. You want those interview shots to be steady.

Remember WOCHU: wide shot, over-the-shoulder, closeup face, hands closeup and unusual. Shoot and move. Action reaction. Allow your subject to enter the frame. And, shoot repetitive action from different angles to help with your sequence.

Location

When planning a news story, visualize a location that would enhance, not detract from, the interview. For example, if you are covering a story about a water shortage, don't shoot your interview in an office complex. When it comes time to edit, you'll be bouncing back and forth between indoor shots and outdoor shots—losing continuity. Plan to shoot your interviews where they fit with the story. Remember Huppert's "groom the cow."

EDITING EFFICIENTLY

It takes time and lots of practice to get to the point where you feel confident with your editing. That means you're going to have to do some of the exploring and experimenting on your own time. That's how we learn.

Editing is more than just joining shots, soundbites and natural sound. It's melding your video and soundbites with the appropriate pace and rhythm—taking the moments you shot and creating a memorable story with a beginning, middle and end.

Editing is deciding what to keep and what to cut. It's how you take the 30 minutes of video you just shot and reduce it to a 1:30 package without losing any of the important details, visuals or emotion.

Editing helps you get your character from point A to point B without slowing the pace of the story. It speeds up or slows down a scene. Those sequences you shot will help you in the editing process and get you out of a jam.

Remember Joe Little's "Pregnant I" we talked about in Chapter 9? When you sit down to edit, the "Pregnant I" helps tie everything together. You've planned your story so that you know you will start with your main character and that you will transition to the broader topic. Then, you will come to the resolution that brings you back to your main character, which is how you will end your story. Little says:

> Because you shot for the character and you wrote for the character, even though I budgeted an hour for editing, I maybe need 20 minutes because I'm now editing for the character. I'm editing natural sound of my character. I got all this great video of my character. I don't have wallpaper video. I have specific, focused video of my character doing whatever it is he does. And now it's all focused on this thing.

This focus allows Little to edit more efficiently, leaving him extra time to get ready for his live shot.

Little has been doing this for a long time, and 20 minutes to edit a package is realistic for him. When you're just starting out, you're going to need a lot more time. That's why staying focused and shooting for the edit is so important.

Here are a few other tips to make your editing more efficient.

Get Organized

1. Organize your files: It starts with organizing your files. Remember in Chapter 9 how you organized your video on your external hard drive or computer desktop? Now you will do the same in your editing program.

    TV stations use a few different types of editing systems. The more common ones include Adobe Premiere Pro, Avid Media Composer, Final Cut Pro, and Edius. There are also dozens of desktop and mobile editing apps.

    Most non-linear editing systems are similar in their process. They use disk space on your computer or external hard drive to store your files. These include video files, audio files, jpegs, etc. It is critical that you organize all of your files so you know where they are, and your editing program knows where they are.

    When you edit, you will not actually be editing or modifying the original files. Your editing software is recording the instructions you give each time you make an edit, and it directs the playback of those files according to your instructions. This is why it is crucial that you keep all of your files organized and in one place to avoid getting the media offline alert.

2. Start a new project: Open the non-linear editor that you will be using. Each time you start editing a story, you should start a new project. Working from your external hard drive, start a new project and give it a name—usually the same slug you used when you wrote your script. Browse to the location on your external hard drive to make sure your project is saving to the project file that you created.

3. Create bins: To keep yourself organized, create bins. These are basically folders that show you where all of your files are. Name one bin "video." Now, go to that project file that you made on your external hard drive and drag all of the files from that video folder into your editing software's video bin. Create a second bin for your sequences or editing timelines.

4. Organize sub-clips: Now, open your video bin and organize your clips into sub-clips. Give each of your interviews its own bin. Organize your B-roll into additional bins by topic.

Now you're ready to edit. Because you've logged your video, indicated the shots on your script, and organized your video files in bins, you've already saved yourself a lot of time.

Starting the Editing Process

The key is to lay down the bones or foundation of your story first, and then fill it in with supporting video or B-roll.

When we talk about foundation, we're referring to the base of the story—like the cement slab under a house. A strong foundation will keep your timeline well organized and make it easier to raise the walls and roof of your story—or in this case the audio track, soundbites, B-roll and natural sound.

Editing Your Project

You will need either a printed or digital copy of your script to refer to as you edit your story. Figure 10.12 is a fictional story that is marked with editing instructions in the left column.

In this example, we are using Adobe Premiere Pro, but all non-linear editing systems have the same basic functions.

Start your story with compelling video and sound. Avoid starting with an interview soundbite unless the anchor intro makes clear that the first voice heard in the package will not be the reporter's.

1. Start by laying down the establishing shot with a NATS pop
2. Insert your first voice track (Audio 2), overlapping the first video so the voice track comes in during the first video.
3. Insert your first interview soundbite (Video 1/Audio 1).
4. Insert some natural sound.
5. Insert the second voice track.
6. Insert the second interview clip (Video 1/Audio 1).
7. Insert the third voice track, and so on.

Don't worry about the B-roll right now. You are only editing the foundation of your story: the voice track, NATS, soundbites and reporter stand-up.

It should look something like Figure 10.13. Note the natural sound pops that help each sound bite flow into the next.

[SOT] [NATS LEAVES] [video of trees and leaves blowing in wind]	{SOT} (rustling sound of leaves on the ground) [00] WITH EACH GUST OF WIND, THE COLORS OF FALL COVER THE FRESNO STATE CAMPUS.
[cu Fatima talking] [SOT] [CG:] [IN: I LOVE] [OUT: YELLOW ONE THERE] [02] [CU THEN WS FATIMA ON BENCH]	{SOT} (Fatima - "I love the yellow one there.") THIS IS FATIMA TEIXEIRA'S FAVORITE TIME OF YEAR ON CAMPUS. SHE HAS A FEW FAVORITE TREES AND STUDY SPOTS THAT
[SOT] [CG: Fatima Teixeira, Student] [IN: just makes me smile] [OUT: it's so pretty] [09]	{SOT} ("just makes me smile. The cooler temps give me more energy. I now spend more time on campus because I think it's so pretty.")
[SOT] [NATS SNEEZE] [CU FLOWERS IN TREE]	{SOT} (Person sneezing) IT'S ALSO TOUGH ON PEOPLE'S ALLERGIES .... ALL THE STUFF GETTING BLOWN AROUND WITH THE COLORFUL LEAVES.
[SOT] [CG: Kelly Bates, Student] [IN: As soon as I] [OUT: for my allergies.] [08]	{SOT} ("As soon as I see the first leaf change color, I grab my allergy meds and keep them with me. This is the worst time of year for my allergies.")
[SOT] [NATS frisbee group]	{NATS} BUT AS YOU WALK AROUND CAMPUS YOU FEEL AN ENERGY. IT'S LIKE PEOPLE ARE COMING OUT OF THE SUMMER HEAT SLUMP AND .... PLAYING.

Figure 10.12 Script Editing Instructions

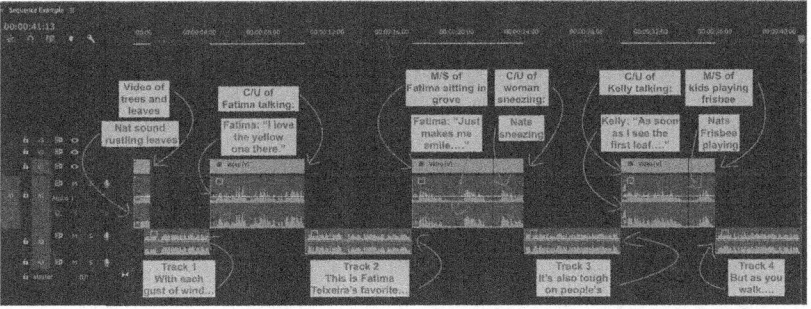

Figure 10.13 Editing Workflow

Some students and beginning MMJs insert random shots and soundbites once they get back from the interview and build their story that way. Avoid this, at least when you're starting out. Once you are an expert editor, you may develop your own editing strategy, but for now, follow this workflow because it helps you stay focused and manage your time well.

In Figure 10.13, notice that all of the interviews are on Video 1 (V1) and Audio 1 (A1) and the voice tracks (without connected video) are on Audio 2 (A2). This setup helps the editor see where sound and/or video is missing (the black areas).

The V1 video track will be filled in with B-roll that coincides with the words being spoken in the voice track. And the A1 or A3 audio tracks will be filled with NATS or background sound.

Once you've finished the foundation, it's time to add the B-roll and additional NATS. Lay down your B-roll with NATS (Video 2 and Audio 1 or 3, as seen in Figure 10.14).

Make sure you don't have any gaps in the timeline without sound and look out for missing video. If you shot sequences, your edit should go smoothly, especially if you shot sequences with a lot of tight and super-tight shots. If you didn't shoot sequences, you may find some of your shots don't go together without causing a jump cut, which breaks the continuity. The antidote for this is more B-roll. That's why you should always shoot enough B-roll.

Your edits should be simple cuts, clean and crisp. Look for opportunities for **match cuts**, when the action continues across two shots from different camera angles.

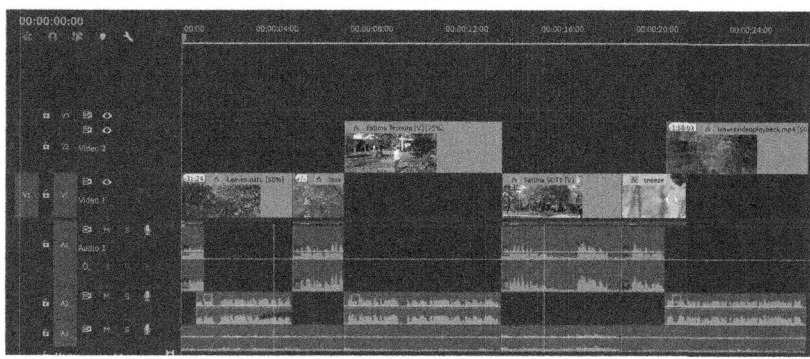

Figure 10.14 B-roll on Sequence

Cross dissolves may look pretty, but they should only be used for a change of scene or time. Most general assignment news stories use straight cuts.

Once you finish editing, take a moment to play back the sequence once or twice, watching the video and listening to the audio levels. Your voice track and soundbite audio should be in the −6 to −10 dB range. Background sound should be in the −20 to −25 range. Look for flashes of black (missing video), flash frames (a brief frame or two of video that causes a "flash" effect) or jump cuts, and correct them.

Once you review your video and make adjustments, you will need to export your sequence into a viewable movie file. Remember, you are not actually changing the video when using a non-linear editor. You are pointing to the video—giving the computer instructions on what the edits should look like once they are exported.

If you were to save the sequence or timeline and try to play it back without properly exporting it, you would get a media offline warning in a big red or black box, which is the last thing you want to see.

Your newsroom will have specific settings based on where your video will air or stream. A common broadcast format is H.264 with the preset High Quality 1080p HD. If you are exporting your video for digital only, your preset may be different.

When you export, clearly name the file using the same slug as the one on your script and in the rundown. Confirm that the file is saving to the output file in the project folder on your external hard drive or in the proper newsroom drive.

REMINDERS FOR SHOOTING AND EDITING
- Remember to keep all of your video, digital photos, audio and logs on an external hard drive organized into separate folders.
- Shoot sequences (XCU, CU, M, WS—try to make it 50% XCU AND CU).
- Shoot a variety of different focal lengths and angles (shoot and move).
- Allow the subject to enter the frame.
- Look for repetitive action and anticipate the next action.
- Look for reaction to the action.
- Avoid crossing the 180-degree line.

- Look for and avoid distractions in the background.
- Use a wireless lavalier microphone for interviews and stand-ups.
- Use a tripod (sticks).
  - Always use headphones when doing interviews and collecting sound.
  - Gather room tone (an old radio technique) for at least one minute from each location.
  - Remember to keep quiet when gathering sound.

QUESTIONS

1. Why is it important to use an external hard drive in the video storage and editing process?
2. What are the five main shots that make up a five-shot sequence?
3. Why should you use a tripod when shooting video?

TRY THIS

1. Pick an object and shoot a five-shot sequence (extra wide, wide, medium, tight, super-tight).
2. Shoot an example of action/reaction.

NOTES

1 PBS News Hour Student Reporting Labs, Retrieved from https://studentreportinglabs.org/tutorials/
2 Freedman, W. (2011). *It Takes More Than Good Looks to Succeed at Television News Reporting*, A Wealth of Wisdom, LLC, p. 138, ebook.
3 https://lesroseonline.com/tips-and-tricks/

Producing for Broadcast and Digital
Part 3

Producing the Broadcast Newscast

Eleven

In This Chapter	
What is a Newscast Producer?	182
Day in the Life of a Producer	184
Newscast Themes	185
Building a Newscast	187
Rating Periods (or Sweeps)	197
Running a Live Newscast	198
Breaking News	199
Reminders for Producing Broadcast News	202
Questions	202
Try This	202

Producers are among the most sought-after employees in the industry. A person can start in a medium to large market right out of college in this position and usually make more money than reporters in their first job.

This position can easily be a stepping stone to management. That can mean finding a market you like and staying there instead of moving around like many reporters and anchors must do to move up in the industry. The only way to make this a secure and exciting career is to know what you are doing.

> **Mentor Moment: Kevin Olivas, News Recruiter, Sinclair Broadcast Group**
>
> "If you know how to be a solid newscast producer, you are going to be in demand. There's a massive need for newscast producers over reporters, and it's been that way for several years."

DOI: 10.4324/9781003137016-11

WHAT IS A NEWSCAST PRODUCER?

Ask any producer and he or she will likely say, "I like to be in control of the newscast." It's usually less of a power trip and more about creativity.

A newscast producer is an artist, counselor, partner, commander and, yes, writer. The producer looks at the big picture while creating the newscast and does so with the stories that are pitched in the planning meeting. The producer pulls from other content sources, looks at a vast array of stories, and decides where they will go in the newscast and in what format.

"I love controlling it," says KNXV-TV senior producer Kianey Carter. "Being able to build it from the ground up myself. Seeing all of the elements and picking and choosing—putting something on TV that's different every day."

The artist part of the job comes in deciding how to effectively tell a story. Will video or graphics be used? Would a live shot be useful in showing something about the story? Should one reporter tell one aspect of the story and then toss to another reporter or anchor to tell a different side of the story? A producer gets to make a lot of creative choices each day.

Part of that artistic creation can also come from another lesson in humanities—history and perspective. You must be a student of history to know if a story is coming back around in a different iteration or if it relates to something else the community is familiar with.

No one can be expected to know everything about everything, so having a file of past stories can help immensely. We've talked about how important it is for assignment editors and reporters to do this. You, as a producer, should, too.

Let's say you have breaking news of a fire in the resort mountain community in your viewing area. Check your file to see when this community last went through this. Have an editor go back through the archives to find the video. Take a few moments to write something from an old script, or send that information to the live reporter. Having insight on a topic makes the reporter look smart. That perspective helps the viewer better understand the impact of the story.

The counselor part of the job comes in helping the reporter find focus with the story. You may also need to inspire or motivate a reporter who is having difficulty connecting to the story. You must see the big picture of the newscast as well as dig into each minor detail of the rundown that will create that theme.

Kevin Olivas describes a good producer as a part-time psychologist.

"Having the leadership skills to know how to 'read' people is important," Olivas says. "Knowing which people on your news staff need that leader who can tactfully but assertively tell them what they need to do and which people on your news staff do better if you just give them an assignment and then back off."

Those leadership skills include moments when you must manage colleagues who are twice or three times your age and experience level. It's daunting. Some veteran journalists will treat young producers as a child and undermine their decisions. This is when a producer must be firm and have a professional conversation with that veteran or, if necessary, take that conversation into the news director's office. You are in charge of that newscast. Period.

It's a balance of trust. A producer is a partner to the newscast anchor in making sure that anchor has plenty of information to accurately and energetically cover a story with proper facts and pronunciation. Just like in finding and sharing more insightful information with the live reporter on the fire, you can help the anchor in the same way.

Your job is to make the anchor look and feel in control. You should always work to make sure the anchor knows how to pronounce tricky words in scripts. A good producer should also look for ways to help the anchor appear well researched on a subject for ad-lib opportunities. Producers hope the anchors will do this on their own, but in any event, your job is to make the anchors shine.

Is his tie crooked? Have the floor director straighten it. Is her necklace out of place? Help her put it back in place. Are the lights creating awkward shadows? Ask the engineer to fix the lights or have the anchor move a little to get in the correct light line.

Yes, this attention to detail helps the anchors look good but in keeping an eye to that big picture, you are working with every player to ensure the *whole* product looks good, sounds good and is helpful and powerful for the viewer so that nothing distracts the viewer from getting important information. Building that kind of team connection is what makes good producers great and newsrooms stronger.

A producer is also a partner with the newscast director in turning creative, artistic ideas into reality with the technical tools at hand.

Once you build the rundown, you must meet with the director. The director will help you figure out if a camera or a monitor or a live feed is feasible when the rundown calls for it.

To use the analogy of painting, the newscast is the canvas, the producer is the painter and the director is in charge of the colors of paint and paintbrushes helping you create the vision on the canvas.

You are also a commander, keeping everyone on track to submit their work properly, on time and in the format needed for that specific newscast. When there's breaking news, you must calmly command the news crews to new fact-finding and information-sharing positions for the live newscast. You regularly communicate with everyone to make sure they're all aware of the plan and any changes that may come during the shift. When breaking news happens during the newscast, the assignment editor traditionally helps.

> **Mentor Moment: Bryan Lenocker, Executive Producer, WABC, New York**
>
> "I have always tried to stay focused on what is important and what needs to be handled right now. Speed is important, but so is focus. Don't jump around too much in the rundown. It leads to things being missed and causes more chaos. By the producer remaining calm it trickles down and you will have a better show. The director. The anchors. The reporters. The assignment desk. You will be a better leader to everyone working on the show."

And, the producer is a writer. You will write all of the stories in a newscast not taken care of by the reporters.

DAY IN THE LIFE OF A PRODUCER

While every newsroom has its own specific flow, rhythm and design, this is a rather standard look at a normal day for a producer. You should understand, though, that in the world of news, *normal* means ever-changing. Be ready for that. The one thing everyone in a newsroom in every capacity can count on is change. Every day is different.

You should come to work already having an idea of what's going on in the world and in that community. That means keeping up with what the station, and other stations in the market, have been reporting on in the hours before your shift begins. When you come to work and the planning meeting begins, you are up to speed on the topics of the day.

Sadly, not everyone takes their job that seriously. KTNV Las Vegas news director Nancy Bauer Gonzales says some of her producers "walk in straight from the street and sit down like they just rolled out of bed."

Bauer Gonzales also has producers who come into the meeting totally prepared.

"They know what networks are offering up. They know what's going on today. And, they know what happened last night. They know what was in our 11," Bauer Gonzales says.

Not all producers stay up to watch the late news. Some, especially those on the early morning shift, record the newscast and watch it as they get ready for work. That's the kind of dedication that's needed for this job.

In this planning meeting, the producers, assignment editors and reporters discuss the content that is available to them, will be covered or needs to be covered. Before this planning meeting, the producer goes through all of the content sources available to that newsroom. Those sources include the feeds the news station subscribes to: Associated Press, CNN, the network affiliate feeds and station ownership feeds.

The other content sources include the stories local reporters are covering, those already posted on the station's website and social platforms, and those trending on social media. This helps the producer know what the big story of the day is and how it will be covered in that specific newscast. Maybe something big is happening in a different part of the state, country or world. How can that story be localized to inform, connect or help the people in your community?

Once those questions are answered and local content is decided upon, you sit down at the computer and create the newscast. This is known as "building the rundown."

NEWSCAST THEMES

Every newscast has its own theme based on the timeslot. Knowing the theme and mission statement of your newscast is critical in choosing the stories that are of most interest to that specific audience. It helps to visualize the viewers in that audience, which will help you choose the stories for your particular newscast.

Morning News

Viewers are just waking up and getting ready for the day. In fact, these viewers are usually listening more than watching because they're getting ready for work or school. They want to know what will help them start their day. What is the weather and what will it be throughout the day? What's happening on the roads that may affect a viewer's commute? What is happening around the community and world? What will be happening today? Is there anything trending or popular that will give the viewer something fun to talk about with friends at work or school? What do parents need to know to help children prepare for the day?

> **Mentor Moment: Kianey Carter, Senior Producer**
>
> "I'm a fan of having a predictable rundown with unpredictable content. By that I mean, at 7:20 we always knew the money reporter was coming on. You could count on that. The viewer knows 'If I hear that segment and I'm still brushing my teeth, I'm late.' Those things work well, especially for a morning show."

Midday News

The viewers for this newscast either just got home from the overnight shift at work, are stay-at-home parents in the middle of late morning chores and errands or are working from home and don't have to wake up early.

These viewers are looking for a news update. Did something happen since this morning's news? Is there a big story I can get a little more in-depth information on? How will the weather be changing in the next few hours? Is something happening later today that I should know?

Mid-Afternoon News

These viewers are preparing for family to return home from work and school. It is likely the last little "me time" a stay-at-home parent will have in the day. These viewers want to know if the weather will be changing between now and tonight. What's happening on the roads that may affect the commute home? Education, family, health, cooking and entertainment news are popular themes for this time period, as well as the big news of the day.

Early Evening News

These viewers are traditionally making dinner and doing homework with the children. As with the morning news, they may be listening while multitasking at home. Common viewer interest is the weather. What's the big news of the day? What happened in the last few hours? What's the next step for that story? What's happening tonight?

Late Night News

These viewers are likely heading off to bed. Again, the weather is traditionally a top concern as they need to know what the weather will be like in the morning. Are there any commute issues the viewer should be aware of? Other big interests include a wrap-up of the day's news and a look ahead to what's happening tomorrow.

This is the mindset for producer Alex White at KFSN in Fresno.

"For the 11 o'clock, I'm fighting the clock with the audience who's wanting to go to bed," White says. "So, what can I give them that is really big off the top and grabs the attention?"

BUILDING A NEWSCAST

Now that you know the content available from the reporters and feeds, and know what the theme is for the show being built, it's time for the artist to come out. A producer chooses a good mix of content keeping in mind what stories should have priority over others, which stories flow well with each other and how the placement of those stories will bring about an interesting, compelling and energetic pace to the newscast.

In building that rundown, the producer meets with the director to note special effects and production concepts, the right time to call for video or graphics and makes sure all of the technical devices are working and available.

> **Mentor Moment: Kianey Carter, Senior Producer**
>
> "I don't think everything has to fit together. I just think you as the producer of the show have to believe in the story. So, if you think your audience wants to hear that Joe Jonas had a baby, then, OK, put that story in and believe in it. It just can't come out of left field for people. You can't have a story about a double murder and then talk about Joe Jonas having a baby."

The Rundown

Figure 11.1 is an example of a newscast rundown. All newsrooms customize their own rundowns, so the one you use in your student newsroom or at a local TV station may look different.

In this example, you will notice several different columns. Moving from left to right, the first column is the page number broken down into segments or **blocks**. For example, with A1, "A" is the first block of the newscast and "1" is the first page, which matches the page number on the script.

The second column is the story **slug** (the brief title of the story).

The next column is the **talent**, the name of the anchor who will read the story. You'll hear that referred to as the "anchor read."

Next comes the shot column. The producer uses this column to indicate whether the anchor is telling the story on a one-shot or on-cam, on a two-shot with a co-anchor, on a three-shot with a guest, or in a box with a reporter in the field. The newscast director uses this column to note which camera will get those shots. The director is also looking at whether another set in the studio might be used for this camera shot.

\multicolumn{10}{c}{Show #7}									
								Under 00:01:03 / TRT 00:28:27	
Page	Story Slug	Talent	CAM/SHOT	Format	Writer	Source	Est. Duration	Actual	Back Time	Front Time
A2	OPEN		(off top)	SOT + music			00:00:30	00:00:01	4:01:03 PM	4:00:00 PM
A3	WELCOME	B/T	2&3/2 BOX				00:00:05	00:00:05	4:01:33 PM	4:00:30 PM
A4	FRESNO ORANGE TIER VO	TASHA	2/1 SHOT	VO	ASHLEY		00:00:25	00:00:25	4:01:38 PM	4:00:35 PM
A5	VERDICT REAX INTRO	BROOKE	3/1 SHOT	INTRO	ASHLEY		00:00:10	00:00:11	4:02:03 PM	4:01:00 PM
A6	VERDICT REAX PKG			PKG	ASHLEY		00:00:40	00:00:00	4:02:13 PM	4:01:10 PM
A7	CHAUVIN VO	BROOKE	3/1 SHOT	VO	ASHLEY		00:00:10	00:00:11	4:02:53 PM	4:01:50 PM
A8	CHAUVIN SOT VO	BROOKE		SOT VO	ASHLEY		00:00:30	00:00:27	4:03:03 PM	4:02:00 PM
A9	STREET VENDOR SAFETY INTRO	TASHA	2/1 SHOT	INTRO	GIO		00:00:15	00:00:16	4:03:33 PM	4:02:30 PM
A10	STREET VENDOR SAFETY PKG			PKG	GIO		00:01:45	00:01:45	4:03:48 PM	4:02:45 PM
A11	STREET VENDOR SAFETY TAG	TASHA	2/1 SHOT	TAG	GIO		00:00:10	00:00:11	4:05:33 PM	4:04:30 PM
A12	JOBS STRUGGLE INTRO	BROOKE	3/1 SHOT	INTRO	WYATT		00:00:10	00:00:07	4:05:43 PM	4:04:40 PM
A13	JOBS STRUGGLE PKG			PKG	WYATT		00:01:48	00:01:49	4:05:53 PM	4:04:50 PM
A14	JOBS STRUGGLE TAG	BROOKE	3/1 SHOT	TAG	WYATT		00:00:10	00:00:09	4:07:41 PM	4:06:38 PM

Figure 11.1 Rundown Example

It's important to work closely with the newscast director and know what the technical capabilities are in making this rundown work. Many TV stations have eliminated a lot of positions and rely on production automation systems, which in some cases the director must operate.

It is not uncommon for the director to double as the technical director (TD), operating the switcher and calling the shots at the same time. Some directors are required to operate the switcher, graphics, audio, video, robotic cameras and cue the talent, all while keeping track of pacing and flow of the newscast. That's taking multitasking to a whole new level.

The next column is for the format of the story. This is where the producer indicates whether the story is a reader, a reader with graphics, a VO, a VOSOT, a PKG, a live shot or an interview.

The next column shows the writer of the story, usually the producer or reporter who originated the story.

The next column is used for the source of the story—a live shot or if the video is coming from a network feed.

The last four columns are used for timing purposes. The estimated duration column is the guestimate made by you or the reporter for how long a story will run. This time will change once the story is edited and an accurate time is known.

The actual time column is the time the computer gives a particular story based on the word count.

The last two are the back time and **front time** columns. The front time counts from the beginning of the newscast and shows when each element should hit if the newscast is running on time. The back time counts from the end of the newscast and shows when each element should hit if the producer is to end the show on time. The computer makes these calculations so the producer doesn't have to.

The number at the top of the rundown shows the producer how light or heavy the newscast is—meaning whether the newscast is running long and something needs to be cut or the newscast is short and ad-libbing may be needed. In the example in Figure 11.1, the producer is going into the show one minute and three seconds light.

Priority

Sometimes stories are placed in chronological order or topic themes such as crime or politics. Some are placed in terms of impact or how much they're being talked about in the community or social media. Others are just the biggest story of the day and are an obvious lead. Knowing your newscast theme can help the producer decide the story order and placement.

You also must take into consideration the timeliness of the story—when it happened. If people have been getting updates on the big story on social media, you can't write the story as if it's new.

"We can't come out of the gate at 11 and say, 'A deadly shooting in Times Square this afternoon,'" says Bryan Lenocker, executive producer at WABC in New York. "We have to say, 'We have new pictures tonight of the person police say opened fire in Times Square, and he's still on the run tonight.' It's all in the wording. It's a different way of thinking, but when you start doing that, it will give your show a different feel."

Pacing

No matter the placement, you must make sure there's a pace and energy to the newscast. Think of it like driving a car. When you push the accelerator, you can feel the power of the car. Pull your foot off the gas pedal, and the car slows. Having a natural flow of fast and slow can work, but make sure it's not so much that it feels disjointed or disorienting.

> **Mentor Moment: Cyndee Hebert, Managing Editor of News Content, WTHR 13, Indianapolis**
>
> "It's not only the words that have to be engaging, it has to be what you're watching. Even your lower thirds have to help tell the story. You don't want boring video in a monitor behind the anchor because that's going to ruin the pacing. Graphics must help tell a story and not just fill a hole."

Flow

If multiple reporters are covering multiple angles of a story, would it look good, and would it be technically possible to show each live reporter in a box on the screen with the anchors? This visual shows the viewer that your team is all over the story. It helps with showing and creating the topic flow of a story. It's also important that you meet with the director to decide how to make these technical things happen.

When creating flow, try to not put stories in silos. By that we mean, if the big story of the day is a local golfer winning the U.S. Open, you don't need to wait for the traditional sports block to run that story. It could be the lead of the newscast with more angles of that story later in the sports segment.

You also don't need to put *all* crime stories together or all fires together. The flow of the newscast comes from what's called the process language.

"The writing is how you bring flow between unrelated stories," says Luis Felipe Godinez, Sacramento Univision news director. "We are in this knowledge that things need to be linked. But what you really need to do is take people through this newscast. Guide them through it."

"Yes, you should put stories that are alike together," Lenocker says. "But that doesn't mean you do six crime stories in a row and then six political stories. Should all of those be together? How can you break them up? Can you combine any of those stories or present them differently?"

Lenocker recommends doing anything you can to break up the traditional way of presenting stories.

Simply put, the producer is always thinking about the viewer benefit with each story placement. Everything you write is for the viewer. It's not for you. Maybe you love video games and superheroes. There may be a place for an occasional story on those topics, or your newscast research may show the viewer is *not* interested in that. Then, you cannot write about it for that newscast. Knowing the key interest and theme of the newscast helps in choosing the stories as we just talked about with newscast themes.

Here are other opportunities for you to add viewer benefit in a newscast which in turn helps build story priority, pacing and flow.

Perspective

Earlier we talked about the importance of adding historical perspective to a story. If a reporter does the "nuts and bolts" of a story, meaning the facts and figures of something, the producer can create a perspective moment after that story. It can be as simple as a graphic or archive video of something from the past that relates to the present. That can either be a few sentences from the anchor at a monitor showing that graphic or video or an anchor toss to a different reporter for that other side of the story.

To use the example of the coronavirus, many newsrooms looked at the similarities and differences between this virus, the flu and allergies so people could better understand the symptoms and when to call the doctor. Newsrooms also compared it to past pandemics like SARS in 2002, Bird Flu of the late 1990s and Spanish Flu of 1918 for perspective on its contagiousness and spread.

Reassurance

Some stories can be unsettling and a moment of calm is needed. Again, that may come from a few simple words from an anchor or some video, graphic or picture that offers reassuring facts or historical perspective. In our coronavirus story example, reassurance was offered with information about handwashing, mask-wearing, social distancing and vaccine opportunities.

Forward the Story

If something else may be happening in the next few hours or days or months ahead relating to a story, it must be added to the newscast. It can be a simple anchor tag to a reporter package or live shot or a quick story with a graphic of what's to come next.

To forward the coronavirus story, anchors gave information about when the president's task force would be updating the country, what new biotech company was working on a vaccine, when and where people could get the vaccine, and as things progressed, the status of a possible booster shot.

Helpful Information

When the coronavirus first started hitting U.S. communities, common stories helped viewers spot the differences between this virus and the common cold, flu and allergies. Other helpful information included places where people could get tested for free.

Where do you get that information? Stan Heist, director of news training and development for Sinclair Broadcast Group, says as our world evolves, so too must our mindset in the newsroom.

"Our viewers have become accustomed to interviews via Skype or Zoom or whatever technology," Heist says. "Producers, who used to do an interview over the phone, can interview someone quickly for a sound bite or digital story over video and suddenly you have a whole new piece of content there."

Community Connection

Some viewers want information and then want to move on. Others need to feel a deeper connection to a story and the people involved.

Your job is to create moments for the anchors or reporters to share that connection.

> **Mentor Moment: Cyndee Hebert, Managing Editor of News Content**
>
> "That's your job to make the anchors feel comfortable on the air and make them look good. Because if I'm working eight hours on a show, I want them to carry it off and look good so we can all be proud of our hard work."

Social media is another part of that community connection. Many news stations include areas on their website or social channels where people can connect and share comments and pictures on topics.

It's always important after a story to include a graphic and reminder for TV viewers to get more information and connect with others on social media. This, of course, is not necessary for every story. Meet with your social media producer and pick one for that specific newscast. And then, be sure to use that interaction and those viewer pictures on the air.

Teases

Once the story slugs are entered into the rundown (with the anchor reads, story format and estimated time for each story), it's time for you to decide which stories should be teased at the beginning and throughout the newscast.

Writing teases early in the shift is a smart move because it's usually when a producer is most creative. Waiting until right before the newscast is a time when the stress level is high, which can eclipse your creativity.

Good effective teases are critical in keeping a newscast audience watching. Writing them early gives an editor time to get the perfect, compelling sound and pictures without rushing.

Good teases make the viewer want to stay to see the story. What makes a good tease? Maybe a piece of sound like, "Woah, I've never seen anything like that before!" Or an unusual piece of video like the inside of a car ripped apart and the script says something about how a black bear got inside this Toyota Prius and what it was looking for. Some stations call that "Shot, SOT, Surprise." Figure 11.2 gives a few examples of the right way and the wrong way to write a tease.

As you see in these examples, in creating good teases, you must look for interesting or surprising video, or compelling sound. Then, write to that video without giving away the whole story. You should always ask your editors, photojournalists and reporters if they have any of this compelling sound.

That quick natural sound (**NATS**) can bring the viewer right to the emotion or sense of the story. Producers can use this nat sound in a **cold open** (a video tease at the beginning of the newscast), in a tease

YES:	FIRE IN DOWNTOWN ORANGEVILLE TONIGHT. SEE HOW A CHILD'S QUICK THINKING KEPT THE FLAMES FROM DESTROYING AN ENTIRE APARTMENT BUILDING.
NO:	AN EARLY MORNING MANHUNT IN A DOVER NEIGHBORHOOD.
YES:	[NAT SOT "come out with your hands up."] 　　THAT'S WHAT WOKE UP PEOPLE IN THIS DOVER NEIGHBORHOOD AT FOUR THIS MORNING. 　　WE'LL TELL YOU WHAT HAPPENED AFTER THAT LOUD ANNOUNCEMENT AND WHY POLICE WERE CONCERNED FOR EVERYONE'S SAFETY.
NO:	ANOTHER CAR BREAK-IN IN SOUTHEAST WILSONVILLE.
YES:	PARK RANGERS AREN'T KIDDING WHEN THEY SAY THROW AWAY YOUR FOOD. 　　SEE WHAT A HUNGRY BEAR DID TO THE INSIDE OF THIS CAR FOR A CANDY WRAPPER.

Figure 11.2 Creative Tease Writing

going to the commercial break or on social media giving viewers a piece of the story that they can see in its entirety on the TV broadcast.

"For every story I tease, in a column in the rundown I write that I teased it." Carter says. "If two stories go together, I write 'connected to story above,' so I know if I kill the first story, I have to kill both or re-write the intro or lead of the one I saved."

Carter doesn't want the anchors to tease a story that got dropped. That makes the anchors look bad. It makes the viewers wonder about a missed story, and it produces a newscast that does not deliver on what was promised. It's a simple mistake to avoid if you pay attention to your rundown.

If there is a graphics designer, now is a good time to meet to discuss what will be needed in the show. If a story doesn't have video, the graphics designer can create a visual to help the anchor explain something. Maybe it's a map. Maybe it's a picture with an address or bullet points of helpful information.

Again, waiting until the last minute is not a good time to ask a graphics designer or any colleague to slam together something creative for the newscast. Keep in mind, breaking news can always happen, so having everything in place early helps everyone create a strong, well-balanced, informative, compelling newscast.

Note: Some producers will ask their talent to shoot a **promo** or **topical** while in the field covering a story. You'll want to get topicals for your best stories to drive viewers to your newscast. These topicals can air on TV and on social media.

The Little Things

At this point, you have built the rundown, and anyone looking at it can clearly tell the story content, who's reading it and in what format. The so-called little things to check are important so no one has any doubt of what's intended. That includes *inside* the story script, too. Let's say you have Tasha's name in the rundown reading the story slugged Fresno Orange Tier. Her name must also be at the top of the story script in the [TAKE ANCHOR] cue. It should read: {1-SHOT TASHA}.

Keeping an eye on the so-called little things includes the spelling in each script including the CG names and locations and full-screen graphics. It includes checking the TRT on all SOTs and packages in the scripts and in the rundown to make sure the newscast is properly timed.

A4 - FRESNO ORANGE TIER VO				00:00:25
NOTES:		Format:	VO	
Writer:	ASHLEY	Talent:	TASHA	
CAM/SHOT:	2/1 SHOT	Source:		

[Tasha]	**{TASHA}** FRESNO COUNTY IS NOW IN THE ORANGE TIER. RESTRICTIONS ARE EASING UP SO MORE PEOPLE CAN GET OUT AND ABOUT.
[TASHA VO] [CG: Fresno County]	**{TASHA VO}** RESTAURANTS AND MOVIE THEATERS CAN INCREASE THEIR INDOOR CAPACITY TO 50 PERCENT. GYMS GET 25 PERCENT CAPACITY INDOORS … SAME WITH WINERIES AND BREWERIES. AND SOME EXCITING NEWS FOR STUDENTS. THE HENRY MADDEN LIBRARY IS NOW OFFERING STUDY SPACES ON THE FIRST FLOOR. THEY WILL BE OPEN WEEKDAYS FROM EIGHT TO FIVE. SEATS ARE FIRST COME FIRST SERVE. JUST IN TIME FOR FINALS.

Figure 11.3 Broadcast News Script Example

And, double-check any work someone else did for you to ensure it was done and done correctly.

Timing

All of the scripts should be completed an hour before the newscast airs. That's the goal.

So, if there's breaking news or something big needs to change, there's time to add that without feeling frazzled.

During this final hour before the newscast, go through the rundown and check for errors. Create better flow between stories if necessary. Rewrite or tweak a lead or story tag. Meet with the anchors to answer any questions they might have.

This is also a good time to meet again with the newscast director to make sure everything technical will work. And, it's critical that well before the newscast begins, you know the timing of the show, which stories could be dropped if you're over, or what can be plugged in to replace something else.

A newscast is literally timed to the second. There is little room to be off, even by a few seconds, because commercial breaks come in at a specific time. The end of a newscast and the next program air at a specific time. The commander aspect of the job must be attuned to the clock, and make sure everyone is aware of the time.

Every producer has a trick or two when it comes to timing. Carter says she's an over-stacker. That means she'll put more stories in the newscast than she has time for. She'd rather kill a story than try to find one to fill a hole in the rundown.

"I'll write a story and in another column in the rundown I'll write 'kill' or 'kill first' to help with my timing," Carter says.

Sure, the computer program of the rundown times the newscast. It will tell you how over or under a newscast is based on the estimated story duration column. But, a good producer also manually backtimes the newscast as a backup. Just in case.

Don't freak out about the math. This is actually pretty easy. Start with the absolute time your newscast must be out. Let's say it's 4:28:30.

If you need 30 seconds after your anchors say goodbye, then they should be finished talking by 4:28:00. If the final story runs 30 seconds, then the anchor must begin reading that story at 4:27:30. You keep back timing all the way up to the start of the newscast or at least up to the first commercial break. It can give a producer a big peace of mind.

RATING PERIODS (OR SWEEPS)

There are four big months of the year when many TV stations work to bring in the viewers: February, May, July and November. These are the traditional times of the year when you are expected to be at work, not go on vacation, get married or get sick.

The ratings numbers (how many people are watching your newscast) help the sales department come up with how much the station will charge businesses to run a commercial during those newscasts based on the number of viewers watching at that time. That money is the main way stations pay the bills, including your salary.

With more markets buying overnight ratings services, ratings months are becoming less stringent, because *every* day is considered a ratings day.

Those overnight ratings numbers show how many people are watching and when those people turn the channel. The producer's job is to keep the viewer from turning the channel.

Many newsrooms have a clock that the producer builds the show around meaning that a newscast must hit a segment or commercial break at a specific time. A promotional producer may work closely with a newscast producer to build an alluring tease that corresponds with a promo that's been running all day for a specific story such as the one in this video example.

> **Author Note—Kim Stephens**
>
> "When I worked at NBC Bay Area in San Jose, I did a story on a design called The Shark Shield—something surfers wear as a shark repellant. The story was teased throughout the day and then teased as the newscast went to the first commercial break. My story led the second block. The next day we looked at the overnight ratings to see if people stayed through the commercial and they did. That was considered a success."

Aside from thinking about the priority, pacing, flow, perspective and community connection of stories while timing the rundown, you must also hit certain times in that rundown according to ratings research.

RUNNING A LIVE NEWSCAST

About five minutes before the newscast begins, the producer gets in place in the control room or booth. At this moment, your mindset changes from writer and show creator to command and control—the captain of the ship.

Here, you and the director talk about last-minute plans or concerns. You will check the anchor **IFB**s, the earpiece anchors and reporters wear to hear important information from the producer. You will check in with the live crews to make sure they can hear you and are ready.

During the newscast, the producer listens to everything going on in the control room to make sure everyone's doing what is envisioned in the rundown. The producer also listens to the newscast to ensure the anchors and reporters are following the plan and are reading the correct words in the scripts.

This can be a stressful time. Keeping focused and calm is important. If something happens that strays from your vision, you must have a Plan B or Plan Z depending on how far the newscast goes off the rails.

The director and anchors will be looking to you for guidance on what to do or where to go next if, for example, a video or live shot freezes, an anchor starts coughing or the wrong story runs. Having a plan can save a newscast and keep the viewer from knowing anything crazy was happening behind the scenes. That's the goal for every player in the live newscast—never let the viewer notice a mistake. It's important to move on immediately and smoothly, and deal with the emotions later, Commander.

> **Mentor Moment: Kianey Carter, Senior Producer**
>
> "My advice for producers is to talk with your anchors about the show. I think one of the most enlightening moments for me was a conversation I had with an anchor when I was new to the job. The anchor asked me why I built the show the way I did. She then told me what she thought I did well and what I could improve upon. If I had not asked that anchor, I would never have learned. It was constructive criticism that I'll always remember."

BREAKING NEWS

When breaking news happens, the assignment desk is the epicenter of information. It's the huddle where everyone on the news team learns their part of the play: who goes where, who covers what angle of the story, etc. That helps keep each reporter focused on his or her story, and it gives the producers a clear roadmap of the topics that will be covered in each newscast.

It's during these intense and exciting times when the producers and assignment editor create the story plan. They may decide to have a reporter cover the nuts and bolts of a story for the 5 p.m. newscast, for example, but cover a different, more creative or character-driven angle of the story at 6 p.m.

During these breaking news events, the assignment editor is also in contact with the network and other TV stations that are asking for live shots and video.

The ability to stay calm is an important attribute. When news breaks during a live newscast, the assignment editor must be in direct communication with the newscast producer so they can decide how to get the story on the air quickly and accurately.

> **Mentor Moment: Tracie Potts, NBC News Washington Correspondent**
>
> "As a live reporter, I need an organized show producer. What time do I hit? Is the anchor asking questions? What are the questions? At least give me topics. How much time do I have? By 'live-VO' do you want me to talk for a minute or do you really envision Q&A with your anchors? Communication is key. A bad newscast happens when I don't know the plan in advance; anchors suddenly toss to me unexpectedly, and I'm in the middle of a key point and get a short 'wrap' because I wasn't told how long to speak."

In many stations, an assistant producer will write the breaking news story and ready the crews or feed. Then the producer will alert the director and anchors. That's a perfect-world scenario. Let's instead talk about everything falling on your shoulders, which is more realistic.

Carter says breaking news is a process that must be done quickly and preferably in a certain order. Once, while producing the morning newscast, she found out about breaking news during a commercial break. She had 30 seconds until the newscast returned, and that was not enough time to get the story on cleanly.

"You've got to understand, yes, I need to get it in. I just can't blow everything up and risk imploding the show," Carter says.

She says because effective communication is key, she used the 30 seconds left in the commercial break to tell the director that live video would be coming from the station's helicopter. Then, she told the anchors.

"Tell the director because that's the first person who has to take it on the air," Carter says. "Tell my anchors so they know exactly what we're going to do. Then tell my photog who's probably already ready, but tell the photog and reporter how long before they're coming up."

Then, Carter looked at the rundown to figure out where to insert the story, typed up a few words and told everyone how much time they had. Sounds pretty smooth.

"No, breaking news hasn't always gone that smoothly," Carter laughs. "It comes with a lot of practice."

It helps if the producer shares a few facts and a source with the director and news anchors. The director will tell the producer when the video or live pictures are ready to go. Carter used the commercial break to alert the anchors when they were able to fully listen. If the newscast was back on, she would have waited for a moment to tell each anchor when they weren't reading a story.

In a situation like that, when the anchors are live on the air, the producer would tell anchor A while anchor B is reading a script. Or, the producer might wait for a package or even a SOT to tell one or both anchors what's happening. If you must break in immediately, while the anchor is reading, a producer must be brief and to the point in the IFB. Make sure you press the IFB button completely before speaking into the mic. No full sentences. Here's an example:

"Breaking news next."
"Fire."
"Sequoia National Park."
"Follow script."
"Ad-lib."

A good anchor needs just a few facts: what and where. Then, once the live pictures appear, the anchor will talk about what is being seen on the screen. The anchor would love to have more facts or a few short words in the teleprompter to help in this ad-libbing. A new, unpracticed anchor might need a full script. If that is not possible, then that's when the commander/producer talks in the IFB sharing information.

A fictional example of this is in the movie *Broadcast News* as the producer, played by Holly Hunter, talks into the ear of the anchor, played by William Hurt. The few facts Hunter shared in this movie scene helped Hurt build an incredible story based on the pictures he and the viewer saw.

This symbiosis can be an amazing and magnetic moment of teamwork in real life as it was in this movie.

> **Mentor Moment: Chad Hypes, News Director, KTVL, Medford**
>
> "It's ALWAYS better to be right than first. It may not always be fair, but people expect us to be accurate 100% of the time. Viewers don't care that this is your first job, and they do not care that you were working on multiple stories. That means that you must make sure you have all the info you need before presenting it to the public. Double and triple check statistics."

REMINDERS FOR PRODUCING BROADCAST NEWS

- Write your teases before you write your show.
- It is a producer's job to make the anchors look good.
- Choose a story or two in your broadcast news rundown that you are willing to float or drop just in case time gets away from you.
- Each newscast has its own theme. That will help with story choice and placement.
- Producers should talk with their anchors for ideas and advice.
- Producers should meet with the newscast director when building the rundown.

QUESTIONS

1. What makes an effective producer?
2. What are three things a producer must consider when deciding the order of stories in the rundown?
3. What's the producer's job when it comes to the news anchors?
4. Why is timing the newscast so important?
5. What should be included to create an effective tease?

TRY THIS

1. Conduct a planning meeting where classmates share story ideas.
2. Build a newscast rundown based on those ideas.

Producing for Digital and Social Media

Twelve

In This Chapter

What is a Digital Producer?	204
Getting Permission to Share Pictures and Video	206
Writing the Web Story	207
OTT (Over-The-Top)	210
Social Media	211
What About the Haters?	218
Trends and Analytics	219
Reminders for Producing for Digital and Social Media	222
Questions	222
Try This	222

When was the last time you watched a television newscast? Fewer people are getting their news from TV now and instead are connecting to news and information through websites, streaming services, mobile apps and social media. Those are the fastest-growing and evolving aspects of news gathering and storytelling. They are ever-evolving and still a conundrum as to how TV stations can make money with digital news compared to traditional broadcast news.

As John Colucci, senior director of social media at Sinclair Broadcast Group, says:

> Social media is a brand-building tool; however, you can't earn money on that alone, and it's difficult to quantify linear TV viewer growth from social. So, the focus for most TV stations is on web traffic, or you could say 'clicks,' since it's hard to quantify driving viewers to a linear TV broadcast from social.

By "clicks," Colucci means anytime someone clicks on a picture or story on a station's website.

DOI: 10.4324/9781003137016-12

There is no way to definitively know, as of this writing, how many people go to watch a TV news broadcast after interacting with the station on the web or through their social media channels.

While corporate, station managers and sales teams figure that out, let's learn how to post, share, engage and build our news product digitally, which means telling and sharing stories across digital platforms.

While we focus in this chapter on the title of digital producer, it is important to know that every newsroom employee is expected to post and share content digitally. Some days this multitasking can feel overwhelming. The newsrooms that have a clear, digital job-flow ease that burden by sharing in the work and the rewards.

> **Mentor Moment: John Colucci, Senior Director, Social Media, Sinclair Broadcast Group**
>
> "One minute, you're writing your own web story assigned from the assignment desk and posting that to social. Maybe the next you're turning on a live stream from a breaking news story and live-tweeting what's happening, or re-tweeting the reporter on the scene doing the same. The next, you're copy-editing and posting a web script from a reporter and the next, coming up for a little air. It's a lot. It's fun, but you have to be open to doing a ton of things at once, and be ready for anything."

WHAT IS A DIGITAL PRODUCER?

Every aspect of a TV station's product on social media and the station's website is this digital producer's responsibility. This person posts stories to the station website then takes those stories and engages with viewers by sharing on Twitter, Facebook, YouTube, Instagram and in some cases Pinterest, Snapchat and TikTok. This job goes beyond cutting and pasting a hyperlink and picture into a social timeline.

News used to be journalists talking to the viewer through the television. Now, we're talking and interacting with the viewer through the computer and cell phones, working as a team to celebrate, bring about change, empower and connect with the community.

Now, news is a multiplatform conversation. Digital content allows a news organization to have an interactive relationship with its audience. It allows the audience to be a part of something in their community.

Digital content also allows for constant communication and updates, empowering people with knowledge at their fingertips. It, therefore, requires relentless follow-up on the part of the journalist and digital content team.

Digital content takes the audience beyond the TV news broadcast offering more information with links and other connections that cannot be included on TV, usually for time reasons.

"Beyond the broadcast" can also mean behind the scenes which is another way to connect with the audience, taking them behind the curtain to see things they don't get to see during a traditional TV broadcast.

> **Mentor Moment: Lisa Argen, Meteorologist, KGO, San Francisco**
>
> "Today, we can reach more people constantly with so many platforms. It's a new outlet that demands ever-changing digital skills, shorter snippets and highly engaging graphics. I'm my own producer and photographer when I communicate on TV, Twitter, or Instagram. We offer more content to our viewers by reaching out to them all hours of the day."

Digital media is now one of the best ways for newsrooms to get story tips and cover stories crews cannot get to. Using viewers' pictures and videos, making those viewers community correspondents, so to speak, strengthens the connection between the newsroom and audience.

The newsroom gets to expand its content with little effort and the audience gets to feel as if it's part of the news team.

> **Mentor Moment: Brandon Mercer, Digital Content Director, SF Gate, San Francisco**
>
> "So often people say so much of journalism is just catering to what the audience wants. Yes, if you're good at catering to what the audience wants. But you can also cater to what the audience needs."

GETTING PERMISSION TO SHARE PICTURES AND VIDEO

We cannot just copy a video or picture from someone's post and share it on our own page or website or in our newscast even if we credit the source. We must always ask for permission.

Some newsrooms will require an official digital form signed by the original photographer as proof. Many people will give permission as they know they'll be credited by the news station for the picture or video. What a thrill to know a TV station is using your photograph. Even knowing that, we must get that person's permission. Period.

If a TV station is tagged in a picture, some stations take that as automatic permission to use that image. Other stations still require official permission. You must know your station's rule on this. It is a breach of **copyright** to ever take someone's image from social media without permission.

There are some places where the pictures and video may be used on TV and shared (with the appropriate courtesy). That's most U.S. government works that are created by a federal government employee as part of their official duties.[1] It's a good idea to check. Again, you must ensure that the photo is from *that* agency and that they didn't get it from someone else. Just because the government agency got permission to use the picture, does not mean the permission transfers to the media.

If the local sheriff's department made a huge pot bust in the mountains, pictures of the bust, even the helicopter video may be used with permission and credited. If the agents posted their own pictures and video, then you *must* get permission from them. The rules, laws and legal interpretation are still fuzzy, so always getting permission will serve you well.

Sarah Light is a digital producer at WNCN in Raleigh, North Carolina. She's part of a team of nine who focus on separate aspects of digital storytelling. Some of her daily tasks include writing stories on the station website.

"I'm constantly looking for new content. We try to post on social media every 20 to 30 minutes," Light says.

Research shows journalists must hook their broadcast audience within the first seven seconds of a newscast or story to keep them watching for the next few minutes.[2]

With digital news, that hook must come in the first three to four seconds of a person seeing a web headline or post. Pictures and **headlines** must be compelling and unique. Content trumps the traditional story format.

> **Mentor Moment: Sarah Light, Digital Producer, WNCN, Raleigh**
>
> "The digital content producer is the glue of the newsroom. Not only do you produce content for digital, but you also oversee all aspects of the newsroom. Be prepared to call and confirm information when needed, and write stories with 100% accuracy, all while monitoring social media and doing other daily work tasks. It can be a high-stress job, but it's rewarding to be able to publish a story the public should know about."

WRITING THE WEB STORY

Reporters are expected to turn their own broadcast stories into web stories. But those stories are just a fraction of what will be posted on a station's website. The rest is done by the digital team.

> **Mentor Moment: Nick King, Sports Anchor/Reporter 3TV/CBS5, Phoenix**
>
> "One of the most challenging parts of television can be time restrictions. A lot of times, I'll feel like the story I'm working on deserves more time than I'm being allotted in the newscast. So, I'll do a longer 'web' version of the story, and a shorter TV version of the story. Or, maybe there's a sidebar, that isn't exactly relevant to what I'm focusing on, but it's interesting in its own right. My general rule with social media is the same one I have with what goes into a sportscast on TV: be interesting, be funny, be memorable."

In the early days of the web, reporters posted their web stories *after* those stories aired on the TV newscast. Now, the trend is to flip that mindset and post to the web and social *before* the story airs on TV. Then, share each of these posts on social media, and after the story airs on broadcast, go back and update the web stories.

"When reporters go out on stories, they aren't just going out and shooting their story and cutting their story," says Nancy Bauer Gonzales, news director at KTNV, Las Vegas. "They're going out and getting still pictures. They're getting information. They're putting it on the web. They're writing the first story for the web and then secondarily comes the television side. If it's huge, then they get on both at once."

Headline, Byline and Dateline

Every station has its own online style which is usually mandated by the station ownership, but each format stems from the foundation of AP style.

The main ingredients of a web story include the headline, byline, dateline, story and media. The headline should be catchy and alluring. Don't tell too much, but don't be so creative that the reader is confused. Sometimes saying exactly what the story is about is best. For example: "Car slams into family's bedroom" or "Baby saved from burning car."

The byline is the reporter's name, the writer of the story or the newsroom staff. The dateline is the location of the story.

Web Story

Broadcast news leads are written in the active voice. They are conversational and focus on the now. It's OK to use active *past tense* writing in web stories. You may be writing this as something is happening or just happened, but you have no idea when the audience is reading this web story. It could be two hours after the story happened, two days or even two months later.

In web writing, there is no place for "happening right now" or "yesterday" or "tomorrow." You must write the time and date. That is "print" writing. Active and conversational writing is still acceptable in web writing. Keep the writing tight, and clear.

Example:

> The free COVID-19 testing site runs for three days at the South Valley Fairgrounds. From 9 a.m. to 4 p.m. January 14 to 16, people can drive up, stay in their car and get the nasal swab test.

Remember when we talked about our broadcast news sentences being short and direct? In web writing, you may include more complex sentences.

Example:

> Most people are reporting mild symptoms like fatigue and a headache. But some people, especially those with medical conditions, develop more severe symptoms, including pneumonia, which can be fatal.

Attribution in web writing is different than in broadcast writing. In broadcast writing, we put the attribution, the name of the person who said something, in front of the paraphrase. In web writing, we place the attribution at the end of the first sentence, according to AP style.

Web example:

> A family packed into their van to get tested. The parents and three teenagers were visibly excited.
>
> "You'd think we were in line to get tickets to a KISS concert," said Frank Jackson from behind the steering wheel of the family van. "We're so excited. We don't feel sick. We just want to be assured that we are all OK."

Broadcast example:

[VO TOP]	{VO TOP} FRANK JACKSON AND HIS FAMILY WOKE UP EARLY TO GET IN LINE FOR THE BIG EVENT. JACKSON SAYS IT'S LIKE BEING IN LINE FOR KISS CONCERT TICKETS.
[SOT:] [IN: We're so excited] [OUT: are all OK"] [Runs: 07] [CG: Frank Jackson, Getting a COVID test]	{SOT} ("We're so excited. We don't feel sick. We just want to be assured that we are all OK.")

Media, Pictures, Links, Embeds

In a web story, the main media is the story package—what aired or will air on the newscast. Again, depending on station style, you may either just upload the reporter package or pull a clip from the broadcast including the anchor intro and tag. That video clip is then included in the web story. Make sure the featured picture of that video is relevant to the story.

Creating a gallery of at least three photos is recommended because each click of a picture is a click on the website, which can mean more money for the station in terms of web ad sales.

If you are short on pictures, be careful with **open-source** graphics or photos. These are found on the internet, free to use, but still may be copyrighted so you still need to get permission to use them. If you don't get permission and get caught, your station could be fined several thousand dollars for copyright infringement.

OTT (OVER-THE-TOP)

Many stations are still working out the details on this one. They have found OTT, over-the-top streaming services, to be a good revenue source. OTT, also known as Connected TV or CTV, allows news and entertainment to be brought directly into your home's smart TV or digital device through a subscription service.

Mercer says it's just about getting "television," also known as video content, through the internet allowing viewers to watch the internet programs on their TVs.

> **Mentor Moment: Nancy Bauer Gonzales,**
> **News Director, KTNV, Las Vegas**
>
> "We have a big OTT platform. If a story is really big like an explosion, then the reporter will go out, set up their camera, and we'll put them on OTT on the air. If the president is going to speak and we're on the air, we'll take it live because ABC will take it. But we'll convert to our OTT platform and still do local news. The viewer can choose between watching the president or watching local news. At any time of the day, viewers can watch whatever they want."

At some stations, OTT doesn't affect the news staff in any way. At other stations, it's another part of the daily responsibilities for reporters, producers and anchors. When reporter Elisa Navarro worked at KXXV in Waco, Texas, she regularly provided OTT content for the station.

"When I was out live covering a story, I'd get a text from a producer saying, 'Hey, can you record a look-live VOSOT for OTT?' So, I would record a look-live VOSOT, end it their way and they'd use it for their OTT rundown. On the morning show, they always had something they would upload to OTT, like the top stories of the day, and I'd help them out anytime they needed content from me."

Navarro says the requests didn't impact her because she was just doing more of what she did all morning for the station:

> When we covered elections, we had OTT coverage and digital coverage all day. So even though we were only on the air at five, six and 10, we were still live on our OTT platform. We had our anchors going back and forth from the shows to OTT. It was just an added show. It's added workload. But it's the same work. You're just replicating it for another platform.

SOCIAL MEDIA

Once the story is posted to your station website, share that web story on your social media feed, and message the newsroom's digital team so they can share it as well. Newsrooms have different protocols on this. Some prefer that all stories are shared first on the station page and then reporters share on their personal or station pages

Social media is more than just posting broadcast stories, saying, "Watch at 5 p.m.," or chronicling your life.

Punctuation, grammar and wording matter. Facts and added value matter. Rumor and hearsay do not have a place here. Flippant, colloquial or boorish posts may be your style on your personal pages, but they are not acceptable in professional posts. It's important to remember you are representing your station as a news professional. Your words, pictures and posts must follow suit.[3]

> **Mentor Moment: Jeff Lenk, News Director, KBAK, Bakersfield**
>
> "It's 4 p.m. and you put something up that says, 'Tune in at five. I'm going to show you this story.' I'm not going to schedule time an hour from now just to watch this story. You've got to give me something good right there on Facebook that hooks my attention. If you want me to watch your full story, give me a piece of it on Facebook. And then I'm going to tune in to the news to watch more of it."

Just because a story was in an earlier newscast and posted on the station's website does not mean your work is done. A creative newsroom citizen will look for creative ways to build on that story, continuing to grow it. Here's some food for thought as the newsroom moves from newscast to newscast.

"If a story played one way during the morning newscast, how will it play and what different angle or **sidebar** will it take on the station's app, its social media, or its website?" asks Kevin Olivas, news recruiter for Sinclair Broadcast Group. "What different aspect, angle, or sidebar to the story can live on each of these platforms?"

These are questions Olivas asks all newsrooms to consider to keep up engagement, stay different from the competition and share diverse viewpoints with the community.

Let's be clear, though. If there is breaking news, the plan changes. KBAK's Lenk says:

> If there's breaking news, we're going to be running a Facebook Live for as long as an hour or two or even longer depending on what's happening in that situation. We're not going to put that up temporarily, and then say, 'Hey, if you want to keep watching this live, go to our website instead.'

Just because you grew up using these apps does not mean you know how to use them for professional journalism purposes. Here are best practices for Twitter, Facebook and Instagram, according to The Poynter Institute:

- Make headlines specific and descriptive
- Write simply: Subject/verb

- Clear writing is better than clever writing
- Find the emotional aspect of the story (quotes can add to this)
- Use active verbs
- No attribution or sourcing in the headline (unless the source is the story)
- Always source and give credit in the body of the story and social post
- Specify location and town. Don't say "local"
- Pictures must depict the theme of the story
- Closeup photos of people work best
- Be responsive. This is a two-way conversation
- When mistakes are made, own up to them quickly.

Each medium should be used differently to get the optimum professional connection with your audience. As Colucci says:

> I have come across many folks looking for social media jobs in the news who think that their personal expertise on Instagram is sufficient enough for the job, and it isn't. I once did an informal interview with someone who had an impressive Instagram presence for her (very cute) dog in addition to her own. She was seeking a job in news and when I'd ask her pointed questions, such as: 'Walk me through how you'd seed a certain news story across platforms,' she struggled to answer.

Mentor Moment: Da Lin, MMJ, KPIX, San Francisco

"My rule is if it's not something you're comfortable sending to your mom or your boss, then you should not tweet it out. And, leave the personal political views out even if it's your personal accounts."

Twitter

Twitter began only offering 140 characters. Now, it's up to 240, but keeping your posts short and sweet is best. Twitter analytics show shorter and better written tweets get more responses than longer ones that aren't particularly well-written.[4]

Twitter is great for breaking news and "new" news. If something big happens, it's often the first place people go for information. Yes, we always like to be first to get information out, but we must make sure the tweet is correct. It's best to add a picture and a link, when possible, for greater likelihood of being retweeted.

If you are continually updating a story, use a thread. That means to keep all of the pictures and information in a thread so a follower can keep up with the whole story.

Nick King says he'll do this if something important is coming out of a press conference.

"Social media is also a good place to share quotes from a news conference in real-time. Certain things can't wait for TV," King says.

> **Mentor Moment: John Colucci, Senior Social Media Director**
>
> "Treat Twitter like a reporter's notebook. As you go along talking to folks and gathering information, note it on social media. It's right there as a record and can also help the folks back at the station compose a web story out of that social media content."

As a morning live reporter and MMJ, Will Tran at KRON in San Francisco tweets all morning long.

"It is as important, if not more, than broadcast," Tran says "It's especially important for big or breaking news. Get a Twitter account. Get it now. It's as vital to a reporter as a microphone. In a way, it's a huge microphone."

Colucci recommends journalists think of Twitter as a live global feed.

"This is where you go first to post breaking news content and keep people updated as it happens. Also, adding photos and video increases engagement. It's OK to repeat information and post more frequently here," Colucci says.

If you are not following a continuing, active story, then it's recommended to limit your tweets to every 30 minutes. You don't want to bombard people.

If your station has a hashtag, use it. It's a great way to get your audience talking and help with station branding. However, limit those hashtags to two on Twitter.[5]

Tweets that contain links receive higher retweet rates than tweets with no links. And remember, Twitter isn't just about what you post.

It's important to follow, like and retweet others to build and continue engagement.

> **Mentor Moment: Chad Hypes, News Director, KTVL, Medford**
>
> "Digital deadlines are just as important as TV deadlines. If you cannot make your digital and social deadlines, it does not matter how good you are on TV. You will not last. You have to understand the importance of unfolding your story throughout the day on digital and social and look at TV as the last piece of the puzzle. People want their news now. They are not gathering the family around the TV at 6 p.m. to watch the news. They see and hear things on digital or social first and then decide if the story is important enough to watch the news."

Facebook

Facebook is a conversation place. Yes, we post news stories and videos there, but it's more than dropping a story in a post. It's about talking about that story, finding out how your followers feel about that story. What's their story? What are their pictures and stories relating to? Ask them to share. And then, you must respond. Again, it's a conversation to connect with people and to share and find emotion.

Asking questions is a big way of engaging that conversation. Adding substantive pictures, videos and links are recommended. Posts with video receive more likes and shares than posts with still photos or without any type of media. Live posts receive the most engagement.

Perspective adds to content, too. A picture of a forest fire is one thing, but including details that the mountain community went through this a year earlier can give this post context and heart.

> **Mentor Moment: Dion Lim, News Anchor, KGO, San Francisco**
>
> "I use it to build my brand and build a relationship with the community. I think of it as a newscast I can control myself and use to my advantage. Nearly all of my exclusive leads on stories about racism and xenophobia toward Asian Americans come from Facebook and Instagram."

How often should you post to Facebook? If a conversation is getting traction let it stay and build. Engage with the posts and react to comments. That can drive the conversation. Don't post over it which means to post a new different topic. Wait an hour or longer before posting again if a post is getting traction.

Professional advice from Colucci:

> I recommend above all, prioritize local stories in your community above national stories. Also, post a few times per day and mix up the post types. I suggest mostly links, but pepper in photos and video. In the post copy, be as descriptive as you can without being too verbose.

> **Mentor Moment: Theresa de los Santos, Ph.D., Associate Professor of Communication, Pepperdine University**
>
> "Facebook is the platform of the people. It has the most users of any social network, and it has the most features for journalists to use. Facebook posts are the longest types of news posts. Research shows that posts of five lines or longer get 60% more comments than shorter posts. Posts that include some type of interpretation are shared 20% more than posts that just state the facts. Soundbites add value to traditional news stories. Use them in Facebook posts, too."

Instagram

Instagram started as a focus on the visual and still is. Pictures are the key here and lead the conversation. This is a medium to share experiences, inspire, be creative and make connections.

> **Mentor Moment: John Colucci, Senior Social Media Director**
>
> "Instagram is meant to be a more uplifting space, so we don't often want to do hard news there. Stick to good photography. Use it to share what's going on, but focus on things with good imagery. Also, if you make a good Story or Reels you can download and repurpose those videos on other social media platforms. Just be careful of music rights."

Here, hashtags rule. To keep posts from getting overloaded with hashtags, it's recommended you make your post and then, in a comment, include your hashtags. Double-check those hashtags to make sure they apply to your post.

> **Author Note—Kim Stephens**
>
> "I posted a picture of my co-anchor and me at work. He has a long Greek name, Prokopios, but shortened it to Kopi for TV. When I started adding a few hashtags, I found one with his shortened name, #Kopi. Oops! In other languages, Kopi means something else. Something quite unprofessional for our morning newscast. I learned my lesson about always double-checking tags."

With Instagram, you also don't want to over-post. One to three posts a day is the suggested number to not bombard your audience. Too much posting can lead to tune out. It's also best to post natively. That means that you go through Instagram to post to Instagram, not a third-party app that posts stories to a variety of platforms. And, *please* remember that journalists are not the story.

Sometimes, we can post our part of the story beyond what will be the broadcast story. Through social media, we have an opportunity to take the viewer behind the scenes of the story and the story-making process.

This "process journalism" is new to the industry, and based on reactions from viewers and followers, it's something people like. This can make a story, reporter and station stand out especially when all of the stations are covering the same story. This is a value-added piece that helps the community connect to the story and the station.

> **Mentor Moment: Kevin Olivas, News Recruiter, Sinclair Broadcast Group**
>
> "Be transparent. Show them how you got the story. How you came up with the idea for it. Or the challenges in getting an interview or getting to the scene of a story."

YouTube

This may likely be the place videos go first before they are posted to social sites. Each station will have its own protocol for YouTube. Make sure you title your video clearly.

WHAT ABOUT THE HATERS?

As we've already discussed there are a lot of ways to positively connect with people through our digital presence. Our posts can empower, uplift, inform, entertain and enlighten people.

But social media also has its haters, liars and people who spew misinformation, disinformation and conspiracies. Journalists must be careful in these waters. You may want to react to an unkind post, or set the record straight. Before you do, take a breath, and talk with your news director. Remember, you now represent a business. Your voice is not perceived to be your own, *even* when you are posting from your personal profile page.

If someone posts something unkind or inflammatory on your professional page, your boss may answer on behalf of the company. Your supervisor may advise you to do nothing. The station may ban the person from the page. It all depends on the situation.

In the case of angry people, no matter how eloquent you are, or factually supported, they will likely not listen to you. So why poke the hornet's nest? Not responding may not give you the most satisfaction, but it may be the smartest move.

Facebook has filter tools to block words or hide comments.[6] Those can be found in Page Settings. If you need to ban or block someone from posting to your page or contacting you through Messenger, go to Privacy Shortcuts. You may want to take screenshots first, so you have proof if you need it down the road. You can also report abusive content, spam or someone impersonating you by clicking Report Post. If you ever feel threatened, you must talk with your boss and law enforcement.

What you post on your personal pages could get you fired. If the post is inappropriate, discriminatory or commercially biased, you could lose your job. Journalistic ethics calls for unbiased information and never selling something. If you want to be an influencer and sell things, go do that job instead. You cannot do both.

TRENDS AND ANALYTICS

Making Money on Digital

TV stations make money airing commercials during the television newscast. They also make money every time an advertisement or online story is clicked on the website. The more clicks, the more money.

Online sales also come from the pre-rolling ads shown before the story. That is why digital teams work to build and consistently update stories on the website then share those stories on social media in the hopes that followers will click the link taking them to the website and click more stories and ads.

> **Mentor Moment: Brandon Mercer, Digital Content Director**
>
> "At some of the websites I've worked for, we got paid every time someone went to a photo gallery. Every single time they click a photo on the photo gallery, we get paid. So, if that's your model, then you need to put photo galleries together. If you're not earning money on photo galleries, then you don't put photo galleries together. It's one of those things if you understand how the business works, you'll be successful in it."

The bulk of a station's revenue comes from TV advertising sales. In the beginning of digital, revenue may have been about 1% but it's growing, Mercer says. TV station budgets are shifting.

"The future for TV is in monetizing video through other means and monetizing their brand via their website, social media, syndication, and other tools," Mercer says. "Reporters need to think about their own personal brand, their name and social following, and how to leverage that for the station to both be successful themselves and make the station successful."

And, remember what makes money and what does not. Mercer says:

> Always push to something the station can monetize—the newscast or the website. Don't give away too much on social media, because no one gets paid for that, and you need to keep the station in business if you want to keep telling stories on that platform.

Colucci agrees that you should know how and where the station makes money with digital and social. "It's also worth noting for some news organizations, ad revenue is made from ads inserted on their video content posted directly on Facebook, Twitter, and YouTube if they have partnerships with those platforms," Colucci says.

Metrics

Digital content managers have ways of knowing what works and what doesn't. You can check your own analytics if you have a professional page and see what posts had more interaction and from where your followers come. This analysis helps managers better understand their audience and see the connection they're having with their community. Colucci says:

> While it's nice to get new followers and likes and comments on posts, which is the barometer one would use to determine personal social media success, I call these 'vanity metrics.' In news, we want people to come to our website and consume content. It's not about the vanity metrics.

Mercer uses audience insights to see what stories viewers are clicking and how they're interacting with posts, videos and photos.

"I realized that when COVID happened, our viewer numbers on the web and digital skyrocketed," says Allizbeth Clavijo, digital producer. "I thought, 'Wow.' Our community depends on us so much to get their information."

Sarah Light says, "When I'm not publishing stories or scheduling social media posts, I take time to research trends on social media or track what is doing well on our website through Google Analytics."

It's an ever-evolving task to understand the audience. The number of clicks is just a start. Following the interaction plays a part, too. But the way a story is written and titled can play a huge role in whether a story trends. That information can help you see when the audience is drinking in a story and when it's had enough. Light says:

> If you're posting just to post content on social media, that can drive people away from your news brand as a whole. You also have to keep in mind that some stories are only trendy for a certain period of time. For example, the

COVID-19 pandemic has been a huge driver of web traffic for newsrooms across the country, but people became fatigued of daily numbers and outbreak stories after a few months. When a situation like that happens, it's time to reevaluate.

A big part of that reevaluation is figuring out a different way to tell the story.

> **Mentor Moment: Brandon Mercer, Digital Content Director**
>
> "You can't make people read boring news. But if you tell good stories, they'll read good stories. I was looking at election coverage and complex issues like that. And you think, we can do a headline that explains the story really well about Proposition 26 bond funds for schools. No one's going to read a title like that. But if you say 'Your kid's education will be dramatically impacted by a prop that may not pass and here's why.' It's a little easier to understand that."

Boyd Huppert posted a social media version of a sweet story on Facebook the day before the broadcast version aired on TV. The story was about a woman who saved all of the empty heart-shaped boxes of chocolate her husband gave her over the years. The story got 1,500 comments and 2,975 shares.

At first, the story on Facebook promoted that night's TV broadcast. Then, once Huppert saw all of the interaction, he linked the story to the website and his franchise, "The Land of 10,000 Stories." He did that because he knew nearly 3,000 people were now seeing his post in their Facebook feed. His goal was to go viral. It worked.

Scan the following QR code to see Huppert's social media post.

> **Mentor Moment: Boyd Huppert, Reporter, KARE11, Minneapolis**
>
> "Likes are like a handshake, comments are like a hug, and shares are like a kiss on the lips. Because that's what I really want is a share. Facebook analytics tell us most shares happen before a story airs."

REMINDERS FOR PRODUCING FOR DIGITAL AND SOCIAL MEDIA

- Be clear, relevant and engaging.
- Always include visuals.
- Journalists are not influencers. The story is not about you.
- Nurture your network. Connect with your audience.
- Verify information before posting.
- Always include sources and context.
- Keep updating information.
- Read out loud to make sure there are no grammar or punctuation errors.
- Always get permission to reuse photos and other media found on the internet.

QUESTIONS

1. Give three examples of how writing for the web is different from broadcast writing.
2. What should you think about when considering using hashtags?
3. Describe two ways a TV station makes money with digital content.
4. Why can a journalist be fired for something posted on his or her personal page?

TRY THIS

1. Tweet about a news story of the day including links, pictures and a source.
2. Post on Facebook about a story you did or one you are working on including pictures and/or video.
3. Post a picture on Instagram about something happening in your class. Link the appropriate people and hashtags.

NOTES

1 www.copyrightlaws.com/copyright-laws-in-u-s-government-works/
2 McSpadden, Kevin (May 14, 2015). *You now have a shorter attention span than a goldfish.* Time, Retrieved from https://time.com/3858309/attention-spans-goldfish/
3 www.careerbuilder.com/advice/social-media-survey-2017
4 www.poynter.org/reporting-editing/2012/what-every-young-journalist-should-know-about-using-twitter/
5 https://help.twitter.com/en/using-twitter/how-to-use-hashtags#
6 www.facebook.com/formedia/blog/safety-tips-for-journalists

The Art of Live and Recorded
Performance
Part 4

Storytelling—Taking it to the Next Level

Thirteen

In This Chapter	
Story Focus	227
Literary Devices	230
Content Wins	233
Drone Journalism	235
Reminders on Storytelling	236
Questions	236
Try This	236

KARE11-TV's Boyd Huppert talks about the dark ages when he recalls the first ten years of his reporting career.

"I didn't really know what I was doing," he says. "I was learning a lot, but I was somewhat unfocused on where I was going with this knowledge."[1]

Then, one day, something clicked. He attended the National Press Photographers Association's (NPPA) News Video Workshop in Norman, Oklahoma, and he had an epiphany.

"It was a life-changing event for me, and it started what I refer to as the period of enlightenment in my career."

What was it that changed for Huppert? In a nutshell, it was focus. He learned how to determine the focus of a story.

Focus is the constant theme for everything a journalist does—from planning and interviewing to shooting, writing and editing. The more organized and focused your shots, the more organized and focused your writing, helping you to create memorable and compelling stories that will engage your viewers.

STORY FOCUS

Huppert's stories focus on a central character—someone who is introduced right away in a "handshake shot."

DOI: 10.4324/9781003137016-13

Scan the following QR code to see Huppert's story about a girl with Down Syndrome who loves playing basketball.

In the story you just watched, you are immediately introduced to Sainora when she says, "I'm good at basketball." The next shot is a closeup of Sainora's face while Huppert says, "Sometimes, all we need is a shot. Sainora Dakoche has been rehearsing for hers most of her life."

This technique helps the viewer immediately connect with Sainora, the central character.

Moments

Many experienced reporters center their stories around moments. They hold back details and reveal them in the form of surprises. But these moments don't happen by themselves.

> **Mentor Moment: Chad Nelson, Director of Photography, KARE11, Minneapolis**
>
> "I spend the majority of my efforts trying to capture moments of people, especially ones an audience can relate to. Everything else is just devices to get you into and out of great moments. The best stories are filled with moments. It's our job to figure out how to use them as transitions to other moments."

For Huppert, moments start with the shooting.

"If you're not looking for something, you're less apt to find it," Huppert says. "I start the process every day determined that I'm going to find these reveals and surprises and that they're going to be built into my story."

> **Mentor Moment: Boyd Huppert, Reporter, KARE11, Minneapolis**
>
> "Look around your room for the color red. What do you see? Now, look around the room for the color blue. Do you see what happens when you're looking for red? Everything else goes away. And when you're looking for blue, everything else goes away. And that's really what focus is. By the way, I didn't make up that analogy. Somebody else came up with it, and it was so good that I stole it. But it just makes me think about how focus works. Once I know my focus, I can't stop seeing it."

Huppert says the real work happens when he's logging. That's when he hears those little details that he missed during the shoot. He spends more time logging a story than he does writing it. He logs constantly—on the way from one shoot to the next; during his lunchbreak while eating in the car; at home until two or three in the morning when he's not doing a **day-turn**.

While logging, he might hear a character say something and then sigh. Huppert will log that sigh. When he writes to it, the sigh becomes a moment.

While some reporters call this a "moment," other newsrooms use the term "surprise" or "reveal," and everyone in the newsroom is asked to look for them. If the reporter or photographer didn't notice a moment right away, the editor is asked to keep an eye out for it.

More broadcast and digital producers, along with assignment editors, are asking the team to give them a "surprise" that can be used in a social media post or a newscast tease.

> **Mentor Moment: Les Rose, Professor of Practice, Syracuse University, Former CBS Network News Photographer, Syracuse**
>
> "If you want to get better, look at a story you love and look at it 10 times, 20 times, 50 times until it's literally part of your DNA. And now it's in your brain and you think, man it's that one shot or one soundbite that I can steal someday. And it's in your memory bank. You don't know when you're going to steal it. But sooner or later you will."

Steal from the Pros

We don't really mean "steal," but one of the best ways to improve your craft and take your reporting to the next level is by devouring the work of others and practicing their techniques.

With YouTube and social media, you have many opportunities to follow and interact with some of the best storytellers in the world. Make a habit of following them on social media and viewing their work daily.

Keeping with this creative storytelling, we're also challenging you to write the story differently, offering a moment or surprise with *your words*. Again, it requires a mental step back from the story to see it a little differently and phrase it with more "sizzle" as KGO's Wayne Freedman calls it.

Freedman likes to use this example of a story that has no "sizzle." It's by a reporter at another station and began like this:

> AT THE LOS ANGELES ZOO, OFFICIALS SAY THEY ARE PUZZLED HOW THIS RARE KOMODO DRAGON ATTACKED A SAN FRANCISCO NEWSPAPER PUBLISHER LAST NIGHT.[2]

Freedman says that was "safe and serviceable," but he chose to begin his story with "sizzle":

> THIS IS THE MOUTH, THAT MUNCHED ON THE BIG TOE, THAT IS ATTACHED TO THE RIGHT FOOT, OF THE MAN WHO IS LEGALLY ATTACHED TO ACTRESS SHARON STONE.

Yes, that newspaper publisher was Sharon Stone's husband at the time. "Good storytelling engages the viewer," Freedman says.

LITERARY DEVICES

Writing techniques or a turn of phrase can turn a ho-hum story into a memorable one. Huppert and Freedman rely on literary devices to make their stories stand out from run-of-the-mill reporting. A literary device is a technique that writers use to produce a special effect in their writing that's different.

You may know these techniques as a metaphor, simile, alliteration, rule of threes and rhyme. There are, literally, dozens of different literary devices.

Huppert says he first learned about the writing techniques in 11th grade English and then promptly forgot about them. But as he began to deconstruct the work of writers he admired, he discovered they were using literary devices.

> **Mentor Moment: Boyd Huppert, Reporter**
>
> "They feel good like putting on a well-worn baseball glove. Or slipping on your most comfortable shoes. Your Saturday shoes. The ones you put on when doing yard work. It just feels good. It's comfortable. It helps give structure to the writing. They entertain, they amuse. They make me go, 'Wow.' That's what literary devices do."

Here are a few examples that Huppert and Freedman have used in their stories:

Opposing Theme

We've long heard "opposites attract." That is true with magnets and in some love stories. Using opposites in your storytelling can be a clever way to make a point. Here is an example from a Boyd Huppert story about a 10-year-old rock and roll prodigy:

"Collin Johnson: blessed with the soul of a rocker – cursed with an 8:45 bedtime."[3]

Scan the QR code for Huppert's prodigy story.

Rule of Threes

People have a tendency to remember things in threes. "Morning, Noon and Night," would be an example of that. Here is how Freedman used this technique in a story about a mass shooting.

"The lucky ones walked out of Santana High School this morning. They were grateful not to be leaving on gurneys, in wheelchairs, or by helicopter after one of their own took a 22-caliber handgun and opened fire in a restroom."[4]

Analogy

An analogy compares one thing to another. It finds likeness in things that may not, on first glance, appear to be alike. In comparing the two things in this way, Huppert said so much more with tongue in cheek.

"A proctologist on his retirement day hasn't seen this many bottoms up."[5]

Metaphor

Many of us learned about metaphors in elementary school and quickly forgot about them. This may be a good time to brush up on that knowledge to elevate your stories to another level.

A metaphor uses an action, thing or even situation to symbolize something else. Here are two more Huppert and Freedman examples:

Huppert: "Life sometimes carries us to deep dark places. This is a story about climbing out."[6]

Freedman: "At Village Wines and Spirits, the quake wasted a lifetime's worth of good drinking. It turned vintage cabs, zins and chardonnays into one big house blend awaiting the mop."[7]

Twist a Cliché

Clichés can turn a good story into a trite one, showing a lack of creativity. A few examples of that are "winter wonderland," "uphill battle," "cold as ice" or "make waves."

However, if you turn that cliché, that can be fabulous. Here's a Huppert example:

"The grass is greenest when neighbors are on the same side of the fence."[8]

Reporters who are just starting out are often overwhelmed by all of the other tasks they must do that they forget about the craft of storytelling. We challenge you to every day find one way to say something that is not obvious or commonplace.

> **Mentor Moment: Boyd Huppert, Reporter**
>
> "My goal is to tell a better story tomorrow than I told you today. To learn another literary device or figure out a better way to introduce a character. That's the great thing about loving my job. When I am working extra hours or working really hard, I say I'm giving the first eight hours to the company and then anything after that I'm doing for me. That's the part where I'm learning to get better and be better at what I do."

CONTENT WINS

In an age where information is at everyone's fingertips, our job is to always stand out for the right reasons. You want to stand out because you cleverly tell stories differently from "the other guys." You provide substance, context, humanity and memorable moments to your stories and newscasts.

You also inform, update and empower. Sometimes, the information is compelling but visually blah. Sometimes the update is critical and must be shared immediately, not later when the newscast airs. Sometimes a piece of information is empowering but doesn't quite line up with the focus of a story. All of this content has a place. It can help a reporter and news station connect with viewers in a unique way. Usually, the place for that content is digital.

A Facebook Live or Twitter thread could be the place to share the compelling information that doesn't have great visuals. Critical content that should not wait until the newscast can also be shared in these ways.

An Instagram post or story could be the perfect place to share a "Wow" moment or surprise. Sharing this content with the audience is impactful and can stir discussion. Then, you can embed those posts into the web story adding more breadth to it.

Basically, we don't want anything to go to waste. Enterprising this content can make you, the story and the station stand out as taking the extra step in connecting with the community.

If we learned anything during COVID in 2020 and 2021, Zoom and FaceTime interviews can be impactful, even if they're not especially visual.

> **Mentor Moment: Tracie Potts, Washington Correspondent, NBC News, Washington DC**
>
> "To be a successful news reporter you have to be curious about everything. My family says I never stop asking questions. You have to read and be a bit of a jack-of-all-trades when it comes to information. In high school I hated history, but as a journalist, I've come to appreciate it. At any given moment breaking news may happen. I have to be ready to go on the air at a moment's notice with little information."

Storytelling changed because of round-the-clock updates of information, resources and perspective. These pieces of content can be used on their own, shared on social, added to digital and included in broadcast stories offering perspective and heart to a topic.

As we discussed in Chapter 6, shooting a video chat interview from a few angles, other than simply recording it through the phone or computer, can add another layer of dimension to the story and offer a little B-roll to help with editing.

Cyndee Hebert, managing editor of news content at WTHR13 in Indianapolis, says her newsroom set up a team of go-to people for an accountability check. They analyze data every day, helping to find trends and important talking points.

"Every day you get new numbers of who got sick and who died," Hebert says. "It's our job to help the viewer understand what that means to me today compared to yesterday. Or three months ago. What direction are we going in? Make it meaningful and impactful."

COVID forced the world to think outside the box. Those ways will likely stay. Greg Vandegrift, journalism professor at St. Thomas University in Minneapolis, says it prompted news briefs to be done on Zoom. Reporters did live shots summarizing what was happening in the community as well as look-lives for constant content sharing.

YouTube is a player in newsrooms as another way to share content. Stan Heist of Sinclair Broadcast Group says many newsrooms streamed live video, especially live press conferences, during the summer of 2020.

"You'd be shocked at the amount of interest, especially during COVID," Heist says.

> **Mentor Moment: Da Lin, MMJ, KPIX San Francisco**
>
> "When it comes to covering COVID and Black Lives Matter stories, the stories can be very sad or emotionally charged. I try to let my interviewees talk about their feelings and emotions. I will stick to the facts. Our job is to report, not add fuel to a fire. Let the people share their feelings because it'll come across more genuine and expressive with their emotions."

Sacramento Univision news director Luis Godinez says his newsroom covered COVID in line with how they approach all storytelling—going beyond numbers and directly speaking to the viewer.

"People not being able to pay rent, and farm workers on the front lines. Covering it from within and in many cases helping people find solutions rather than just reporting stories," Godinez says.

This mindset is taking storytelling to the next level, every day, sharing diverse viewpoints and perspectives, always with the eye to inclusivity.

DRONE JOURNALISM

Speaking of the next level, many reporters and photographers are finding a niche opportunity with drone journalism.

CNN photographer Carmaine Means remembers the day in 2013 when a drone salesman walked into her newsroom at WLS in Chicago.

> **Mentor Moment: Carmaine Means, Photographer/ Drone Pilot, CNN, Chicago**
>
> "It was at the time the drone was very simple. It had a housing area where you could put a GoPro. There was no gimbal. All you could do was a hot air balloon shot. It would go up in the air, and you're just capturing the images as it goes. I don't even think it tilted up and down. It just sat there. And when he displayed it, I was like, 'Man! If they could put a gimbal on this thing, this is going to be a game-changer in our industry.' And I was right."

Means saw an opportunity, and she got busy. She bought two drones and got her drone license in 2014 and started posting drone photos and videos on her social media accounts. By then, she was freelancing for WBBM. She and another photographer at that station were the only two licensed drone pilots in the Chicago news market. When her operations manager asked her if she wanted to fly drones for the station, the answer was easy.

Now Means is a drone pilot and photographer for CNN in Chicago. With drone regulations changing and allowing flights over crowds and at night, she says more news organizations will start using drones. That means more opportunities and jobs for photographers and MMJs who are licensed to fly a drone.

REMINDERS ON STORYTELLING

- Choose conversational words and phrases that connect with the viewer.
- Be clear about the focus of your story and stick to it throughout.
- Always look for memorable moments and surprises.
- Literary devices help transform a story from good to memorable.
- Clear writing is always better than overly clever writing.
- Focus on the humanity, emotion, oddities and humor of stories.

QUESTIONS

1. What's the best way to find a story's focus?
2. Think of the big story of the day in your area. What content would you recommend sharing with your community (in what form) and how?
3. What are three literary devices that you could use to improve your storytelling?

TRY THIS

1. Watch a local newscast and take notes on three moments or surprises you saw.
2. Either take a story you recently wrote, or for the next one you write, use at least one literary device.

NOTES

1 Huppert, B. (2016). Storytelling workshop, California State University, Fresno.
2 Freedman, W. (2011). *It Takes More Than Good Looks to Succeed at Television News Reporting*, A Wealth of Wisdom, LLC, p. 85, ebook.

3 Huppert, B. (2016). Storytelling workshop, California State University, Fresno.
4 Freedman, W. (2011). *It Takes More Than Good Looks to Succeed at Television News Reporting*, A Wealth of Wisdom, LLC, p. 232, ebook.
5 Huppert, B. (2016). Storytelling workshop, California State University, Fresno.
6 Ibid.
7 Freedman, W. (2011). *It Takes More Than Good Looks to Succeed at Television News Reporting*, A Wealth of Wisdom, LLC, p. 246, ebook.
8 Huppert, B. (2016). Storytelling workshop, California State University, Fresno.

Live Reporting

Fourteen

In This Chapter	
Good Live Shots	240
Setting up the Live Shot	245
When Things Go Wrong	246
Writing the Live Shot Script	249
Anchors Asking Questions	249
Breaking News	250
As-Live/Look-Live	252
Digital Live Shot	253
Reminders for a Great Live Shot	253
Questions	254
Try This	254

It's so true. We hold on to failure and let it eat us up inside. We let it define us and we let it ruin us. We let it keep us up at night. But we are here to help you learn from failure and move on.

Many examples in this book come from failures and mistakes. It's why we wrote this textbook, to help you learn from others' mistakes so you can start your career on a stronger foot. You will make mistakes. Some will hurt deeply. They may make you question your career choice and ability. These are opportunities for you. They are moments in your life to learn from, build from, grow from, share and, as we said, move on from and survive.

Author Note—Kim Stephens

"I was sent out to a plane crash one hour before our newscast. This was before cell phones or the internet so the only way I could get information about this crop duster plane crash was at the scene. The photographer and I got to the scene maybe five minutes before

DOI: 10.4324/9781003137016-14

> my live shot. The public information officer was a mile away at the crash site. I had no updated information. All I was thinking about as I put in my IFB was what I didn't know. The anchors tossed to me as breaking news at the top of the newscast, and I got flustered right at the beginning. Then, I said, 'Wait. Let me get my thoughts together.' I wanted to cry. I did when I got home. It was then, in my misery, that I decided I was going to stay in this business, and I was going to have a plan if this kind of situation ever happened again. It was a terrible moment and the best moment of my career, because I learned from my failure."

KGO-TV news anchor Dion Lim recalls a challenging live shot at a house fire. She had no information before she went live in the newscast. Without any facts, she described the scene.[1]

"Surround yourself with details," she advises.

Because she had no facts from the fire department's public information officer, she described what she saw, smelled, heard and felt as ash fell on her face and eyelashes. She also described neighbors' facial expressions and body language as they watched from across the street.

"The magic to ad-libbing is this: Take a moment, whether it's a split second or a few minutes, to plan out how you're going to start and end your ad-lib," Lim says.

Mentor Moment: Tracie Potts, Washington Correspondent, NBC News, Washington DC

"The best way for me to do a live shot is not to memorize anything. I do 25 plus live shots every morning. I never write a script. I jot down a few bullet points that I don't want to forget, especially numbers. But the key is to tell the story, not recite it. To tell a good story, you have to know your story well. Read, read, read! And listen. If you know what you're talking about, you don't have to remember what you or someone else wrote hours ago. You can just talk about it."

> **Mentor Moment: Alicia Acuna, Correspondent, Fox News, Denver**
>
> "Some people like to write out a whole script, and then that script owns them. And you have to be careful if you're not *really* good at delivering a script. If you know the information, say what you know. This isn't brain surgery. It's simple storytelling. And if you try to get too complicated, you're going to lose the listener."

Preparation and practice are key to doing good live reports. Working through situations in your head, talking out loud to yourself and improvising helps a lot. We recommend you do this often at home, in front of the mirror, recorded on your phone or with a friend whose advice you respect.

GOOD LIVE SHOTS

> **Mentor Moment: Joe Little, MMJ/Director of Storytelling, KNSD, San Diego**
>
> "Get in front of the story. Stay with the story. Be aware of what's behind you. There's no reason to pan. I like to reach through the lens, grab the viewer by the hand and take them on a journey."

Little says there are four things reporters should consider when going live. Your background, your framing, being demonstrative and using a wireless lavalier.

First, make sure your location (your backdrop) is relevant to your story. Don't stand in front of a pretty skyline when you're talking about school lunches. You need to be at a school.

Second, you don't have to start your live shot on a medium shot. Little says mix it up. Think outside the box.

"I did five straight live shots, lying on my chest on the ground because the story was on the ground," Little says. "It was a story about straw wattle—those little erosion devices that are on hillsides and construction sites. They're made out of plastic, and the students wanted them banned because they were killing the fish."

So, Little got down on the ground where the wattle was.

Little's third tip is to be demonstrative. Demonstrate things. Show how something works. Use props. Be interactive.

And, most important. Little says throw away the stick mic:

> All humans talk with their hands. We can be more human with our hands. We can communicate with our hands. We can point; we can touch; we can lift; we can push; we can do anything with our hands. You remove the ability to be human if you put a stick mic in your hand and turn yourself into a billboard for your station. You're no longer having a conversation. You put up a barrier. Put a lavalier on so the viewer can focus on you or what you're pointing at. And you can point now because you got rid of the thing in your hand.

Interactive

The goal of every live reporter should be interactivity—giving the viewer a guided tour or demonstrating something.

Live reporters from the Black Lives Matter protests around the U.S. in 2020 walked around city intersections showing people marching arm-in-arm, putting up tents, painting on the street or hanging signs over an entrance to a police station.

After a devastating fire in Paradise, California, live reporters walked up driveways to show where a home's front door once stood. They walked along the still-standing front fence to show the charred backyard arbor next to what used to be a homeowner's pool and was now a big, dirty collection of water and debris.

Live reporters have also ridden roller coasters while interviewing someone in the front seat. They've gone down water slides in big inner tubes and thrust themselves into a rushing river to show how water rescue teams save lives. Or, less dramatically, they've chopped vegetables in a restaurant kitchen with a popular chef. Either way, these live shots were energetic, interactive and helped the viewer truly experience a moment in time.

Mentor Moment: Da Lin, MMJ, KPIX, San Francisco

"Don't stand in front of a place and not reference why you're there. There's a reason why you're doing your live report at the location that you picked. Let us know why and use the space and the environment as part of your live report."

Cyndee Hebert, managing editor of news content at WTHR13 in Indianapolis, says a live shot decision should be made with the producer and reporter together. She agrees with Lin that it has to be purposeful and active.

"People can *see* a fire," Hebert says. "You need to describe what you are feeling, seeing, smelling. What's the activity level like? What can you tell them beyond what the audience can already see? It can't be 'duh' TV."

Energetic

There needs to be energy to a live shot. If there's immediacy, that's great, but if nothing is happening all around you, you still need to show some sort of emotion or action that makes the viewer feel something.

Especially in those emotional moments, it's important to stay to the facts and stay calm. Acuna says:

> You've got to collect yourself. Take some breaths and not get caught up in the excitement of the situation, which is really easy to do, especially when you're new. Take a second and breathe. Don't tell people it's tragic. Don't say 'it's sad' when 10 people are shot. Just give them the information.

Will Tran, an MMJ at Kron in San Francisco, says:

> I think it's OK to say, 'these are scary times' when reporting about COVID. I think it's OK to say it's scary to be out here reporting, but we are making sure we are as safe by maintaining social distance and wearing a mask and that you need to as well if you're coming down here to get tested.

Tran says when it comes to protests such as Black Lives Matter, stick with the facts.

"If a cop is doing something egregious and you're reporting it, make sure you attribute it to the critic *and not you*," Tran says. "You may even feel a crime has been committed by the cop but you can't opine on such stories. Attribute, attribute, attribute."

Being real is important. You cannot pretend to not have feelings. You just need to find a balance in situations like this.

NBC News correspondent Tracie Potts says she tries to avoid showing emotion because that can impact the audience's opinion:

> But we do have to remember that reporters are people and realistically, sometimes it's impossible to hide our emotions. In fact, sometimes it's good to share them. People are not looking for robots to report. When a child dies, it's appropriate to feel and express sadness. With the national outcry that Black Lives Matter, it's impossible for me as a Black reporter not to feel and sometimes show my emotions.

Clean

When we say a live shot should be clean, we don't mean that no one swears. We mean that the anchor toss to the live reporter is tight, makes sense, flows and has no technical problems. Then, during the live shot, the reporter is on track and has a clear beginning, middle and end.

Some reporters use notes, others, like Tran, do not. He says it helps him sound more conversational.

"I make sure I know my information, say what's the latest first, get to the point quickly, and work hard not to ramble," Tran says. "End the report with a good fact or something poignant like, 'The vaccines will eventually get to the rest of the public by spring. Until then, wear your mask and social distance.'"

That can be scary at first, and Tran says things didn't always go as planned when he first started in his career. Now, he says he can ad-lib anytime, anywhere.

"It has served me well. When I anchor and the teleprompter is not working, I can ad-lib through that spell," Tran says.

KGO reporter Wayne Freedman occasionally uses notes but only keywords, not sentences. He recommends live reporters speak naturally and not use clichés such as, "As you can see behind me," "even as we speak," "let's take a live look," or "we can report." He calls those a waste of breath.[2]

If the reporter and producer checked in with each other and planned the live shot, the odds are much greater that the live shot will be clean, informative and energetic because each will know the expectations of the other when it comes to timing and topic.

Safe

Sometimes, in the rush to go live, we may not notice the environment changing around us. A former morning reporter in Detroit, Michigan, rushed to the scene of a neighborhood shooting. It was five in the morning. He and his photographer rolled up to the scene, quickly set up the live shot, explained the scene, interviewed a police officer and then answered some questions from the anchor. Once the live shot was over, he realized the police left and angry neighbors were beginning to surround him.

The producer had planned for that reporter and photographer to stay there for more live shots throughout the morning, but the live team realized the situation had become unsafe. They packed up the car, quickly left and called the station from the road saying they had to pull the plug for their safety.

The adrenaline of being live, as many reporters experienced during the summer of 2020 with nationwide Black Lives Matter protests, kept them right there in the streets. They were close to clashes with police, in a melee of tear gas and in a tidal wave of emotions.

It's important to quickly weigh the journalistic value of the moment. Ask yourself—is your presence, the camera and microphone inciting people? Is it attracting violence?

The Poynter Institute shares a few reminders for journalists in these situations:

1. Report what is happening while adding context as to the why.
2. Fact check. Emotional people may say things as fact. It's your job as a journalist to not perpetuate untruths, misinformation, and disinformation.
3. Do not enable bad behavior by giving attention to attention seekers.
4. Be careful and clear with your words. Note when protesters become rioters.[3]

In these situations, it's human to get caught up and align with a side. As a journalist, you may not. It's also easy to get scared. When an energized situation turns to danger you need to move. Is there another place you can safely be and still report on the story? Can you move to an upper balcony or second-story window?

Always be aware of your surroundings when going live. When you are focused on the story and are in the moment, it's difficult to notice a dangerous backdrop. Don't disregard your safety for the sake of a story or a live shot.

SETTING UP THE LIVE SHOT

A Live Signal

Technology allows journalists to do live shots from virtually anywhere with something as simple as a cell phone. No longer are news crews tied to a microwave or satellite truck that was expensive to use and limited live shot locations.

If you've ever tried to post a great Instagram shot at the top of a waterfall or in the middle of the desert, you know that cell phone signals can be unreliable. But it's the best, cheapest technology we have right now.

When you go live, you may find yourself alone with your cell phone and tripod or with a photographer. Either way, you must communicate with the station to make sure the sound and pictures are ready for air. That usually requires a brief conversation with the assignment editor or producer.

IFB (Interruptible Feedback) Connection

The **IFB** is the earpiece worn by people out in the field and in the studio. It's called interruptible because the person wearing this earpiece can hear the programming of the newscast but the producer or director can interrupt that sound to give valuable information like time cues.

This is also important because the in-studio anchor may ask the live reporter a question and the reporter must be able to hear it to answer it.

Reporter Is Ready

Heads up. Producers need live reporters to be ready before they're ready. It is expected that if the producer can see the reporter in the camera that the live reporter is ready. So, don't be singing, picking your teeth, fixing your hair or gossiping with your photographer. You may be live before you realize you are live.

"Floating or not making your assigned slot is very bad," says Lin. "You do that enough times, and you won't have a job."

If for some reason the live reporter wants to start on something other than his or her face, that must be clearly explained to the producer ahead of time so the producer doesn't assume there is a problem with the live shot. This information also needs to be shared with the anchors so when they toss to the reporter and instead see a burned-out car, they don't assume there's a problem or have an uncomfortable toss to the reporter.

WHEN THINGS GO WRONG

Sometimes the signal fails right before or right as the anchor tosses to the live shot. What do you do? Do you pretend it didn't happen or does the anchor say something? This is when ad-libbing abilities come in handy. Here are some options.

Say Nothing

The situation dictates this reaction. The news anchor doesn't need to say a thing if the live shot was planned but the producer had to scrap it right before the anchor tossed to it. In this case, the viewer has no idea what happened behind the scenes. If this happens cleanly, there is nothing to say. Just move on with the show.

Acknowledge and Move On

If the anchor tosses to the live shot and it has bad audio, bad video or the reporter isn't ready, the anchor must acknowledge it and say, "We'll go back live in a moment."

That may also be a moment for the anchor to ad-lib something about the topic of the live shot and then continue. When the live shot is back up and running, the reporter may want to say something about the issue if it's applicable. For example, if the reporter was at a protest and just got pepper-sprayed and couldn't do the original live but is now able to, explaining what happened would be important. It's *nearly* always a good thing to share what's happening behind the scenes.

> **Mentor Moment: Alicia Acuna, FOX News Correspondent**
>
> "There were these miners trapped in a mine in an explosion in Utah. There was a rescue attempt and during the rescue there was another explosion. It was awful. We were wall-to-wall with the Greta van Susteren show, and it started to rain. And we were on the side of a highway and all the networks were set up there. But the wind was

blowing hard and everything started to fall apart around us. We were losing our tent. Our lights were going out. And then Greta asked, 'Can you show us around?' And I said, 'Yes.' Because the answer is always yes. But my photographer was stuck in the cables because they had come down on him. He went to move, and we were live and he's looking at me, and he said, 'I'm stuck.' And so I had to say, 'My photographer's stuck. We're having some problems.' We were honest about what was going on around us. You make people a part of it when you do that. So that's really important because things aren't always going to go right. Don't feel like you have to be this robot that's perfection."

Anchor Ad-Lib

If you are already in the middle of your live shot and you experience technical problems or, if you're at the bar after "the big game" and people are misbehaving, the live shot must be pulled immediately, and the news anchor must relay the information that the live reporter could not.

This is where ad-libbing and preparation come into play. The anchor and producer must have a backup plan. That plan may include video and a full script ready for the anchor to read. Or, the anchor has notes ready to ad-lib the information.

Author Note—Kim Stephens

"One of the biggest news stories in Fresno was when a man was convicted of killing his children and grandchildren in June 2005. The plan was that I would begin the breaking news with what was happening and then toss to the live reporter. The live signal went down. There was no live reporter to toss to. So, I just pretended this was the plan all along and started ad-libbing the background of the story and what was happening with the sentence being announced at that moment in the courtroom. Thankfully, the producer had a backup plan and so did I. I had my notes on the anchor desk. The producer ran video taking our viewers back to the arrests and other previous stories. I explained the pictures our viewers were seeing."

What if you, the live reporter, freeze, lose concentration or just decide to end the live shot earlier than planned? Oh yes, this happens, and it's embarrassing for everyone involved.

You must remember you have an important job to do. That job is to not only tell the story effectively, energetically and truthfully but also to stay within the allotted time.

The producer fully expects you to stay on track so the entire newscast is timed correctly. If you freeze and fail to do your job, it can throw the control room and the timing of the show into a tailspin. The opposite is the same. You cannot go as long as you want, again, for timing reasons that should be clear from the producer before the live shot even begins.

No Reporter IFB

If you start talking and hear an echo in the IFB, that means there is a mix-minus problem with the audio board at the TV station. Mix-minus is an audio signal that prevents audio feedback and echoes. Some people can still talk and ad-lib through the echo in their ear. If you are one of those people, then carry on with the live shot and tell the producer about the problem after the live shot.

Most people cannot ad-lib through the echo, so the only choice is to pull out the IFB. It's hoped the producer and director are paying attention so they know what's going on and can inform the audio technician about the problem. So, when you put the IFB back in your ear at the end of the live shot, all is clear, echo-free and an anchor can still ask you a question.

If you have no IFB and no communication with the control room, there are a few things you can do. Step out of the shot ahead of the planned live shot and call or text the producer and say there is no IFB and see what the plan is.

If the photographer has communication with the control room, then he or she can cue you from behind the camera. Or, the photographer can show the live scene without you, and the anchor is the one who speaks about the live shot explaining what the viewer is seeing. Again, that requires the anchor and producer to already have their backup plan to adequately tell the story.

WRITING THE LIVE SHOT SCRIPT

At many stations, if the live shot is not breaking news, the live reporter is responsible for writing the anchor script.

This is what a live broadcast script looks like:

[ANCHOR]	{ANCHOR} FRESNO STATE STUDENTS ARE OUTRAGED ABOUT A COLLEGE PROFESSOR AND HER TWEETS. A CROWD IS GATHERING ON CAMPUS TO PROTEST THE ANNOUNCEMENT THAT THE PROFESSOR GETS TO KEEP HER JOB. WILSON BABB IS LIVE AT THE FREE SPEECH AREA ON CAMPUS TO SHOW US WHAT IS HAPPENING.
[TAKE LIVE] [CG: WILSON BABB, FRESNO STATE FOCUS]	{TAKE LIVE}

A script like this can take about three minutes to write. The key is to have a good strong intro and the proper formatting which includes the {TAKE LIVE} cue as well as the CG.

You'll notice there is no script for the live shot itself, only the anchor toss. You, the live reporter, may have notes on a notepad or phone but for the most part, the live script is ad-libbed.

If you plan to use video in the live shot, that would need to be scripted, as well as a roll cue for the director to know when to roll the video. It's all about communication so everyone can have a clean, informative, interactive live shot.

ANCHORS ASKING QUESTIONS

You should be ready for *any* question an anchor asks you during your live shot. This is a big reason why having a clear IFB is so important. This communication can make a live shot exceptionally compelling. If done well, it can also be a great thing to add to a resume reel. The art of the ad-lib is something bosses are always looking for.

Many news directors require anchors to ask a question with every live shot. So, you must be on your toes. These questions offer a few opportunities. They offer a moment for you and the anchor to share expertise on the subject or the history of the situation being covered. Sometimes there's something going on behind you that you cannot see, but the anchor can, so the anchor may ask about that. Maybe the anchor will ask how close something is to your location. This gives you and the photographer a great opportunity to move around, share interactivity and give perspective.

This next piece of advice may seem obvious. The news anchor in the studio must listen to the live reporter. NBC Correspondent Tracie Potts says that can help avoid awkward moments.

"For a live reporter, nothing's worse than wrapping your report with, 'The mayor will speak about this issue at next week's council meeting.' Then the anchor asks: "Do we know when we'll hear from the mayor on this?"

BREAKING NEWS

> **Mentor Moment: Randy Forsman, Newscast Director, KCRA, Sacramento**
>
> "Live shots are an integral part of any newscast, but breaking news is where the real fun begins. You're often forced to make drastic changes to your rundown and often throw your rundown out altogether. You may have to make gut decisions on the fly without having time to prepare. It is within those constantly changing, high-stress moments that a newscast can truly shine."

These stressful, ever-changing moments of news, specifically breaking news, are a rush many people love. There is guilt in getting a rush out of what is usually a tragedy. But the rush is mostly fueled by the desire to get out the information correctly, quickly, creatively, interestingly and visually. When it's your job to report the breaking news out in the field or from the anchor desk, staying calm and focused is key.

Checklist

It helps to have a checklist to keep focused and organized. Here are a few things you should think about before going live:

Checklist for Breaking News Live Shots

- Facts
  - You may only have the What and Where.
- How much time do you have until you go live?
  - Right after the commercial, after this next story, as soon as you park and get the camera set up?
- How long do you have to report this breaking news?
  - Is the producer giving you all the time you need, and how long is that? Two minutes? 15 minutes?
- Is there team coverage? Will all of the reporters covering this story be seen in on-screen boxes as the anchor introduces the breaking news?
  - If that's the case, then you must look at the camera for a while without saying anything because you are on screen.
- Working IFB
- Background information
  - Is someone in the newsroom able to do research for you?
- Video or graphics
  - Is the producer, editor, director or graphics designer able to put together some visuals from past stories on this same topic?

Once you know these answers, it's time to get your thoughts together. Find the story focus. Remember, a lead for breaking news is just like any other story lead. It is an enticing piece of information about the topic.

"Hook your audience with a bold statement—one you make definitively and with conviction. Get to the point. Nothing loses an audience like rambling sentences," Lim writes in her book.[4]

Once on the scene or when you're driving to the scene, think about the visuals—where to safely stand and how to show the viewer around. If a lot of things happened in a short amount of time, you could take the viewer through the situation chronologically. Graphics and video help if your team was able to create some.

Always be thinking about your senses. What do you hear, see, smell, feel or even taste in the air around you? Can you get an interview? It's always best to briefly pre-interview someone before going live so you have some idea about what the person will say.

After you cover the immediate facts of the situation, is there any historical perspective that you can add? If this is a fire at a vacant house, is this the fourth this week or this season? If police shot a person, what's been going on in the community or nation recently concerning this situation? If this is a grass fire, what's the drought situation in your area? Adding perspective like this can be an exceptional addition to help your viewers truly understand the topic.

> **Mentor Moment: Alicia Acuna, FOX News Correspondent**
>
> "End on something strong. A lot of times people don't listen, but they pay attention to the top and bottom. If you can, bring home a point that's not just, 'back to you.' The tag is not a throwaway. You're better than that. Give a little more information and make it a reason to pay attention."

Finally, it's crucial that you know how to end your live shot. What nugget of information will you end with? If you will be staying on scene and have another live report in 20 minutes, say so. Also, tease ahead to the next newscast and say you will have the latest updates "on-air and online." Then, give your name and your station's tagline. ("In Malloryville, Cooper Finnley, Your 24-Hour News Source.") Then, stay there. Be ready for a question. Wait for the producer or photographer to say you are clear. Don't ever walk away from a camera until you've received the "clear" sign from the photographer, producer or director.

Inevitably, you will go over the live shot in your head when it's done and think of things you should have said or could have done better or differently. Do not beat yourself up over could haves and should haves. Make a mental note, and do those things for your next live shot on the air or on social media, or share the information with the crew who will take over the story for the next newscast.

AS-LIVE/LOOK-LIVE

Some live shots are called **as-live** or **look-live**. That means they are done in one take with no editing as if they were live, but they are recorded. Why would we do that? There may be technical problems that preclude the live shot from happening. Maybe there's a cellular signal issue. Most current live shots are done with cellular service using a backpack streaming device, so if the reporter is in the mountains or a place with spotty or limited cell coverage, this is an option to still get the information and visuals on the air.

Instead of canceling the live shot, which messes up the timing, flow and information of a newscast, you could do an as-live or look-live and send the video back to the newsroom so the "live shot" can still make air. Doing an "as-live" also helps keep up the energy for the story which is great for the overall energy of the newscast.

DIGITAL LIVE SHOT

Much of what we just covered translates between broadcast TV live and digital live on any social medium. With digital, however, if done on a cell phone, you may be able to see the responses from your viewers immediately. Speak to those in your live shot. Answer those questions and comments right then and there. That's what this is for. It's a live conversation.

Many reporters will be asked to do digital or streaming lives in between the TV live shots. This may include an interview. If that interview is only available during the digital live, communicate that to the station. Part of that digital live can be recorded, uploaded and used for an upcoming broadcast. It can also be used in social posts or added to the web story. We are in the business of news and storytelling no matter the medium.

A neat thing about doing a digital live, say on Facebook or Instagram, is that your followers will be alerted and may watch and interact with you. This is why your digital live should last at least ten minutes. That gives viewers time to stop what they're doing and watch.

And remember to hold the cell phone horizontal so your shot is landscape and not vertical, making it easier to repurpose for TV.

REMINDERS FOR A GREAT LIVE SHOT

- Be demonstrative and interactive when doing a live shot.
- Always have your IFB with you.
- Use a wireless lavalier. Have an extra lav for your interviewee. Let the control room know if you will be using two remote microphones.

- Live reporters should write their anchor script before heading out if possible.
- Anchors and producers should always have a backup plan with information and video if the live shot falls apart.
- Live reporters should be ready for any question from the anchor.
- If the live reporter wants the opening shot on something other than his or her face that must be communicated to the control room.
- When going live, always be aware of your surroundings.

QUESTIONS

1. What are four characteristics of a good live shot?
2. Name two live shot problems and two solutions?
3. What are two reasons an anchor would want to ask the live reporter a question?
4. What is an as-live or look-live?
5. What are four things to remember as you prepare to cover breaking news?

TRY THIS

1. Write an anchor intro and record your own: 45 as-live.

NOTES

1 Lim, Dion (2020). *Make Your Moment, the Savvy Woman's Communication Playbook for Getting the Success You Want*, McGraw-Hill, p. 131, print.
2 Freedman, W. (2011). *It Takes More Than Good Looks to Succeed at Television News Reporting*, A Wealth of Wisdom, LLC, p. 182, ebook.
3 www.poynter.org/reporting-editing/2020/dos-and-donts-of-covering-protests/
4 Lim, Dion (2020). *Make Your Moment, the Savvy Woman's Communication Playbook for Getting the Success You Want*, McGraw-Hill, p. 26, print.

Newscast, Sports and Weather Anchors

Fifteen

In This Chapter	
What the Public Sees	255
Anchor or Influencer	257
Building Credibility	258
Voice Health	261
Facial Expressions	265
Clothes, Hair and Makeup	267
Live on the Anchor Set	274
Sports Anchor	276
Weather Anchor	279
Community Engagement	282
Social Media	284
Personal Protection	285
Reminders in Anchoring	285
Questions	286
Try This	286

Turn on the news and you will see a face talking back to you. That's the news anchor.

You may think, "What a cool job. What an easy job." You are right—partly. It is a cool job. It is, however, not an easy job.

WHAT THE PUBLIC SEES

News anchors are the face of the TV station. That means they represent the station in the community. Viewers want the anchor to come to Grandma's 93rd birthday party. Viewers want the anchor to come to their child's elementary school and help kick a bully out of school. Viewers want the anchor to speak at their event, find their lost dog and pay their rent because this month is hard to make ends meet. Seriously, we get requests like these more often than we can count.

DOI: 10.4324/9781003137016-15

If a technical director presses the wrong button on the control board and a picture of the sheriff comes up when the anchor is talking about a sex offender, the viewer or the sheriff blames the anchor.

If the producer has an incorrect fact in a story, the viewer loses trust in the anchor who read that story.

If the floor director cues the anchor to the wrong camera—well, you get our drift—it's the anchor who looks inept.

Depending on your station, these scenarios happen infrequently or all of the time. It's partially because the anchor's face is in the viewer's home every day, and viewers feel a certain familiarity with the anchor. Because the viewer doesn't "know" the technical director, producer or floor director but "knows" the anchor, the anchor is seen as the one in charge. We know the anchor is *not* the one in charge of the newsroom. The news director is the boss, but the viewer doesn't know the news director either. Being the face of the station is a big responsibility.

Viewers want the anchor to tell them what's going on in their community and world. They want the anchor to have a heart but be strong. They want the truth, all of the facts, no opinion, but still, they want to know how the anchor feels. They want the anchor to dress nicely, not have a wayward hair sticking out, wear something different every day and speak clearly, concisely and effortlessly. They want anchors to talk to them through the TV, not read to them. They want anchors to be at ease and not look like they have a metal rod stuck up their spine.

So, where were we on that "it looks easy" part?

First a caveat. This chapter devotes a lot of time to looks and appearance. It purposely comes after the writing, reporting and storytelling chapters because those are the foundation of this career. You cannot get to the presentation and appearance part without proficiency in writing, reporting and storytelling.

As much as we would like to tell you that looks don't matter, they do. But so does substance. You must maintain your integrity. It's the basis for your credibility.

> **Mentor Moment: Nick King, Sports Reporter/Anchor, 3TV CBS5, Phoenix**
>
> "Good anchors are clear and decisive. They're able to identify the heart of a story and tell it in a succinct manner. The best

> anchors are able to convey why the information they're sharing is important. Just as importantly, the best anchors are part of a team. They're not above anyone else in the newsroom. They're friendly and approachable to people behind the scenes, who are often paid far less and likely less experienced. Nobody likes working with a prima donna."

ANCHOR OR INFLUENCER

Many people want to be influencers. There are two types. One is more commercial. Another is more journalistic.

We often see the commercial influencers on social media striking a pose or flexing, endorsing a product. Selling or promoting any for-profit good is sales, not journalism. Journalism is unbiased and not for profit.

Another type of influencer *does* have a place in a news anchor's world. It's the kind that directly speaks to substance, community, ethics and leadership. Some examples of that include topics such as social justice, mental health, racial equity, suicide prevention, the environment, healthy living and community activism.

This is positive, unbiased, fact based, community based, empowerment type work. It's like a reporter beat. These anchors build a following on social media and on-air based on their study and expertise of a certain topic. This can be a powerful platform leading to great stories and contacts. These kinds of influencers make a difference in their community through journalistic ethics and *not* promoting a for-profit business.

When interns tell Cyndee Hebert, managing editor of news content at WTHR13 in Indianapolis, they want to be on TV, she asks, "'Who are your senators and representatives? Who is your mayor? What are the top three stories in the news?' You can want to be on TV. To be a good anchor, you also have to want to *live* news," Hebert says.

> **Mentor Moment: Will Tran, MMJ, KRON, San Francisco**
>
> "Journalists are not the center of the story and never should be. They're choosing the wrong field if they want to be loved, because most people these days don't care or even hate reporters."

Doing a selfie at the TV station in a blue dress that looks great on you and posting, "Feeling blue on this September 11th" is more about attention than substance. This post may get tons of likes and follows, but it also etches away at a news person's credibility. It's what Sinclair senior social media director John Colucci calls a vanity post. Advice: wear that awesome dress to a fun event, take a picture with someone getting a special award, and write all about that deserving person. *That* is your job as a journalist.

BUILDING CREDIBILITY

Most anchors start out as reporters. That's because reporters are on the front lines of connecting with the community. They drive all over the area meeting people, covering breaking news and telling stories. They know the audience well. The natural progression is a promotion to anchor to further connect with the viewer because of the vast knowledge he or she has gained in the field.

It is that knowledge that is often called upon in writing interview scripts and deciding the best questions to ask. The anchor's discerning eye can make sure the crux of the story is complete and the "why care" and community perspective are included.

> **Mentor Moment: Chris Alvarez, Sports Reporter, KGO, San Francisco**
>
> "Talent will get people so far, but how much are you willing to work for it? Do you love what you do? Are you having fun? Believe it or not, those types of things show up in your performance. The biggest compliment I can receive is someone telling me that they can tell that I love what I do just based on how I am during my sportscasts, reports and social media posts."

Pronunciation

While re-reading scripts (an hour or more before the broadcast) the anchor's job is to ensure correct pronunciation. Do you know how to pronounce the name of every community, business and street in the area? One way to learn is to go through months of web stories or archived TV stories to find words you don't know how to pronounce and ask.

Do not accept the answer, "Oh, I think it's...." Find someone who knows for sure. Mispronouncing words is a quick way to lose credibility. If no one in the station knows, call the office of the person or the town.

> **Hint:** most city and county offices have a recorded welcome message. In that message, the town or official's name is said. Voila! Now you know how to pronounce it.

Plenty of online sources offer audio pronouncers. Make sure those sources are reliable because some are not.

Mispronunciation becomes less of an issue when an anchor pre-reads the scripts a few times. That not only helps you catch words that are a challenge to pronounce but also to catch any grammar, spelling or punctuation errors.

Dion Lim remembers a time when she didn't catch those errors before going live:

> I was afraid of telling my writers there were major typos and factual errors in the scripts. This led me to stumble on camera and spewing not-quite-right information to the masses. Nobody knew it was the writer who did it. I was the fall guy and face of the bad work. But I learned over the years how to approach someone about their work and to offer suggestions and guidance in a way that was constructive and didn't come across as bossy or authoritative.

Breaking News

Anchors must be able to ad-lib at a moment's notice if there's breaking news or if a last-minute story needs perspective. News anchors must be up on what's going on around the world and the community. If your producer says we're breaking out of a story to go live to the health department because of a person with the flu, the anchor needs to already know what is going on with the flu. Is the flu really bad this year? Is there another virus that people are dying from? This is how things began in the winter of 2020 before the coronavirus became the big news of the year.

If the breaking news is a landslide, is this the same area where there was a devastating wildfire last year? Rain after a wildfire is of concern because the land can easily slide.

If the breaking news is a house fire, is this the same location where police have been trying to get homeless people to stop squatting? This is the community and world perspective news anchors must have.

> **Mentor Moment: Scott McGrew, Anchor/Reporter, KNTV, San Jose**
>
> "Spend some time being a producer. Nothing will prepare you better to understand how a newscast flows and why sometimes you just have to do something a certain way because it makes sense. The other stuff is obvious: practice your scripts, practice empathy, listen to what people are saying, and above all realize you ain't fancy. You're just the final cog in a big machine."

McGrew makes a good point. Knowing how to produce and why a producer makes a particular decision is helpful. This speaks to the bigger picture. To be a good (enter newsroom job here) you should do a lot of *other* jobs first. This offers perspective, understanding, a discerning eye and knowledge about how and why the news gets on the air or online every day.

If the anchor has reported before, he or she understands the chaotic scene during a breaking news live shot and can ask relatable questions. That anchor can also verbally jump in if a reporter is getting flustered or is missing a piece of information.

If the anchor has produced before, he or she can assist with story flow and appreciate tense communication from the producer in the control room during breaking news.

If the news anchor has forecast the weather before, she or he can help explain a news story about a tornado, flood, ice storm or haboob (a big sand storm common in desert areas around the world). Even if an anchor used to do traffic reports or sports reports, that expertise may come in handy.

> **Mentor Moment: Dion Lim, News Anchor, KGO, San Francisco**
>
> "This business is terribly subjective. I've had news directors not hire me because of my voice, while others will offer me jobs because of it. The way I tell stories is different from my colleagues. It doesn't mean one of us is the better storyteller, we just have different styles."

VOICE HEALTH

Talking may come easy to you. Open your mouth and out comes sound. But there's something different about projecting your words. That doesn't mean yelling. You have a microphone on your shirt or jacket. You only need to talk loud enough to be heard on that device.

Projecting is to speak concisely, clearly and with energy. If not done correctly, you could sound high pitched, nasally or breathy. At the worst, you could strain your vocal cords.

Let's take a moment and explain how sound comes out of our mouths. It can help keep you from losing your voice and help ensure your voice is pleasant to listen to.

The Diaphragm

It starts with a breath. Take in a deep breath. Keep pulling in that breath—deeper. The deep breath needs to come from way down in your belly as your midsection pushes out when you inhale. That's your diaphragm.

Deep breathing from your diaphragm can help you pump a little more weight at the gym. It may help you get a deeper pose in yoga or Pilates. It can also help calm you if you start to get anxious about an exam, interview or anything that's causing stress. That calm can also help keep your voice in a controlled, lower pitch that equates to an anchor's credibility.

Do you remember that first time you heard your recorded voice you thought, "Ick. That's how I sound?" For a lot of people starting out, the voice can sound high-pitched or just unfamiliar.

If you breathe deeply, the voice pitch will come down because you're speaking from your diaphragm and not your throat. When we get nervous, we tend to have shallow breaths and speak from the throat. That brings up the pitch of our voice because the muscles in the throat are pulling on the vocal cords.

"Like a guitar string. Pluck it, it vibrates," says Dr. George Hsu, an otolaryngologist, also known as an ear, nose and throat doctor. "Too much tension, the string, or vocal cord, doesn't vibrate well. Each person has a natural resonance frequency where it vibrates the best."

Hsu likens the vocal cords to a rubber band. "The vocal pitch changes with pressure. When stretched, the pitch goes up," he explains.

The Larynx and Vocal Cords

Deep breathing can put less stress on the voice box, which is also known as the larynx. It's like a big brother putting his arm around his little brother, the vocal cords. If the big brother (larynx) is hurt in any way, the little brother (vocal cords) is put in a tense situation. The cords are pulled tightly, and the voice starts to change. When the larynx is healthy, there is no adverse tension on the vocal cords, so they can make the sound they're supposed to.

Healthy Voice Box

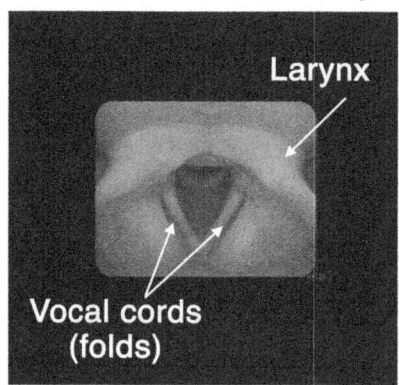
Folds are open when we breathe

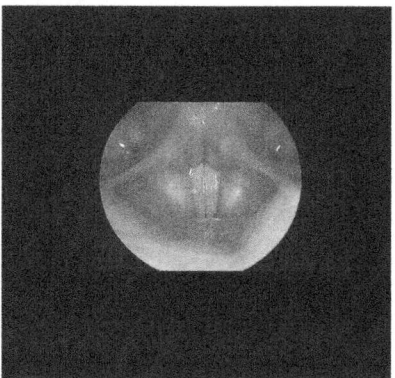
Folds close when speaking and vibrate to make sound

Damaged Voice Box

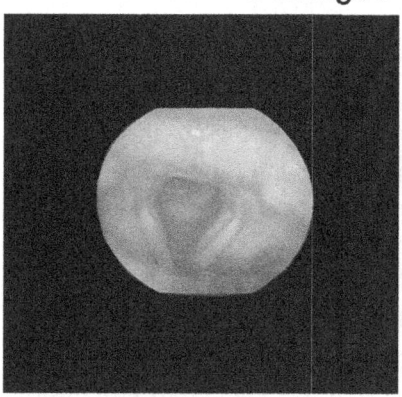
Inflamed larynx pulling on the vocal cords

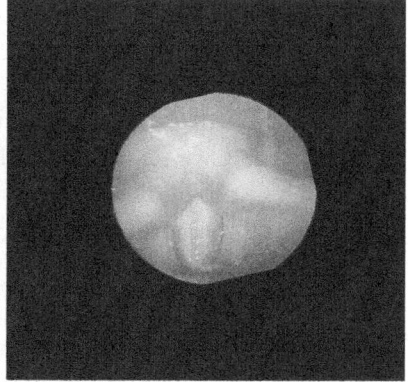
Vocal cords unable to vibrate because of inflamed larynx

Figure 15.1 Larynx and Vocal Cords

There are a few ways the larynx gets hurt. One comes from talking too much or talking too loudly. That can hurt the voice because it strains the muscles around the larynx which in turn puts tension on the vocal cords.

Air passes through the vocal cords each time we make a sound and take a breath. If we're dehydrated, that air can heat up the voice box and change the vocal quality.

"Air goes through the vocal cords at 200 cycles a second for women and 100 cycles per second for men," Hsu says. "So, hydration is important."

Hsu is talking about good vocal hygiene. Water is the best way to hydrate. Stay away from caffeine or anything acidic.

The voice box is at the important junction between the airway through which we breathe (known as the windpipe or trachea) and the esophagus where our food travels to the stomach.

We can hurt the larynx by what we eat and drink. If we eat a lot of junk food, acidic food and soda, the stomach can create extra acid. Some people feel the pain known as heartburn. Others don't feel any pain at all. But stomach acid or vapors can move up the esophagus and burn the larynx.

If you notice you're having heartburn often, you may want to eat less acidic foods or at least don't eat or drink it before you perform. That includes soda, alcohol and caffeine. Hsu recommends you drink a lot of water. Tea, honey and lemon work well too. Lemon may be acidic outside the body, but when it's ingested, it becomes alkaline, the opposite of acidic.

Don't eat and then go right to sleep. Allow your body to digest food before lying down. That cuts down on the acid vapors inflaming the larynx.

What if you notice you're losing your voice?

"Don't talk. Not at all," Hsu says. "Rest prevents you from developing tension in the larynx. Relax the voice, especially on weekends."

Hsu also says you should avoid coughing, as difficult as that may sound.

"That traumatizes the vocal cords. Clearing the throat does too. Yelling and whispering are both bad. Whispering is just as bad as yelling because you are putting a lot of tension on those muscles," Hsu says.

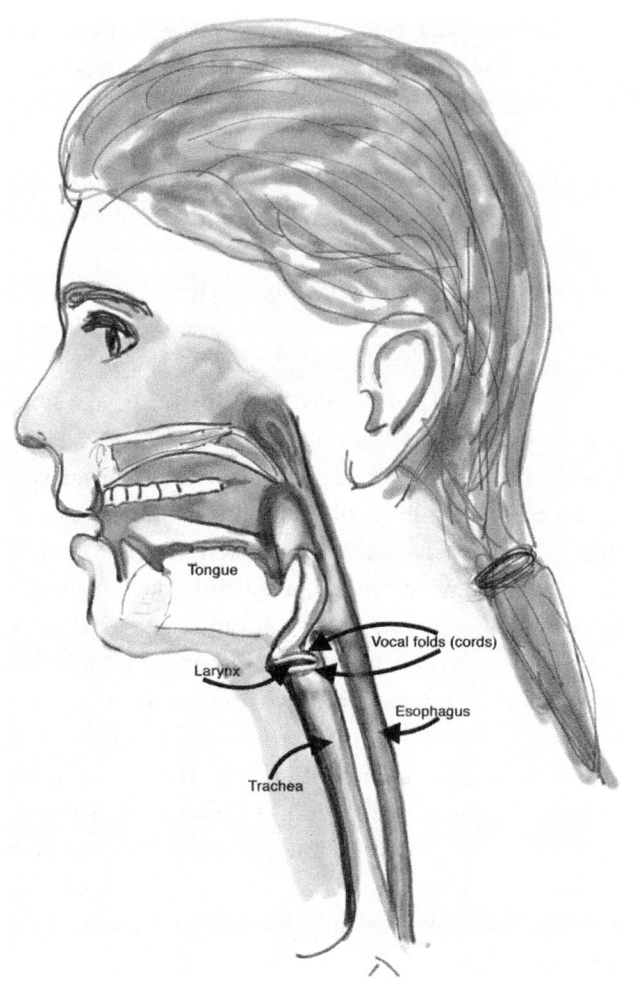

Figure 15.2 Voicebox

Breathe

We already talked about diaphragmatic breathing. Now let's look at how you use your breath while speaking.

Have you ever had to stop to take a breath in the middle of a sentence? Or, maybe you were belting out a favorite song as you were driving in the car and ran out of air and had to take a breath when you were supposed to be singing more words. We need to get control of our breath so we can breathe at the right time while we're talking. Frankly, this just takes practice.

One of the easiest ways to practice this is to read out loud. If you are taking a newscast production class and get to read scripts, use those. Or, go to your favorite news website. Read a story out loud. Project with your voice. Again, we don't mean to yell, we just mean to speak with strength and authority. Pause where there's a comma. Pause where you think there should be some inflection or emphasis. It's OK if you run out of air occasionally. Figure out what made that happen and keep reading. The more you do this, you'll gauge your lung level and know when to appropriately pause for a breath.

FACIAL EXPRESSIONS

While you are reading that story out loud, look at yourself in the mirror, or better yet, record your face. Figure out how to read the story with an expressive face. No, widening your eyes and lifting your eyebrows is not the only move here. Does the nature of the story call for a look of sadness, horror, dismay, disappointment, exasperation, excitement, anticipation, hope or joy? These are just a few emotions anchors need to learn to *feel* in the face so they can express them while delivering stories.

The face has 43 muscles. That's a lot of expressions. It's important to become familiar with what they feel like so you can share them on command when the script calls for it.

If you play golf, you know muscle memory is important for when you address the ball at the tee. How deeply do you bend your knees? Your arms? Your lower back? Knowing what that feels like will help you hit more consistently and stay in the fairway. If you are a diver or basketball player, skater or piano player, muscle memory is important in how you perform. If these athletes and musicians practice over and over to increase their consistency, anchors must, too.

When you practice reading, write the emotion of the story at the top of your page. For example, if you are reading a story about children graduating from kindergarten, put a happy face on the script. Remember to smile while reading this story. If the story is about a fire destroying a campus apartment complex, write "serious" at the top. Look down, imagine the students who lost everything, then look up and deliver that story.

Why are we spending time on this? Remember, we talked about how we want our scripts to be written conversationally so they sound like the anchor is just talking to the viewer and not reading. The expression will help further this comfortable storytelling.

Showing Emotion

If your heart and spirit feel emotion, how can your face not follow? You may wonder if showing emotion hurts your credibility. Recently, our students asked whether they can maintain impartiality if they feel for the stories they're reporting. Yes, though it depends on the emotion and the story.

As with many things, there is a gray area. It is understandable for an anchor to be choked up after an emotional story about the death of a mother alone in a hospital room. During COVID-19, this was a common occurrence. Families said goodbye through a cell phone as that mother took her last breath. The death of a loved one is terrible. A person dying alone is heart wrenching.

In the example of Black Lives Matter protests and reporting of how George Floyd died under the knee of a police officer in Minneapolis, the emotions of anger and sadness are universal. We anchors and reporters know to keep our opinions to ourselves, but we *can* share context and perspective.

While reporting on Floyd's death, NBC Washington correspondent Tracie Potts had to make a split-second decision when an anchor unexpectedly said, "Can I ask you a personal question?" during a live shot. Potts remembered her journalism professors' lessons to never give an opinion. But based on her years of engaging with viewers through social media, she has also learned viewers want to know who you are.

So, she answered as the mother of a teenage son and a woman of color. She says it felt cathartic and that sharing her perspective as an African American was her responsibility.

Potts wrote an article about that exchange for the USC Annenberg Center for Health Journalism.

"Reporting on race can be stressful," Potts wrote in the article. "But it's necessary. In this critical moment in our nation's history, no one can tell this story like those who have lived it."[1]

Potts describes this as bias versus perspective:

> My bias, we all have them, should never impact how I tell a story. My job is to be fair and objective and tell all sides, whether I agree with them or not.

But my *perspective* as a person of color, as a mom, as a Christian, as a Southerner, as a college graduate, as a woman, are helpful in providing insight to my viewers.

If anchors and reporters are truly a mirror to the community, then how can they not feel in the stories they report?

Dion Lim received an Emmy® in June 2020 for her work on one of the most challenging days of her anchoring career.

> **Mentor Moment: Dion Lim, Anchor**
>
> "When the Gilroy Garlic Festival shooting happened in 2019, and I was at the anchor desk for three hours by myself, absorbing interview after interview of kids recalling what it was like to see their relatives shot or hearing from terrified festival-goers who hid underneath tables to escape the gunfire. I started tearing up after hour two because it was just so heavy and tragic. I couldn't keep it in any longer. I think if an anchor did not react in this way, or at least with some semblance of sadness, then they're not human. They're robots."

CLOTHES, HAIR AND MAKEUP

Every newsroom has a different style. That style is usually a mirror of that newsroom's community. Some are more conservative than others. You need to know your station's on-air look. For the purpose of helping you learn the business and get a job, we are going to describe a uniform that is on the more conservative side because this is the foundation from which everyone begins.

We call it a uniform for a reason. It is what you wear to work. It's not what you wear to go out with friends. The anchor uniform is not designed to cover up or take away your personal identity and style. It is designed to make the anchor look clean, crisp, vibrant and undistracting while imparting important information.

Tailored clothes work best. Tailored means form-fitting but not so tight that you see undergarment lines or rolls of the tummy.

Solid colors traditionally work best. A small, tiny moiré print does not work well. The camera can't figure out what to focus on and shows a strange-looking, wavy pattern. Examples of tiny print would be a lot of thin lines, small polka dots, chevron print or tiny flowers. If those lines or designs are bigger, about the size of a dime, the camera will work just fine. Simply, the recommendation is to dress presidential.

"You never see a U.S. president wearing a black suit, black shirt, black tie, or a suit with crazy big stripes, or odd-colored shirts," says Desiree Hill, a mass communication professor at the University of Central Oklahoma and former TV news consultant.

For women, she suggests the female elected official look.

"They tend to wear basic suits or professional dresses that do not distract. Traditional lawyer-wear also can work for on-air talent," Hill says.

Men

Blazer: It's pretty easy for men to dress like a news anchor. Wear a medium-weight material blazer. Usually, that means wool, which can come in heavy or lighter weaves. These weaves are not likely to wrinkle and that's what we want—no wrinkles. Steer away from cotton and linen on the anchor desk. They may be OK out in the field.

Some body types may work better with double-breasted jackets. The key is to sit and see how the jacket fits when trying it on in the dressing room. If it bunches in weird ways, find a different cut. A blazer must lay well on the body as the person sits and stands.

Solid colors work best for TV, but it's usually OK if the blazer has some light lines of other colors. An example of this is a navy blazer with faint lines of yellow, red and/or light blue. Those lines are not likely to make the camera freak out. The same goes with a square pattern in faint colors. Those usually work well, too.

Big, bold white lines on a dark-colored blazer do not work well with the camera.

Sorry, you may look "clean" in real life, and you can proudly wear it outside of the news studio. The pattern just doesn't work well for news anchors.

Sports anchors can usually go a little bolder with their clothes. Check with the boss.

Usually, news managers prefer men to wear blazers in colors ranging from gray and navy to brown, taupe and dark khaki. A light gray or light blue can work in the warmer months. Red, burgundy, pink, gold, purple and green blazers do not work well for TV news.

They may be just fine for weather and sports but not for news because they can be distracting.

Think of it this way. If the news anchor is on camera and someone is walking by the TV at home, the first thing that person should notice is the news anchor's face, not the clothes.

Shirt: TV consultants say white is the universal best color for men of all skin tones. It acts as a frame to highlight the face and, again, the face is what we want the audience to look at to see all of those expressions for each story.

There are a few other colors that can work on TV, too, like light blue, light yellow, any light color. We say light because it's a hint of color, not something that just pops out. If you can barely notice what color it is, that works.

A few shirt colors that do not work well for a TV news anchor are black, navy blue or dark brown. Again, this may look fabulous as you head out to a friend's wedding but not on TV as a news anchor.

It's fine to show off your personality, but there's a fine line between that and insubordination. Take a moment to think whether this is the "hill you want to die on." That means, are you willing to possibly throw away your job and have a fight with the news director over this topic?

Tie: This is where you can show some personality. You may choose virtually any pattern or color you want except, as we said, tiny little designs like polka dots or chevron lines. Other than that, go for it.

If you are a bow tie guy, maybe hold that for Fridays or holidays or something that people can look forward to and know that it's special. Bow ties can be considered distracting for news mostly because they are considered to be dressier than a standard tie. However, if you really want to wear bow ties to stand out, have a conversation with your boss and work something out. It could be a cool, memorable thing that helps the audience connect with you.

Jewelry: If you are a man with an earring or necklace, most news managers will ask that you do not wear them on set. The reason is not to take away your individuality but to keep from distracting the viewer from the important news you are sharing. If you are doing weather or sports, you may be able to keep the jewelry in plain sight. It all depends on the overall style of the station and community. It requires a conversation with the news director.

Hair: Slicked-back hair is not a common look for TV news. If you prefer your hair like this, find a product that holds but doesn't look wet or greasy. If you prefer a messier look, find a way to have controlled, messy hair that you can replicate every time you are on the air. News anchors' looks should not change from day to day. Consistency is key.

The same goes for facial hair. Anything extra on the face can be distracting on a tight shot of a TV news anchor. If you wear a mustache, keep it groomed. Full or tightly trimmed beards are not common in TV news, but that doesn't mean they can't work. There are examples of newsmen with facial hair, including your mentor in this book, Nick King. Wolf Blitzer is another whose beard has become his trademark. It all depends on what your news manager likes.

What if there is no hair? Los Angeles makeup artist Robin Slater has a secret weapon to combat the shine of the stage lights: "Ban Roll-On Antiperspirant & Deodorant Unscented," she says.

Makeup: This is not a comfortable topic for most men, but it must be worn when you're at the anchor desk, and in many cases, in live shots. You do not need to wear a lot of makeup, but just the right kind and the right amount will even out the skin tone and keep the bright lights of a TV studio from showing the blood vessels that sit under the top layer of skin.

Depending on whether you have dry or oily skin, you'll need to decide whether to use a powder, liquid or gel foundation. Going to the makeup counter and working with a professional who understands TV lights is key. Not all makeup works under these conditions.

"Always keep natural powder and a mattifier," Slater recommends. A lot of companies make mattifiers that help fight shine on the face. It's used under the makeup. You do not need to add color to the skin, just a protective layer to even out the skin tone.

If you choose to wear a little bronzer, make sure it doesn't turn orange under the lights. Use it sparingly and in strategic places, where you would naturally tan—not under the eyes, for example. Make sure your face and hands match.

Some men have naturally rosy lips making it look as if they are wearing lipstick on TV. In those cases, men may want to put foundation over the lips or find a light tone lipstick to lighten the natural color of the lips.

If you have light-colored brows, you may choose to add a little color. Brows help frame the eyes, which is where we express the nature of the news stories. So, a light brow pencil or brush may be a good idea.

Finally, some men may choose to wear a light coat of mascara. It opens up the eyes—again, the focal point for our communication. A light application can be helpful. It's up to you.

In the early 1990s, Ted Hall was in a public restroom getting ready for WBIR's Live at Five On-the-Road show. He was putting light powder on his face and then started putting on one coat of mascara. He was wearing his suit, tie and dress shoes 15 minutes before the show went live. A young boy walked into the men's restroom, saw Hall putting on the mascara, and ran out yelling, "Mom!" Hall openly shares that story when explaining how strange and funny it is to be a news anchor.[2]

Women

Blazer: This is an easy go-to look for women. It's a look of strength and professionalism. Just like for men, the best fabric is a light to medium wool or fabric that does not wrinkle and has structure. Silk can work, just make sure it's steamed, unwrinkled and not shimmery. One-hundred percent cotton and linen don't work well on set because of the wrinkle factor. Cotton blends are usually OK.

Just as we advised with men, make sure the blazer hangs on the body without bunching. Yes, sitting in the dressing room can help make sure those clothes will fit smoothly with the blazer buttoned. That button helps to streamline the structure of the blazer giving a slimming effect like the capital letter V. The top of the V is the shoulders. The button is the bottom of the V.

A properly fitting blazer has nothing to do with weight. Size does not matter. Do not let the size of the clothes, be it a blazer, dress, pants or shirt, alter your buying decision. The *only* thing that matters is how it fits on your body. You may need to size up so the outfit lays smoothly.

Be honest with yourself. Will you need to wear shapewear? No one should *ever* see an underwear or bra line under the fabric. Ever. Shapewear could help with that. Adding a padded bra could also help. Seriously. Sometimes the only thing that takes away an odd bunching in a dress or blazer is a little more oomph in the chest area to smooth away a distracting line of the fabric.

The colors and patterns of blazers for men hold true for women. But for some, the blazer is not a good fit for the body, as Dion Lim remembers from her earlier days in the business:

> I used to wear these big boxy suits in not-so-flattering shades of black, brown and gray. It wasn't me. I'm full of life and energy and color. A news manager once told me to wear Skittles® colors because they'd pop on TV. I did, and it worked for me. It became my signature. As long as my outfit was clean and tidy and not distracting, people would appreciate the professionalism, notice the brightness and move on to focus on what I was saying, not my clothes, which is the point.

Blouse: Just as for men, the color of the shirt can add a pop of color to frame your face, or like a man's tie, add a little personality. Make sure it does not show cleavage. Remember, you're trying to wear clothes that don't distract from the stories you are sharing.

Also, make sure to tuck in the top. When standing up, the look should be a clean pop of color seen at the neckline of the blazer which flows into the pants or skirt that hangs below.

Dresses: A popular look for anchorwomen is jewel-toned, sheath dresses. Jewel tones are vibrant colors, or as Dion Lim's boss described, Skittles® colors. They look great on a TV screen and under the studio lights. These vibrant colors work well for dresses, blouses and blazers for most women.

If you have great arms, wearing a sleeveless dress may work well. If your arms are not toned, this may be a distracting look. Because of lighting and shadows, a woman's arms may look less toned on TV than in person. Also, some newsroom managers forbid this look on the newscast. Under a blazer, a sheath dress nearly always looks flattering.

Dresses are another style of clothing that must be checked in the dressing room for lines, wrinkles and bunches when you sit or stand. Shimmery satin may be pretty, but on TV it does not work well.

Jewelry: A little sparkle or spot of color is good but anything that yells out "look at me!" does not work for the TV anchor uniform. Just as we wrote for the men, if a viewer is walking by the

TV and notices your jewelry, or anything other than your face, that's distracting.

The other thing about jewelry is to make sure it won't hit the microphone. If you are wearing a crew neck, make sure the necklace does not fall where the mic will be clipped.

Earrings should add a pop of color or sparkle but not to a distracting degree.

Bracelets are great for color and sparkle; however, if they make any noise as you move your arms on the anchor desk, you'll have to take them off. Same with a watch. Bangles and charms rarely work because they can be noisy. Stretchy bracelets may work better.

Makeup: Women are used to wearing makeup. Be warned. More is not better. As we described with men, not all makeup can hold up to studio lights. Usually, that will mean no illumination makeup. You don't want the lights of the set or live shot to catch every little sparkle on your face. That dewy look a favorite actress and model wears may look fabulous on her, especially when she performs at the halftime show of the biggest football game of the year, but under the studio lights, it can look unflattering.

> **Mentor Moment: Dion Lim, Anchor**
>
> "If people are paying more attention to your oil slick than the words coming from your mouth then you've got problems. My makeup bag is stocked with an endless supply of oil blotting sheets and powder."

Contouring can be helpful in a limited way. It's best to practice. The key areas are the jawline, under the cheekbones and possibly along the bridge of the nose. And, as you are working the jawline, make sure to extend the makeup and color of the face down to your neck. The face, neck and hands should be the same color.

Watch your eyeliner and lashes. Remember this is to enhance or open up your eyes to best communicate, not mimic the latest high fashion. Slater says keep the cat-eye look for the weekend and the big bold fake eyelashes for your friend's wedding.

> **Mentor Moment: Robin Slater, Union Journeyman Make-Up Artist, Los Angeles**
>
> "Study your market. Just as make-up for dramatic film, documentary, soap opera, everything has its place. Don't study drag makeup. That's become an extremely bad trend. That heavy makeup, strong contour, shimmery highlights, glitter, thick eyeliner, and big lashes are not appropriate for news. But there are some exceptions in the Latino market. Subtle lips with natural colors are good. Avoid gloss and heavy liner."

LIVE ON THE ANCHOR SET

Your day as a news anchor may begin six hours before the newscast begins. You may have spent that time covering a story, speaking at a community event or reading through scripts and working with the producer or even producing your own newscast.

By the time you are called to the studio, none of that matters. Tired, hungry, angry, thinking of something else? Forget it. The viewer knows *nothing* of what you did before the studio lights went on. This is the moment that matters. Get in the headspace. Make sure you give yourself enough time to fix your face, hair and clothes. Have your water next to you. Put on your microphone and IFB. Check with the control room that they both work. Take a deep breath and sit up (or stand up) straight.

At this moment you should know what's next. In fact, you should know your next three steps—your camera, the story you're reading first and the story you will read next. That brings calm and control. Even if it's breaking news and you don't know what the pictures will be, you know you're going off script. See, even though there may be a lot you don't know, you always know *something*.

While you are on camera telling these stories, you are showing the emotion of the story in your face and body language. You are using your head, shoulders, chest and even arms to tell the story. You are looking to your co-anchor every once in a while, if you're on a two-shot.

Remember what the audience sees. Viewers are looking at two people looking back at them. Think of it like you're at a party. You and your co-anchor are talking and a person walks up to you both and joins the conversation. Now, you are looking at both this new person and your co-anchor while telling your story. At a party, and on the anchor desk, it's just that—a conversation.

On-Set Interview

If an interviewee is added, in person or through a monitor, your job is to continue that conversation. Either the producer or anchor will write the script for this on-set interview. It will include a lead sentence or two about the topic, followed by an introduction.

Introduce this person by looking at the camera—your audience. That's how you'd do it at a party, looking at each person as you introduce them. There may be thousands of people watching you, but you must think of the audience as just one person.

Once you introduce your guest, ask your first question and then let that person speak. Those questions need to be researched and decided upon ahead of time. Even though you have those questions, you must listen to the answers for the opportunity to learn something new or to ad-lib a totally different question.

These interviews are conducted much the same way as taped interviews, but a live interview has a specific time constraint.

So, let's review. As an anchor, you are looking at the camera, using good posture, reading the teleprompter, sharing emotion and expression in your face and body. You are occasionally looking at your co-anchor and a monitor if that's included on the set. You are listening to interviews, asking questions, some ad-libbed and not on your list of prepared questions. You are paying attention to which camera is next or which monitor you need to walk to for the next story. And, you are projecting energy to your viewer. It can be exhausting. Thirty minutes can feel like an eternity when you just start out. It's a marathon, not a sprint, and requires all of the preparation you've read about in this chapter to do well.

Once the broadcast is done, thank your crew. Commend your co-anchor and producer. Have a debrief to talk about what went right and what could be fixed for next time. Always keep an eye to the positive. Always keep an eye to learning how to do better.

SPORTS ANCHOR

> **Mentor Moment: Nick King, Sports Reporter**
>
> "No matter what genre you're covering, the goal is to be memorable and make people feel. Make them laugh, make them cry, make them think. Find the human emotion in stories, that will stick with the people watching long after the newscast ends."

Sports is more than highlights. Those are still a segment of the job, especially for that stunning over-the-wall catch in right field, the last-second goal or the 50-yard Hail Mary pass for the winning touchdown. But the reality nowadays is that people are able to access those plays on their phone in an instant.

Phoenix sports anchor Nick King says his job is to give the viewer the full story of that highlight, the how and the why.

"This goes back to two words—curiosity and memorable," King says:

> We have to go beyond just watching a game and look for the details on the field and behind the scenes that tell great stories. Personally, I've found that this background makes the highlights so much richer when you're able to put real meaning behind them.

King considers himself a storyteller, not just a "sports guy." He prides himself in making his stories relevant and noteworthy:

> I would argue sports stories provide even more opportunities to inspire. Not simply because of the amazing talent on the field or the court but because of the real-life hardships people overcome to reach college athletics, professional athletics, or even the end of a local marathon.

> **Mentor Moment: Chris Alvarez, Sports Reporter**
>
> "Be willing to be versatile and make sure you can do it all. It's not just showing up on set and being on-air. You have to be able to shoot, write, edit, be good on social media, and have an on-camera presence. A lot of jobs especially in that first small market will be a

> news/sports combo or weather/news combo, so even if sports is your passion, be willing to take a job that is both to get your foot in the door."

Many people in your community participate in amateur sports such as running, cycling and swimming. They're Little League coaches, ballet teachers and soccer moms and dads. There are thousands of untold stories in your community that have all of the elements of good storytelling—a strong central character, compelling video and great nat sound (NATS).

King considers every aspect of his job storytelling, even highlights of a Phoenix Suns basketball game.

He asks himself, "What are the plays I need to show that tell the story of the game?" He includes an amazing play or a play that was a deciding factor in how the game turned out. That's how he tells the story of the game to his viewers:

> It's not just what's happening in that moment. It's a combination of what you are saying with context. Where in the game are we? What's the score? How many points did that person have in the game? For example, I'd say, 'Second quarter Suns up a point. Devin Booker. Two of his 36 points of the night.'

Alvarez calls that "Situation. Action. Results." Sometimes you write the highlight based on a game or on a singular player or action.

"For example, the Warriors were down a bunch last night. Then they made a big run in the fourth quarter. We started the highlights in the fourth quarter because we're in the market of San Francisco and we care about the Warriors so we focus on them," Alvarez says.

If he worked at a national sports channel the highlights might look different to reach the broader audience.

Knowing your market is key. You may personally be a New England Patriots fan, but if your audience in Milwaukee roots for the Packers, then you cover the Packers.

"For most places, the NFL is king," King says. "For us, the Arizona Cardinals are just OK, but pretty much anything that happens with them is our biggest news. Almost nothing beats that."

At the time he said this, the Suns were doing well, so the local basketball team was the number one focus.

"Unless something happens with the Cardinals," King says. "If they sign a player or make a trade, that is still the most important thing."

The only story that could possibly top that, is if something crazy happened in the world of sports that has people talking. Being flexible is an important part of the job.

Both of these sports anchors log big plays as they watch multiple games at a time. They write down the time code of each play. Then, they pick a few of the top plays from that list and write their highlight VO. Then, they edit that VO. After that, they re-read their script as the video plays to make sure the words match the video and vice versa.

When something big in the world of sports happens, these experts are called to action and work in tandem with the news crews. Like on February 23, 2021 when Tiger Woods crashed his SUV down a hill in Los Angeles. Alvarez recalls that day:

> I was getting calls quickly. I came in early. I talked with the news producers about how to cover this. Tiger went to Stanford. There were a lot of local connections. We decided news reporters would cover the nuts and bolts of the crash. I would cover the sports world, the outpouring of support. The PGA golfers were in Florida. They were speaking. Some were crying. I focused on how the sports world was reacting.

Both Alvarez and King are sports anchors on the weekend in their markets. During the week they focus on a different type of sports reporting known as human interest stories. Their stories may be about an athlete but they focus less on stats and more on connecting with the humanity of the story.

"The grandmother who doesn't know about sports but can connect with the story. That's the goal," Alvarez says. "Good sports is more about human interest compared to who threw for 250 yards in the first half."

> **Mentor Moment: Nick King, Sports Anchor/Reporter, 3TV CBS5, Phoenix**
>
> "'Nothing' writing drives me nuts. You must say something interesting. I could do a live shot before a game, say who's playing and at what time. That's essentially nothing. Or, I could find something statistical or a trend or something to keep an eye on."

That kind of viewer connection is what drives Alvarez and King to keep working during games and events their friends are watching and enjoying together at home:

> You think you love sports; you're going to find out how much you love *working* in sports. Weekends and nights. That's when the important things are happening. Often, I get texts or calls from friends. They're together watching a big game on a Saturday and having fun. I'm in my office, by myself, watching the game, taking notes, not totally able to enjoy it and a little stressed out because I know the game is going to end like three minutes before I need to be on TV to talk about it.

Alvarez says, "This business is not for everyone. You miss things, birthdays and holidays. I wouldn't want to be doing anything else. I love what I do. It doesn't feel like a job."

If becoming a sports reporter or sports anchor is your goal, it's this type of storytelling that news directors and sports directors will want to see on your resume reel.

Scan the following QR code to watch King's story that won a regional Edward R. Murrow award.

WEATHER ANCHOR

If our job is to communicate and do so conversationally, then this is another prime position for that viewer connection.

> **Mentor Moment: Lisa Argen, Meteorologist, KGO, San Francisco**
>
> "My first job was in Knoxville, Tennessee. This was a great college town and a big step away from my upstate New York roots. I knew back in 1990, I would have to be willing to traverse

> the country if I was dedicated to really learning how to do my job. Living in different cities allowed me to learn firsthand about how geography affects weather patterns. Knoxville is influenced by mountains and a great plateau. My next job in Chicago, I was by a huge Great Lake. Today I forecast next to the vast Pacific Ocean."

Argen says her job is about much more than temperatures and jet streams.

"Weather affects everyone and many businesses," Argen says. "My ability to connect with people through conversation and weather tidbits within two to three minutes is certainly challenging, but faced with severe weather and changing viewer habits, I have had to adapt."

> **Mentor Moment: Lisa Argen, Meteorologist, KGO, San Francisco**
>
> "Right now, we're in a drought, and last year's wildfires have left an indelible imprint on our communities. There has never been a more important time for communicating the impact of weather on our lives and livelihoods."

Everything must be relatable. Are those temperatures well above or below normal? Has the area not experienced that temperature in a long time, or is it a record? Do the viewers need to make changes because of the incoming winds, freezing temperatures, rain, snow, intense heat or bad air quality? Is this changing weather coming from a big weather event that happened many states away?

In some of those cases, the story and the weather forecast move into a whole different category. It can become a lifesaving moment as former WBIR meteorologist Marti Skold remembers from May 18, 1995.[3]

"That date is etched into my mind forever," Skold says.

The TV station in East Tennessee had a brand new radar system. It was a big deal. This technology allowed Skold and the other meteorologists to track storms down to the neighborhood and street level. You may consider this commonplace now, but back in 1995, it was a new way of telling the weather story of the day.

"When I saw the first hook echo of the supercell, I knew that this would be a devastating outbreak," Skold says.

On the radar screen that was filled with green, which signifies rain, there were other colors she was honing in on. Orange and red showed intense rain. When she saw the red hook, which signified a tornado, she knew she needed to jump into action.

This was well before social media. The only way to inform the public at the time was by breaking into television programming. Did you catch the date? May 18th. Ratings.

In fact, on this night, it was the season finale for one of the most popular comedies on TV, "Friends." This was also before you could rewind a broadcast and re-watch a favorite scene. This was before you could watch a show On Demand. Back in this day, we got one chance to see a TV program and then would have to wait for re-runs at a much later date. Barbaric, right? How did we live back then?

Back to the tornado and the meteorologist.

"I was focused on making sure that our viewers were warned in time to get to a safe place in their homes. When the tornado was tracking right into populated areas, I reached out to the evening producer, the news director, and the general manager and said we have to break in now!" Skold remembers.

They understood the magnitude of the storms and trusted her judgment. Skold says:

> We broke into 'Friends' at a big moment in the show, but I knew that lives were at risk. I never hesitated or had a second thought about what was on. I knew people needed to take action immediately. Management stood behind me. They trusted me. The viewers trusted our station, forecasts and tracking system. The next day one of our reporters was on the scene of the homes that were damaged, and one family said their lives were saved because they were watching TV at the moment we broke in. They ran to their safe place. Their living room where they *had* been sitting was destroyed. Those are stories that tell us how making a decision can save lives. I have always been grateful to have had wise managers who trusted their staff.

Yes, some people, who were not in the tornado's path, were mad that their favorite TV show was interrupted. And they let the station know with phone calls and letters. Station management ran the episode a few days later, in its entirety.

COMMUNITY ENGAGEMENT

A well-respected news anchor must strike a balance between delivering news, much of which can be bad or distressing, and positively representing the community. As we've said, it is a big responsibility and rests almost solely on the shoulders of the anchor.

Mistakes are seen by many and that can hurt one's pride. Being yourself may rub a viewer the wrong way and that can hurt, too. Some days you can do everything right and feel like a winner, and the next day you can feel like the ultimate loser based on viewer comments.

A successful news anchor must have thick skin. As Don Miquel Ruiz writes in *The Four Agreements*, don't take anything personally.

In his second agreement, he writes: "Even if others insult you directly, it has nothing to do with you. What they say, what they do, and the opinions they give are according to the agreements they have in their own minds."[4]

In other words, Ruiz is saying people project their own beliefs, and it's not about you.

Lim advises while growing that thick skin, concentrate on what matters, but she admits sometimes mean comments hurt.

"Hurtful emails used to make me cry or spend sleepless nights staring at the ceiling for hours," she says. "The quicker you can learn to brush it off and laugh at some of the ridiculous comments, the faster you can get on with your life and focus on your job."

Don't base your self-worth on the opinions of strangers, co-workers or even bosses. Nor should you base your self-worth on the number of awards you receive.

Some news anchors can share a story of when a news director said, "You will never be an anchor in my newsroom." Guess what happened? Those employees were promoted to news anchor when that news director left.

This is a subjective business based on what a news manager likes or what a **Q-rating** reports.[5]

Even news anchors who are Emmy® recipients year after year find themselves in the general manager's office being told their contract is not being renewed. Do your best. Be honest with yourself. Make yourself proud.

Navigation

One of the first things a new news anchor or any newsroom employee should do upon moving to a new community is drive around and get lost. Get to know the region. You must know where cities and towns are in relation to the TV station.

Learn about the businesses and industries in the community. Know the social makeup of the area, main thoroughfares, population, cost of living and common concerns. Be aware of the bigger picture of the state and region. That takes studying, reading and asking questions.

Who to ask? Meet with city, county, state and industry representatives. Learn about them and their industry and make great contacts along the way.

Public Engagements

Remember at the beginning of this chapter we told you about viewers inviting news anchors to Grandma's birthday party? News anchors are also asked to speak to Bible study groups, read to second graders, speak to college students and emcee big fundraising events. It can be a challenge deciding which events you have time for or which ones are journalistically appropriate and ethical to attend.

The best first step is to have a conversation with the news and promotions managers. Some stations require all community requests to be cleared by the station. That can take some pressure off the news anchor.

> **Mentor Moment: Dion Lim, Anchor**
>
> "Nobody will believe what you're reading or saying if they don't see you as part of the community. Understanding what issues matter to them and being able to back it up gives you credibility and the ability to tell the story genuinely. It adds context and trust. When others trust you, they'll share things with you. Most of my stories these days come to me as tips from people I've met in the field and at events. It's the fastest way to immerse yourself in a new community and why I average around 30 events a year."

Doing community engagements *is* part of the job. In fact, it's often specified in the news anchor's contract. Yes, it's an added responsibility outside of the station and can take up many a Saturday night.

The anchor walks in the door of the classroom, church, birthday party or convention center as a representative from the TV station. That's a big deal to the people receiving you. Remember, they're inviting the news anchor, so dress and act like the anchor they know from TV.

SOCIAL MEDIA

Community engagement also includes connecting with people through social media. When you work for a TV station and have a public persona, you will likely be asked to create a public account for Twitter[6] and Instagram.[7] With Facebook, you add a public page to your private account. You and the station become administrators to this new, public page, which can have an unlimited number of followers.[8]

It's your name and your responsibility to keep up, but once you leave the station, the page goes away along with every interaction, message, post and picture. It is the property of the TV station. Remember that every time you post on it.

Some stations allow employees to use an existing public profile as their station account. If it's your own account that you bring with you, you have control over it. You are the administrator, and it stays with you no matter where you work.

Facebook limits the number of "friends" to 5,000 on a private profile. But, the number of followers on a public profile is unlimited. The number of likes on a professional page is also unlimited.

It can be challenging to remember which page you are posting to and from which account. We recommend you decide what you want each account to be known for. What will your voice be? That may help you decide what you post.

Now that you are a news anchor, frankly, the minute you decide to become a journalist, your opinions must stay private. The news anchor's job on social media is to inform, share and link stories from the station website, engage in conversation, and share a little of your life behind the scenes. Your voice must always stay above the fray even when your followers sink well below.

Connecting is the key purpose. In those connections, you may likely get story ideas, build important contacts and maybe generate more viewers to your TV station and website.

PERSONAL PROTECTION

The downside to all of this community connection can be a viewer or follower who gets delusional. Viewers welcome you into their lives and homes, and over time, may feel like they know you even if you've never met in person. In rare cases, they may try to visit you at the station, send notes, flowers or other gifts. They may boldly ask you out on a date. You must be careful. Not everyone has your best interest at heart.

Sometimes people will say things that make you uncomfortable. Before the #MeToo movement, many women said they just took the comments and moved on. #MeToo reminded women they do not have to take those comments. It also reminded the people saying those comments that they must watch their words.

In her book, Lim writes you should set an early precedent.[9] It can make for an uncomfortable moment in the short term but can be empowering in the long term.

"If you let someone call you 'babe' for two years, you've set a precedent that it's OK because you haven't done anything about it," Lim says.

Even when you are living your own life outside of the TV station, when you are off the clock, you must pay attention to your surroundings. First of all, people may recognize you. So, be generous with a smile and don't get bent out of shape when someone says, "You should not go to the grocery store in your exercise clothes," or "You really should put on your face before you go out."

Oh, the things people will say! Aren't you glad you're on TV?

REMINDERS IN ANCHORING

News anchors:

- Represent the TV station at all times.
- Are unbiased and do not sell or promote any product.
- Must have an understanding of the market.
- Must know how to pronounce community names/places.

- Should take care of their throat health to keep a strong voice.
- Know that facial expressions play a big part in communicating news stories on TV.
- Acknowledge that public engagements are a big part of the job.

QUESTIONS

1. Why should a news anchor avoid acting as a commercial influencer?
2. What could cause someone to lose his or her voice?
3. What fabric patterns should news anchors avoid?
4. What three things should news anchors remember about social media profiles versus pages?

TRY THIS

1. Watch a newscast and look at a news anchor's face during a reader story.
   a. First, turn off the sound.
   b. Then, put a piece of paper up to the screen and cover the anchor's face from the nostrils down.
   c. Can you tell the nature of the story strictly by the facial expression?
2. Follow two news anchors on social media, and list five examples of how they connect with viewers, share behind the scenes info, and show impartiality.

NOTES

1 Potts, Tracie (June 22, 2020). *Journalists of color are part of the story of racism in America. That raises tough questions on the job.* Center for Health Journalism, Retrieved from www.centerforhealthjournalism.org/2020/06/19/journalists-color-are-part-story-racism-america-raises-tough-questions-job
2 Hall, Ted. Author's personal recollection, 1993.
3 www.weather.gov/mrx/may1895tornadoes
4 Ruiz, Don Miguel (1997). *The Four Agreements*, Amber-Allen Publishing, p. 49, print.
5 https://variety.com/2016/digital/news/youtube-stars-traditional-celebrities-data-1201799487/
6 https://help.twitter.com/en/managing-your-account/managing-multiple-twitter-accounts
7 www.facebook.com/formedia/blog/best-practices-for-facebook-and-instagram
8 www.facebook.com/help/104002523024878
9 Lim, Dion (2020). *Make Your Moment, the Savvy Woman's Communication Playbook for Getting the Success You Want*, McGraw-Hill, p. 94, print.

Local Journalists and Journalistic Practices
Part 5

Ethics, Law and Deciphering Fake from Fact

Sixteen

In This Chapter	
Ethical Considerations	290
Codes of Ethics	291
Legal Considerations	296
Fake News	300
Reminders about Ethics, Law and Fake News	302
Questions	302
Answers to Ethical Questions	302

In the movie "Broadcast News," when the producer, Jane, discovers the news anchor, Tom, staged a scene in a news story, she shouts at him: "Working up tears for a news piece cutaway? You totally crossed the line between what's ethical and what is garbage!"

Tom shouts back, "It's hard not to cross it; they keep moving the little sucker, don't they?"

> **Mentor Moment: Al Tompkins, Senior Faculty, Poynter Institute, St. Petersburg**
>
> "In that movie, the line for ethical editing was not moved—he moved it for the sake of theatrics. Ethics is always situational. There are very few YES and NOs that apply in every situation. Ask if you would be willing to explain your decision to the public. Who made it? Why did you make it? How did you make it? If you are not willing to explain the process, you probably are not ready to make a decision."

More than three decades after the release of "Broadcast News," that scene is still relevant. During your career as a journalist, you will be confronted with many ethical challenges.

DOI: 10.4324/9781003137016-16

Something as seemingly minor as instructing an interviewee to walk down a hallway so you can get B-roll is staging. You shouldn't do it. Our job is to record life as it happens without interfering or directing. As we discussed in earlier chapters, we do this by anticipating what is going to happen next, so we're in place and ready to shoot when it does happen.

Ask your subject what he or she will be doing next and ask for permission to record them while they're doing it. That's not staging.

> **Mentor Moment: Jake Milstein, former News Director, KIRO7, Seattle**
>
> "The lesson is to lean into curiosity. Ask a lot of questions. Get to the truth of the matter – and then explain it to the audience. It's also OK to update your reporting. A great news director I worked for coined the phrase, 'the best available truth.' As you report more, the truth might change. Explain that to the audience; don't hide from it. Corrections come from a place of strength, not weakness. Call out falsehoods when you see them. Also, it's OK to question other journalists in your own newsroom. It takes teamwork to get a story right."

ETHICAL CONSIDERATIONS

Here are some ethical dilemmas to consider: Should you conceal a source's name? Use an inflammatory video from social media without verifying the source? Report a death before it's been confirmed by the coroner or next of kin? Do a live shot for your station's client and not disclose the association or that the station received compensation? Release the name of a rape victim? Stop a person you're covering from hurting or killing himself? Use sentences or information from someone else's news report without first getting permission? Accept free passes to an amusement park or concert or a free cup of coffee? Read a "must-run" editorial on the air that mimics a news story? Accept products from a company and promote them on your social media platform?

You may be unsure how to answer some if not all of these questions. That's because often when it comes to ethics, it seems like there's a gray area. Fortunately, several journalism organizations have published guidelines, known as codes of ethics, to help you answer these questions. You'll find a list of links to codes of ethics at the end of this chapter along with answers to those ethical questions we posed.

CODES OF ETHICS

Most broadcast journalists follow the codes of ethics from the Radio Television Digital News Association (RTDNA) or the Society of Professional Journalists (SPJ) or a combination of both. Here is a simplified version of both codes—similar but different.

The RTDNA code offers resources to journalists through three guiding principles:

- Truth and accuracy above all
- Independence and transparency
- Accountability for consequences.

The SPJ code offers these guidelines through four main pillars:

- Seek the Truth and Report It
- Minimize Harm
- Act Independently
- Be Accountable and Transparent.

Both codes emphasize "truth" as the most important goal in journalism.

SPJ qualifies it by saying, "Journalists should be honest, fair and courageous in gathering, reporting and interpreting information."[1] That includes verifying information, identifying sources, seeking diverse sources and always attributing.

SPJ recognizes that some reporting will cause harm. You will be reporting stories about people that they don't want reported. That is why SPJ cautions journalists to "balance the public's need for information against potential harm or discomfort."[2]

Most codes of ethics urge journalists to act independently—something that is not always easy to do. There's a lot of pressure on journalists from all sides—your TV station, advertisers, donors, businesses that want to give you gifts, even personal ambition. Avoid conflicts of interest. A journalist should never allow personal bias to alter the facts or intent of a report interfering with a fair and objective story.

> **Mentor Moment: Alicia Acuna, Correspondent, Fox News, Denver**
>
> "It's important to read the articles, not just the headlines, and to also get competing perspectives. When people tell me they only watch Fox News, I say it's a good idea to watch CNN; it's a good idea to watch MSNBC; listen to NPR. There's a reason why we're so divided in this country, and people can assign those responsibilities to many different people and organizations. People tend to sift out the information they get to a place that makes them most comfortable. And if you are just getting information from a place that makes you most comfortable, as a human it can be dangerous. As a journalist, it's a sin."

And finally, accountability and transparency—that means that you should be accessible to the public to explain the ethical choices you've made.

That's what National Press Photographers Association instructor Brett Akagi faced shortly after returning from an ethics fellows training at the Poynter Institute. He was working as the director of photography at KARE11 in Minneapolis, when he and a reporter were sent to interview the family of a teenager who was killed in a car crash. Akagi says no one likes to ask grieving families to do an interview, but it's part of the job.

The teen's parents were still at the hospital when Akagi and the reporter got to the house. But the grandmother was there. Akagi remembers what happened like it was yesterday.

"We left the camera in the car and had a conversation with her," Akagi says. "We asked her if she wanted to go on camera to talk about her granddaughter, and she said yes. So, we did the interview. We got back to the station, and we got a call within about half an hour. It was a lawyer for the family. And the lawyer was pissed off and accusing us of being 'dogs sneaking under a tent to get in under the wire to get information.'"

The lawyer told Akagi he didn't want the story to air. Using ethical decision-making, Akagi and the station's news director weighed the options. They decided the tensions were so high, they would do something most news stations never do. They offered to let the lawyer hear the grandmother's soundbite that the station planned to air.

> Not to influence the story. But to let them understand this is what we were going to use. We're doing a story about the tragedy of losing a teen in a car crash, and from our point of view, it was important that we talk about the tragedy and that people understand it's a real person, it's not just a number. That we put a face on this person.

That's being accountable, accessible and transparent. In the end, the station aired the story, and the family and attorney were satisfied.

> **Mentor Moment: Michael Carr, General Manager, KFSN, Fresno**
>
> "The most important thing is dialogue. It's collaboration and having discussions. When we do have those challenging stories, it comes down to having that conversation and listening to everybody who's willing to give their input. There are rarely perfectly right answers. Ultimately, you have to make a decision on the direction that you're going to go."

SPJ says in an ideal world, ethical questions should be discussed in groups of people.

"Much of ethical decision-making involves back-and-forth testing of ideas. A lot of it is just good instinct. Newsrooms should have more ethical discussions, and those discussions would benefit from some input from outside the newsroom as well."[3]

Al Tompkins, who oversees the Poynter Institute's ethics fellows training, says reporters should reach beyond the gut feeling or "good instinct" and instead use reflection and reasoning.

Tompkins teaches students a four-step process to evaluate stories and resolve ethical dilemmas. Whenever you're trying to determine whether a story or information is legitimate, you should ask yourself the following four questions:

1. What do you know?
2. What do you need to know?
3. How do you know what you know?
4. What other ways should you look at this?

Tompkins uses the 2020 murder of George Floyd in Minneapolis, Minnesota as an example. Floyd, a black man who had been handcuffed, died after a white police officer knelt on his neck for over nine minutes. The first reports that came out said Floyd died of medical complications. That was wrong.

Tompkins breaks it down this way:

What do we actually know about the information we've been given? We know that originally the Minneapolis police department said Floyd died of medical complications.

What do we need to know in order to make a decision? "We need to know whether there's been a medical diagnosis," Tompkins says. "Is there a coroner's report? Is there a medical examiner's report? Might there be anybody else who saw or heard something contrary to that? Were there any eyewitnesses? Are there body cameras? We need to know whether the police are telling the truth. We need to know whether there's more information that didn't come from one source but from multiple sources."

How do we know what we know? What was our source of information? The police department. Immediately after Floyd's death, there was only one source, which Tompkins says is "bad journalism."

Is there any other way to look at this? Yes, as body camera and eyewitness video started coming in, we got a clearer picture of what happened, Tompkins says. But that takes time. We need to ask ourselves whether there is a possibility that the initial information isn't accurate, true and complete.

Tompkins says the problem is exacerbated by the information that comes from official sources.

"Sometimes we don't ask," he says. "We just report and leave it. And that can be hazardous."

Mentor Moment: Brett Akagi, Owner, Akagi Media, Kansas City

"We work in this gray area. Some things are black and white, and some things are gray. And you have to figure it out. But if anyone operates without good ethics, it's problematic because then you worry about their decision making when it comes to other choices. How do they conduct themselves in public? You've got to have a bedrock foundation of good ethics."

Keeping factual means using clear, concise language. Controversial issues can be emotionally charged, and non-factual language can add to the drama. Take the abortion issue. Is it pro-choice or abortion rights advocate? Is it pro-life or anti-abortion? The Associated Press says: "Use the modifiers *anti-abortion* or *abortion-rights*; don't use *pro-life, pro-choice* or *pro-abortion* unless they are in quotes or proper names."[4]

When in doubt, consult the AP Stylebook.

Mentor Moment: Scott McGrew, Anchor/Reporter NBC Bay Area, KNTV, San Jose

"Freedom fighters are another person's terrorist. Terrorists are another person's freedom fighters. An officer-involved shooting is when a police officer shoots someone. He wasn't just involved. Separations are layoffs. So, too, is a reduction in force. A navigation shelter to help the homeless find helpful services turns into a homeless shelter if it has beds. Limited military strikes are still military strikes."

You can learn more about ethical decision-making by subscribing to the Poynter Institute, SPJ, RTDNA and newsletters written by other industry organizations. Take a media ethics course at your university. Media law and ethics are required courses in most journalism programs. If they're not required at your university, take the classes anyway. You'll benefit in the long run.

LEGAL CONSIDERATIONS

While there is a gray area when it comes to ethics, with media law, it's more black-and-white. If you make a mistake as a reporter and cause harm, you and your TV station could be sued or you could even wind up in jail.

> **Mentor Moment: Will Tran, MMJ, KRON, San Francisco**
>
> "Know the law. I took media law in college and it has served me well all my career. Know what you can and cannot do. From time-to-time I've been told I can't film here or stand there. Many people have no idea how the law works when it comes to the media. Knowing what's public property is key because so many think they can tell you not to film that scene or them."

Journalism is the only profession that is protected by the First Amendment of the Constitution. It states that Congress shall make no law… "abridging the freedom of the press." However, it doesn't give journalists special rights or privileges that members of the public don't have. We still need to follow the law.

Something as simple as stepping onto private property or refusing to reveal the source of a story can lead to your arrest.

Fortunately, there is a quick and easy guide that has condensed just about everything you need to know about media law. The Associated Press Stylebook, required by your professors, has a Briefing on Media Law that can be a lifesaver when you're in a jam. It would be a good idea to brush up on it and refer to it when you have a question about a specific area. Here's a brief rundown.

Privacy

Invasion of privacy is the unjustifiable intrusion into the personal life of another without consent. There are four ways to invade someone's privacy.

- **Public Disclosure of Private Facts**: Publishing details about someone's medical or school records or any private information that is known only to the individual or close family and friends. The information in question must be highly offensive and not of any legitimate public interest.

- **False Light:** Running a photo or a headline of someone that is incorrect or shows them in a false light. This also applies to attributing a statement to one person made by someone else.
- **Misappropriation:** The use of a photo of someone, usually a celebrity or famous person, without their permission. This doesn't generally affect reporters because misappropriation deals with the commercial use of a person's name or likeness.
- **Intrusion Upon Seclusion:** This is getting information illegally or unethically. For example, if you record audio of someone without their permission in a state that requires two-party consent, you can be sued. That's why it's so important that you always ask for permission to record video or audio.
  - Intrusion by Trespass: You have every right to be on public property, but the same does not apply to private property. You might be covering a story about a storage facility owner who is accused of ripping off customers. If you walk on that property without consent, you could be breaking the law. On the flip side, you may be told that you can't photograph someone from where you're standing on public property. As a general rule, as long as you are in a public location where there is no reasonable expectation of privacy, you have every right to take video and audio recordings. That includes taking pictures inside a business or home if the interior can be seen from public property. And that includes taking video of protesters.

Shield Laws

Journalists are protected by the Federal Privacy Protection Act and, in most states, by shield laws. That means that you are protected from giving up your notes, videos or confidential sources. There are some caveats, such as knowing about or witnessing a crime, which could cause you to lose that protection.

Contempt of Court

If you use an unnamed source for a story on a crime and you have first-hand knowledge of that crime, you could be forced to divulge your source. Refusal to do so could bring a contempt charge against you, which could land you in jail.

Defamation

You could get sued if you publish something that's false and damages a person's reputation. The best defense against libel is the truth. If the story you broadcast or post is true, it can't be libelous, even if it damages someone's reputation.

If your story is about a public official or someone who is in the public eye, you have a little more protection. In order for a public official to win a defamation case against you, she or he must prove that you published the story knowing it was false or that you published it with reckless disregard for the truth. That is known as actual malice, holding public officials to a higher standard.

Often, reporters will use information that comes from a privileged source, such as a court hearing or an official government proceeding like a city council meeting. This is not an absolute privilege meaning it's not 100% protection. But as long as you strive to do responsible reporting of a government proceeding, you will have qualified privilege.

Another defense is fair comment and criticism. This one is a little more difficult to support because as reporters, we should not be offering our opinion unless we are a restaurant, theatre or music critic. But opinion writers can say just about anything, as long as they can prove they are giving their opinion and not implying what they are saying is fact.

One other landmine to watch out for: republication of a defamatory statement. If you take something from the internet and use it as part of your story, and it was defamatory, then you can also be held accountable. This is why you should always verify information before you repost or report.

Closed Courtroom

There are limits as to when the media have access to courtrooms, but those limits are specific. Generally, juvenile hearings and grand jury proceedings are held behind closed doors.

In rare cases, when an attorney says media access would violate his or her client's right to a fair trial, a judge may consider whether to close the courtroom. Before the judge does that, it must be determined that there is no reasonable alternative to closing the courtroom and that any limitation is as narrow as possible. Because closing a court proceeding is a First Amendment issue, reporters have a right to have their objection heard. It is important that you consult legal counsel if you are ever in this position.

Open Meeting/Open Record

Many investigative reports have been written about violations of open meeting/open record laws. All states have open meeting or sunshine laws, which require transparency in government business. This also includes virtual meetings and even email communication. But these laws vary by state.

City, county and state government boards are required to hold open meetings whenever they have a quorum, usually a majority of members on a board. The only exceptions, in most cases, are executive sessions, when the board needs to discuss a personnel matter or potential litigation (lawsuits).

If you feel that you are being illegally excluded from a meeting, or that a meeting that should have been open was held privately, you should immediately alert your news director.

Attorney Tim Buchanan says an open meeting violation is not as clear as an open records denial. If a meeting is held in private, Buchanan says you may demand corrective action. If that doesn't work, your station can file a court petition to have whatever action the board or council took voided.

"If the court agrees and grants an order, the body then would have to redo the hearing, discussion, or determination in public. If there was a violation but no action was taken, there is no order that is obtainable," Buchanan says.

You can find your state's open meeting and open records laws online. News industry organizations also provide demand letter templates like the following one from the California News Publishers Association.[5]

Scan the following QR code for an example of a demand letter.

Freedom of Information Act (FOIA)

The Freedom of Information Act gives the public the right to know what the government is doing. What used to be a long, drawn-out process has been simplified because many federal government agencies post their Freedom of Information publications online.

Before you submit an FOIA request, you should check foia.gov and foiaonline.gov, the National Online FOIA Library. You can search previous FOIA requests and access records that have already been released without having to submit any paperwork.

Should you decide to submit your own FOIA request or public records request, check the Student Press Law Center's public records generator.[6]

> **Mentor Moment: Bryan Lenocker, Executive Producer, WABC, New York**
>
> "If we aren't asking the tough questions and fighting for people and trying to find the truth — who will? We are more divided than ever right now, but it has helped me become even more focused on what I am doing here and the importance of good storytelling and helping our community. I have always believed in local news. I think the work we do in our cities and communities is so important. People trust us, they turn to us. They may not always agree with us, but I feel strongly in our mission."

FAKE NEWS

Fake news has taken over social media and has spilled into mainstream media. During the COVID-19 pandemic in 2020 and 2021, millions of people relied on information from social media to learn about the virus, how it was transmitted, how it could be prevented and how it could be cured. However, many of those posts were inaccurate.

An Italian epidemiologist began collecting social media data in the early days of the pandemic. His team analyzed 127 million tweets. The results were startling. In just one day in March 2020, they found 46,000 Twitter posts linked to COVID-19 misinformation.[7]

Some of the false claims included information that drinking bleach cures the coronavirus and 5G technology caused the disease.[8]

> **Mentor Moment: Scott McGrew, Anchor/Reporter**
>
> "Understand there is a truth around facts. And be prepared to be accused of bias by telling the truth. My favorite phrase about that is if one person tells you it's raining and another says it's sunny, your job is not to report both sides. Your job is to look out the window and determine who is right."

Verification

Journalists need to be particularly careful when they come across videos and photos from unknown sources because it is so easy to alter them now. But there are also many ways to verify them. You can verify photos with Google's reverse image search to see if there are duplicates and if the original photo has been altered. Videos are a little more difficult, but there are tools such as YouTube Dataviewer or the InVID Verification Plugin. Use fact-checking sites like snopes.com and FactCheck.org. Google has Fact Check Explorer, which searches fact check results from the web about a topic or person.

Never re-post or publish anything from social media unless you have verified its authenticity.

> **Mentor Moment: Theresa de los Santos, Ph.D., Associate Professor of Communication**
>
> "Especially during the emotionally-charged events we are living through right now, I recommend scheduling news consumption from specific sources and strategically limiting overall exposure, while still gathering necessary information to stay current.
>
> Particularly, when someone encounters emotionally provocative news content and realizes that emotional manipulation may be occurring, they should pause. By slowing down our thinking and reactions, we can take time to verify information, understand why we are worked up, and be more responsible about the information we spread further."

Codes of Ethics

- Society of Professional Journalists: spj.org/ethicscode.asp
- Radio Television Digital News Association: rtdna.org/content/rtdna_code_of_ethics
- National Press Photographers Association: nppa.org/code-ethics
- Online News Association Code of Ethics and Social Newsgathering Ethics Code: journalists.org/tools/social-newsgathering
- Public Relations Society of America Code of Ethics: prsa.org/about/prsa-code-of-ethics
- Public Media Code of Integrity: publicmediaintegrity.org/code-of-integrity
- Associated Press News Values and Principles: ap.org/about/news-values-and-principles

Figure 16.1 Codes of Ethics

REMINDERS ABOUT ETHICS, LAW AND FAKE NEWS

- Consult a code of ethics related to your field when considering an ethical dilemma.
- Discuss ethical questions with others in your newsroom.
- When deciding how or whether to cover a story, ask yourself what you know, what you need to know, how you know what you know and what other ways you should look at the question.
- Remember when you are on public property and there is no reasonable expectation of privacy, you have every right to record video and audio.
- Always verify sources.
- Truth is the best defense in a defamation case.

QUESTIONS

1. What are the four questions you should ask when evaluating the accuracy of information for a story?
2. You've been contacted by a cosmetic company that says they love your look and want to send you a free product. All you have to do is create posts about the product. How should you respond?

ANSWERS TO ETHICAL QUESTIONS

Here are the answers to those ethical questions we posed at the beginning of the chapter. First, a caveat. There are no hard and fast rules when it comes to ethics, only guidelines. We are answering these questions

- Should you conceal a source's name?
    - Identify sources clearly. The public is entitled to as much information as possible to judge the reliability and motivation of sources.
- Use an inflammatory video from social media without verifying the source?
    - Take responsibility for the accuracy of their work. Verify information before releasing it. Use original sources whenever possible (SPJ)
- Report a death before it's been confirmed by the coroner or next of kin?
    - Balance the public's need for information against potential harm or discomfort. Pursuit of the news is not a license for arrogance or undue intrusiveness (SPJ)
- Do a live shot for your station's client and not disclose the association or that the station received compensation?
    - Distinguish news from advertising and shun hybrids that blur the lines between the two. Prominently label sponsored content (SPJ)
- Release the name of a rape victim?
    - Show compassion for those who may be affected by news coverage. Use heightened sensitivity when dealing with juveniles, victims of sex crimes and sources and subjects who are inexperienced or unable to give consent. Consider cultural differences in approach and treatment.
- Stop a person you're covering from hurting or killing himself?
    - The right to broadcast, publish or otherwise share information does not mean it is always right to do so. However, journalism's obligation is to pursue truth and report, not withhold it. Shying away from difficult cases is not necessarily more ethical than taking on the challenge of reporting them. Leaving tough or sensitive stories to non-journalists can be a disservice to the public (RTDNA)
- Use sentences or information from someone else's news report without first getting permission?
    - Attribution is essential. It adds important information that helps the audience evaluate content and it acknowledges those who contribute to coverage. Using someone else's work without attribution or permission is plagiarism (RTDNA).
- Accept free passes to an amusement park or concert or a free cup of coffee?
    - Refuse gifts, favors, fees, free travel and special treatment, and avoid political and other outside activities that may compromise integrity or impartiality or may damage credibility (SPJ)
- Read a "must-run" editorial on the air that mimics a news story?
    - Expose unethical conduct in journalism, including within their organizations (SPJ)
- Accept products from a company and promote them on your social media platform?
    - The acceptance of gifts or special treatment of any kind not available to the general public creates conflicts of interest and erodes independence. This does not include the access to events or areas traditionally granted to working journalists in order to facilitate their coverage. It does include "professional courtesy" admission, discounts and "freebies" provided to journalists by those who might someday be the subject of coverage. Such goods and services are often offered as enticements to report favorably on the giver or rewards for doing so; even where that is not the intent, it is the reasonable perception of a justifiably suspicious public (RTDNA).

Figure 16.2 Answers to Ethics Questions

by quoting excerpts from the RTDNA and SPJ codes of ethics. It's up to you to interpret what they mean.

NOTES

1 SPJ Code of Ethics, Revised September 6, 2014. Retrieved from www.spj.org/ethicscode.asp
2 Ibid.

3 Brown, Fred, ed. (2020). *Media Ethics: A Guide for Professional Conduct*. Indianapolis: Society of Professional Journalists, print, p.40.
4 www.apstylebook.com/ap_stylebook/abortion
5 https://cnpa.com/legal/brown-act-letter/
6 https://splc.org/lettergenerator/
7 Bruno Kessler Foundation. (2020). *Fake news in the time of C-19*, Retrieved from www.tortoisemedia.com/2020/03/23/the-infodemic-fake-news-coronavirus/
8 Ibid.

Getting That Job
Seventeen

In This Chapter

Building Your Digital/Social Media Brand	307
Internships	308
Networking	310
Applying for a Job	312
The Demo Reel	315
Do You Need a Website?	318
Resumes to Impress	320
The Job Interview	321
Negotiating a Contract	323
Starting Your News Career	324
Agents, Consultants and Recruiters	327
Why Your Mentors Love Their Jobs	328
Reminders on Job Opportunities	335
Try This	335

College goes by quickly, especially the final year or two. This is when many students are getting the best hands-on experience. They're doing an internship, working on the student-run newscast or putting together stories in class.

This work is far more than just homework and class assignments. It can go on your resume reel and website. This is the body of work future employers will be looking for. The minute you know you want to be in this field, you should be building your portfolio.

> **Mentor Moment: Adrian Luevano, Sports Reporter, KIFI, Idaho Falls**
>
> "I treated my sports internship like I was already a third member of the team. I came in and I was ready to go. I'd say, 'I'm here. Send me with a photog.' And they were like, 'We're not going to

DOI: 10.4324/9781003137016-17

send you with a photog.' But I worked to demonstrate that skill. I think having a relationship with the sports director helped. He was like, 'Let's test it out. I'll have you write these games.' I would go with him to certain games, and then I would write my own script. And then he would compare it to his script. After two weeks of that, I was going out on my own. I was doing my own notes. I'd come back and write the highlights. I would pull the feeds from the Central Coast and from Bakersfield and then I would write the scripts to those. When they came back to the station, I had four games already done for them."

It doesn't matter if you think you want to be a producer one semester and then decide later you prefer directing, doing weather or reporting. Having a varied body of work is helpful. What counts even more is your ability to work on a team, work on a deadline and be self-reliant.

Mentor Moment: Brett Akagi, Owner, Akagi Media, Former News Operations Mgr. KCTV, Kansas City

"A student who only wants to be a reporter will ask, 'Why do I need to know how to shoot, edit and master tech?' I don't know of any media newsrooms that want to hire people who specialize in one thing. The more you know and can do makes you a better job candidate. The same is true for photographers asking, 'Why do I need to know how to write or even be in front of the camera?' Hiring managers want people who they can plug into different situations, depending on the needs of the organization."

Here is a list of what news recruiter Kevin Olivas from Sinclair Broadcast Group says he looks for:

- Works wonderfully with others
- Great at taking constructive criticism and using it to become a better storyteller
- Great writer.

Notice nothing in this list is specific to reporting, anchoring, photography, weather or sports. It's about the person's attributes and work ethic.

> **Mentor Moment: Chad Hypes, News Director, KTVL, Medford**
>
> "I think it's crucial for college students to keep up with technology and learn how things work in a newsroom. The more 'tech-savvy' grads we have hired always do better. They can communicate easier with the team because they have an understanding of how things work, and they can troubleshoot in the field which makes them more reliable."

You may hear journalists say they're in this job because they want to give a voice to the voiceless. When your newsroom is reflective of your community, reporters and MMJs seek out those voices and can be more effective in the way they cover their community.

> **Mentor Moment: Michael Carr, General Manager, KFSN, Fresno**
>
> "There is something to be said about people seeing someone that looks like them or that comes from a background they are familiar with. It sends a signal that there are no glass ceilings. There are no, 'You can do X, Y and Z, but be careful because you can't do A and B.' It makes it clear that the best people will rise to the top regardless of where you come from and what you look like."

BUILDING YOUR DIGITAL/SOCIAL MEDIA BRAND

All through school you should be building your foundation. That starts with building your digital and social media brand. Simply put, be active and professional on social media. Follow people in your field, and communicate with them. Don't just like or share other people's posts. Instead, create your own content and tag others. When you do share, add a nugget of insight from your perspective or a picture or video to add to the topic.

You don't have to change your feeds you've had for years, but if there are posts you don't want a boss (or your grandmother) to see, then start a new profile and feed that.

Consider it a weekly assignment of yours—a diary of what you're learning in class and where you're seeing it applied in the world. The earlier you begin building this foundation, the better time you'll have finding a job after graduation.

Future bosses will always look at an applicant's social profiles. If you just started building a profile a few weeks before interviewing, that will be a red flag. The boss may wonder if you truly are committed. Others who feed and grow their brand could get the job instead of you. Yes, your social media channels play a part in the hiring process. Make sure they are presentable. If there is anything questionable, it's best to be upfront about it.

INTERNSHIPS

An internship is lifechanging for most students. It plops the student right into the reality of the business. An internship can be inspiring. It can also be a rude awakening that the job you always thought you wanted isn't what you thought it would be. Great! What an opportunity. Finding out what you *don't* want is just as important as finding out what you *do* want. No time in a newsroom is a waste.

Allizbeth Clavijo interned the summer before she graduated. During her final semester, she worked on her university's student-run newscast. Two weeks before graduation, a news director hired her as an assignment editor and digital producer. Even with the hands-on experience from her internship and school newscast, she says the frenetic pace of the newsroom surprised her. She quickly learned how to adapt.

"Understanding every position and their needs is important because it's a team thing," Clavijo says.

Even though an internship is a class, it's also a job in the real world. Interns are expected to be early. On time is late. Interns are expected to dress the part of a professional, not that of a casual college student. Interns are expected to be prepared.

> **Mentor Moment: Adrian Luevano, Sports Reporter**
>
> "You've got to treat it like you're trying to get a job. You've got to dress up in a shirt and tie or a nice shirt and slacks. I was always ready to fill in if the sports director or sports reporter got food poisoning. That was my logic. I'm ready to go. If you guys need me, I'm here."

If you know you are going out in the field with a reporter, make sure you're dressed for it—boots and jacket for the snow or the farm story. Bring snacks and water. Refer to the go-bag in Chapter 9. This applies to you, too. This is not the kind of job where we get to take an automatic lunch break. And, you never know when there will be breaking news, so always be prepared.

When you get the chance to go out in the field with a reporter, ask if you can shoot a stand-up or a look-live. Be proactive. Create your own story after you watch the reporter do his or hers. Remember you are there to drink in the real-world knowledge.

You should never get in the way of the news crew. When there is an opportunity for you to try some things in the field, that team will likely help you out. Most journalists are willing to pay it forward. We were all interns at one point and know how important it is to get hands-on experience.

When you are in the newsroom watching producers, directors or assignment editors, it may *feel* boring to you just sitting and watching someone else work. Take notes. Ask questions. Ask if you can do anything to help. This kind of motivation and interactivity goes a long way in positive networking. People are hired based on how they work in their internship. If you are easily forgotten because you sat back passively, you are not likely to be recommended for a future job.

Alex White, a newscast producer at KFSN in Fresno, remembers her first internship in southern California as an uncomfortable experience that she regrets not learning from at the time. She says one of the news anchors never spoke to her. Ever. She learned something from that anchor.

"It taught me if I ever come across her again, I don't want her to think I'm the intern who just throws her scripts down on the desk," White says. "Taking the high road is not always fun, but if I ever face someone like her again, I would kill her with kindness."

And there's a good chance White could come across that anchor or someone like her sometime in her career. This news business is a small world.

"Your internship may not be perfect," White says. "Looking back, I watched the anchors get ready for the show. I watched the producers coordinate with the editors. That's stuff I could have used in my interview that I didn't even think of."

Michael Carr got an internship in 1997. After graduating, he worked in San Francisco and Sacramento. Then, he returned to the station where he interned. He worked as a weekend producer in 2000 and executive producer in 2002. By 2012, he was the news director. From intern to news director in 12 years! You never know if the next intern you work with will someday be your boss.

Getting a TV news internship is not always easy. Each station has a finite number of openings. If you cannot get an internship in a TV newsroom, keep looking. There are radio stations, newspapers, online news organizations, companies with their own production and marketing departments, city and county government, state and federal legislators, and production companies where a student can get real-world experience.

An internship lasts only a quarter or semester, so if you love it, work hard at it. If you don't love it, work hard at it anyway, and be thankful you learned something you don't want to do. Remember, there is still great value in that and in the people you will be meeting.

NETWORKING

If you are already feeding and building your social media channels, and you are being an interactive, proactive and energetic intern, then you are naturally networking. Slamming people's inboxes at graduation time is not the right kind of networking.

Think of networking like a spider web. The most successful web is one with lots of threads. Students should be building that web through the years. No all-nighter can build an efficient network.

> **Mentor Moment: Bob Butler, Reporter, KCBS Radio, SAG-AFTRA Broadcaster Vice-President, San Francisco**
>
> "You have to be proactive. Reach out to news directors in markets where you want to work. They won't always answer you, but if they get back to you, that is a contact that you have made. You can develop a relationship with that person by sending them a writing sample: 'I wrote this story for my class; I wrote this for my TV newscast. I'd like to get your feedback on it.' If you do that, after a while when they see your stuff they'll know who you are. They'll see your email in their inbox, and they'll say, 'Oh, that's Janie from Fresno State. She's a pretty good writer.' Do that for four or five different markets. Basically, you're increasing your odds of getting a job."

Alex White's advice is to always be nice. Not just because you want something but because "it's a fundamental thing. It's part of being an adult. You always want to be respectful even if you have differing opinions. Because as a journalist you'll face that every single day."

What if you do not get an opportunity to intern? That was the case for many students during the COVID-19 pandemic of 2020 and 2021. However, there are still online opportunities to network. Professional organizations offer seminars, workshops, conventions, mentoring and scholarship opportunities. You just need to look for them.

Here are a few organizations worth checking out:

- Asian American Journalists Association (AAJA)
- Association for Education in Journalism and Mass Communication (AEJMC)
- Association of Health Care Journalists (AHCJ)
- Association of LGBTQ Journalists (NLGJA)
- Investigative Reporters and Editors (IRE)
- Journalism and Women Symposium (JAWS)
- National Association of Black Journalists (NABJ)
- National Association of Broadcasters (NAB)
- National Association of Hispanic Journalists (NAHJ)
- National Association of Television Arts and Sciences (NATAS)
- National Federation of Press Women (NFPW)

- The National Press Photographers Association (NPPA)
- Native American Journalists Association (NAJA)
- Online News Association (ONA)
- Radio Television Digital News Association (RTDNA)
- Society of Professional Journalists (SPJ)

> **Mentor Moment: Alicia Acuna, Correspondent, FOX News, Denver**
>
> "Whenever I talk to people who are going into this business, I tell them the people you are sitting around right now are the people who are going to matter in your future in this business. You never know who it's going to be. Stephanie and I went to college together. We worked at the college TV station together. It's not like we were best friends, but we knew each other. She called me one day and said, 'I'm getting married, but they won't let me out of my contract unless I help find my replacement. Are you interested?' I said, sure. I went for the interview and Eric Hulnick hired me for the 5 p.m. show. There's really no rhyme or reason to this business. You never know what phone call or moment is going to change the trajectory of your career."

APPLYING FOR A JOB

> **Author Note—Kim Stephens**
>
> "I mailed out packages to stations around the western United States. Each package contained my resume, cover letter specific to each station with the news director's name on it, and a ¾ inch tape of my resume reel. I had no idea if there were openings at these stations. Then I got in my car and drove from Eureka, California down to Bakersfield, California, trying to have meetings with news directors who all said no, but one, who hired me at KERO in Bakersfield in July 1988. Things are much easier nowadays."

Cyndee Hebert, managing editor of news content at WTHR13 in Indianapolis, had no idea what she wanted to do when she graduated from University of Missouri. She had reported for her school classes and hated being on camera. She knew she did not want to do that. It wasn't until after graduation that she learned that she was interested in producing. Hebert says her first boss in Port Arthur, Texas, took a chance on her and hired her to be the 6 and 11 p.m. newscast producer. Her first day was memorable.

"We had a hurricane warning," says Hebert, who learned by doing. "It was hurricane Andrew."

> **Mentor Moment: Scott McGrew, Anchor/Reporter, KNTV, San Jose**
>
> "Take any job anywhere for your first job. If you're not willing to do the overnight weekend shift in Broken Bow, Oklahoma, get out now. It's hard to get that first job. Understand you will never get rich, though, if you're very lucky you may get comfortable. Understand, 'being on TV' is interesting for about a year then just becomes what you do. So, if 'being on TV' is your primary motivation, you're going to spend a lot of years being unmotivated. And for God's sake, don't post a selfie Instagram at a murder scene."

The first thing any student should do is talk with professors and advisers to find out about job openings. Your journalism professors are usually well connected to the industry and are continually informed about openings. You should be serious about the job search, because once your professors reach out to news directors on your behalf, the process has started and you are expected to follow through.

Next, search the web for TV station ownership websites to read the job openings. Be ready to be overwhelmed and excited about the many opportunities before you.

Reporters and anchors will need to begin in smaller markets. Producers, directors and photographers may be able to start in medium-sized markets.

What do we mean by market size? Each market is measured by the size of its Designated Market Area (**DMA**). Nielsen Global Media measures TV viewership in roughly 200 markets. DMA is calculated by how far the TV station signal goes and how many viewers can be reached by that signal. New York City is the largest TV market in the country. Glendive, Montana is the smallest at 210, according to Nielsen DMA Rankings.

Many TV stations are owned by big corporations. Some are owned by private companies or even families. One of the easiest ways to look for job openings is to go to the website of each company and check out their list.

The top 15 companies based on revenue, according to TVNewsCheck, are: Nexstar, Sinclair, Tegna, Fox, CBS, Gray, NBCU, ABC/Disney, Scripps, Univision, Hearst, Cox, Meredith, Graham and Quincy.[1] There are more, but these are a good place to start looking.

The application process is now completely online. Most companies require you to upload a resume, and in many on-air cases, a link to your resume reel.

After submitting the application, contact the news director. If you haven't already started a relationship with the hiring manager, send an email introducing yourself. Say you just applied for a specific position and why your resume should be considered. Contacting people in the newsroom through social media may also help.

This process can take time. It starts with corporate and then works down to the individual station. Each hiring manager is busy running a newsroom, and even though that manager is looking for a new employee, that does not mean it's the most important thing in that person's day, as it is for you. Just because you don't hear anything doesn't mean you're out. Be patient. Be persistent. Do not put all your hopes in one station. Branch out.

> **Mentor Moment: Jake Milstein, former News Director, KIRO, Seattle**
>
> "If you want to be a journalist, don't listen to the folks who say it's a bad career choice for all sorts of reasons. It's a great career choice. And, the job you have out of college is not the job you'll have two years later."

Before and after you apply for the job online, you must do your homework on the news happening in that market and the stories that specific station is covering. You need to know about the big names in the community and TV station so when the hiring manager does call you,

you can have an informed conversation. If a news director asks you what you think about their news and you respond that you haven't seen it, do not expect the interview to last long.

> **Mentor Moment: Chad Hypes: News Director, KTVL, Medford**
>
> "What could cause someone to *not* get the job? A few things actually. First, being late for or missing an interview. Unless you have a really good excuse, you are not going to get a second chance. I am a busy man, and I need to spend my time on people who want to work here.
>
> Second, dressing or acting too casual in an interview. I once interviewed a woman who was in her workout clothes in a crowded café. I couldn't hear her, and she couldn't hear me. The interview lasted about two minutes. Please be prepared for the interview. Do a little homework about the station and location. And always dress and act professionally.
>
> And third, questionable social media profiles. Yes, we are checking. Please clean up your social media before applying. I understand you are in college, but that's not an excuse."

THE DEMO REEL

You should have a reel for every position you apply for. This shows prospective employers what you can do. Photographers share the stories they've shot and edited. Reporters include the stories they've covered. Producers, directors and anchors share the newscasts they were involved in including digital stories and videos. Your reel should correspond *exactly* to the job for which you are applying.

> **Mentor Moment: Jeff Lenk, News Director, KBAK, Bakersfield**
>
> "The ones who really want to be journalists should have a reel that is focused heavily on storytelling. They're going in-depth and showcasing their best work with great interviews and great stories. The people who want to be 'on TV' have reels with a lot more production value to them. I've seen a video montage set to

> music of a reporter doing stand-ups in 10 different locations. It's flashy and cool. It definitely catches the eye, but it doesn't convince me that you want to be a journalist. It convinces me that you like being 'on TV.'"

Lenk says the first 10 to 15 seconds of your reel are critically important. Usually, that means a montage of stand-ups with a quick variety of stories. Each clip should be strong, active, energetic and show strength, creativity and command. It should demonstrate what you are capable of. Yes, that applies to applicants in front of and behind the camera. If you want to put your name and face at the beginning of the reel, have it up for two seconds max before the montage.

"Then I want to see at least two different stories with two different fields to them, start to finish. Without a full package that you've put together, I can't say if you're a good storyteller or not," Lenk says.

Remember, news directors like Lenk get a lot of applicant reels. Your reel could be one of 50.

"So really put a lot of strength and, again, a lot of confidence in that first 10 to 15 seconds and prove to me in that opening that you are a journalist and that you are going to be doing strong journalism," Lenk says.

> **Mentor Moment: Nancy Bauer Gonzales, News Director, KTNV, Las Vegas**
>
> "I like a person to give me their best stuff because I want to see what they think is their best stuff right out of the gate. I looked at a demo reel the other day. The woman was incredible. The first shot on her demo reel, she has her glasses on. Her hair's a mess. But she put it on there because it was breaking news. And I knew that after I watched the rest of her tape. But I thought, 'Oh my God, why did you do that?' I didn't say anything to her. And I'm probably going to offer her a job, but I think you have to put your best foot forward. Because nine times out of 10, you get 10 seconds. And if you can last 10 seconds, you'll get another 10. And if you can last 20 seconds, you'll probably get five minutes. So, you're going second by second on that demo reel."

What comes next? Examples of that strong storytelling on a variety of topics.

"They don't need to be headline grabbers or feature well-known people. They just need to be well told," Olivas says.

That means using what you have learned in this book already—writing short, declarative, active, conversational sentences. Olivas recommends incorporating multiplatform stories.

"If you came up with a great story, post it to your social media and then take a seven to 10 second clip from that site," Olivas says.

Stan Heist, director of news training and development at Sinclair Broadcast Group, agrees. "Today it's perfectly acceptable to insert video from a Facebook live in that stand-up montage as well as showing any mobile journalism."

Always use nat sound (NATS). Show your video shooting and editing skills, and use compelling soundbites. If you have video from an internship, put it on the reel, but be clear that it was from the internship and not on the air.

Any example of how comfortable a person is on camera is important but "avoid saying things so many others say, like the phrase, 'As you can see behind me,'" Olivas says.

> **Mentor Moment: Chad Hypes, News Director, KTVL, Medford**
>
> "I am always looking to see if the person is a 'reporter' or a 'storyteller.' I will always choose the storyteller. Anyone can recite a list of facts and call it a story, but a storyteller tells me how or why something happened. That's something a viewer can connect with. You also want to show your personality a little. Nothing's worse than a reel that only shows the person's headshot at the beginning and then it's just a few tracked packages. People connect with your face and your voice."

So, you started with a montage followed by two stories. In those stories, did you show creative stand-ups? Yes, even MMJs who shoot their own stories can be creative. Those people are more likely to get a hiring manager to watch longer.

Photographers and editors should show creative, well-framed shots and edits with strong NATS.

Producers should show energetic storytelling using a mix of on-camera, video, NATS, soundbites and graphics. Same for directors.

> **Mentor Moment: Kevin Olivas, Recruiter, Sinclair Broadcast Group**
>
> "For producers, in particular, you want to have a demo reel ready to go. I'm often asked, 'How do I create a producer reel?' If you've produced any newscasts in college, the newscast itself can be a producer reel. Pick one that you're really proud of. If it has mistakes in it, that's OK. Mistakes happen."

Anchors should demonstrate an ability to ask a hard question or ad-lib and cross talk with the other anchors on set. You must show depth and give a sense of your passion for journalism not just your desire to be on TV.

This reel can run anywhere from three to seven minutes.

Heist says the best reel leaves the manager saying, "I want to learn more about this person."

If the hiring manager asks for more, make sure you have it. Maybe you have a collection of newscasts you produced or directed, shows you anchored or stories you reported. Send a log with time codes explaining each piece in that collection. The hiring manager will likely scroll through the content, so make it easy for someone to move through your body of work.

Once you are happy with your reel, what do you do with it? Heist says YouTube is a great place to post because it is the second most popular search engine in the world.

Anything you put on YouTube must be organized. Do not send a link to your channel and expect a hiring manager to search through all of your videos. You must send the link for the specific reel for the specific job. If you update a reel, take down the old one. If that old link is on your resume or website and it's broken, that is not good. You have to be on top of your stuff.

DO YOU NEED A WEBSITE?

That is up to you. Frankly it may be work to create on the front end, but it can help you keep everything together in the long run. And, Heist says, it could help you land a job.

"It's common for managers, who may like your work but don't have an opening, to bookmark your website and go back to it when they have an opening," Heist says. "So, keep the URL and keep updating the site."

Heist says if you send the hiring manager to your website, you can change the video a million times and the URL will never change.

The website doesn't have to be extravagant.

Here are a few tips:

Create a homepage with an "about you." It's like your cover letter—a way to introduce yourself—and should include a professional picture.

Then, create a tab for your reel. You could have sub-tabs for a reporter reel and, if relevant, one for producing or anchoring. Clearly mark the difference.

If you are a producer candidate, post a whole show along with a PDF of the rundown. If you are going for a director job, post a whole show along with your director track.

Have one tab for your resume and another for other work you did in school such as newspaper articles, radio reports, scripts, web posts and social media work. Again, clearly mark your work, and include a text box to explain any picture or video you include.

> **Mentor Moment: Theresa de los Santos, Ph.D., Associate Professor of Communication, Pepperdine University**
>
> "Students should have professional social media pages where they post news information frequently and should absolutely put their reels on YouTube. Several of my students have received calls from news directors who discovered them through their reel on YouTube."

If you don't have a LinkedIn page, this is the time to start one. Post your resume and a link to your reel on your page. Then start making connections with people you know, such as your professors and employees at stations where you've interned. When a media professional guest lectures to your class, follow up with a LinkedIn invitation. If you go to a journalism conference, invite the professionals you meet to connect with you. Many students have been recruited for jobs through their LinkedIn profiles.

RESUMES TO IMPRESS

This may seem obvious, but the first piece of advice: be truthful.

> **Mentor Moment: Kevin Olivas, News Recruiting Manager, Sinclair Broadcast Group**
>
> "Don't lie. Not on your resume. Not in your reel. Not in your stories. Not in anything. We are in the information-gathering and verifying business. Sooner or later, the lie will catch up with you."

There are a lot of different styles for resumes. Clarity is important. Put your name at the top along with an email or web address. Any other personal information such as phone number or home address is not recommended. Resumes are often included on websites or social media, which is not private.

Next, list your talents and skills. Hiring managers understand students have limited experience, but all through school you've built up skills. List them. What equipment are you proficient in? Cameras, computers, audio/video controllers and boards. What software and apps can you use? Adobe, Avid, Final Cut, FiLMiC Pro.

> **Mentor Moment: Theresa de los Santos, Ph.D., Associate Professor of Communication**
>
> "Make any school-related or professional experience that can be translated to the positions they are applying for, stand out. I do think the order of skills matters on resumes. They should be listed in order of relevance to the position a student is applying for. A person applying for an MMJ position should list camera and editing skills first. While someone applying for a newscast director position should list control room equipment they know first. If a student is bilingual, when relevant, it should be part of their title. For example, Bilingual Journalist/Reporter. It could also be listed under skills."

The ability to speak different languages and understand different cultures is important in any newsroom. These attributes stand out for news director Luis Felipe Godinez.

"One thing I do look for is if you're bilingual *and* bicultural," Godinez says. "Because that for me is important as well as understanding both cultures. We're noticing that a lot with our audience. They're bilingual and bicultural."

He also recommends putting "bilingual" in the skills area of the resume and clearly on the reel. Also, add "bilingual" to the "about me" on your website.

If you are looking for a job in journalism but have no paid experience, list your skills that *do* apply to the career. That may include class projects or volunteer work relevant to the industry.

"Many students run social media for clubs, sororities, fraternities, even at non-media jobs, such as retail stores and restaurants. This can be tweaked on a resume to be more media-centric than retail oriented," says Desiree Hill, associate professor of communication at University of Central Oklahoma.

If you worked to put yourself through school, include that in your cover letter or the "about me" page of your website. If you had summer jobs that had nothing to do with your career, those can go in your cover letter if they help describe the kind of professional you are.

Maybe one summer you were a Blackjack dealer at a casino or a hot air balloon pilot. Those could be included in your "about me" because they're a talking point for the interview.

THE JOB INTERVIEW

For the college student applying for that first job, there is no reason to apologize for the lack of experience. The news director is well aware of that.

The hiring manager is interviewing you for your level of self-motivation and your ability to communicate, work on a team, solve problems and adapt.

"In the interview, you have to sell yourself," White says. "You sell what you do as a student athlete or if you're working to pay for college all while balancing good grades. Talk about your time management. That's huge in news because we're always under a deadline."

> **Mentor Moment: Chad Hypes, News Director**
>
> "I am constantly looking for new and upcoming college graduates to join our team. This can take a lot of my time, but hiring the right people is one of the most important parts of having a successful newsroom. During the recruiting process, I wear all kinds of hats. This is a big decision for a college graduate and many times they are taking the job sight unseen. I play the role of therapist by helping them weigh the pros and cons of working here at KTVL. I play the role of realtor by providing them with info about our area and even doing virtual tours of potential apartments."

Some common interview questions you should be ready for include:

- In what areas do you excel?
- What ethical dilemmas have you faced in your college career?
- Where do you think you need improvement and how do you plan to do that?
- What challenging stories have you covered and how did you overcome those challenges?
- Tell me about your best story and your worst story.
- What is it you want to get from your *next* job?

Remember, the interview process is a two-way street. You need to ask questions, too. Olivas recommends you ask about the job interview process. Ask if training, feedback, constructive criticism and professional development is offered for employees.

"Ask who are some of their success stories from the past when it comes to journalists who may have started in their newsroom and perhaps went on to a larger market," Olivas suggests.

The interview shows a lot about a job applicant. To prove that you did your homework, ask about a big story the station is covering or something you saw on the website or social channels or broadcast. Explain how and why *you* would be committed to that community.

Olivas reminds you to be realistic about where you apply.

"I can't tell you how many times someone coming out of school took aim on major markets when they were seeking their first full-time job," Olivas says. "Bigger does not necessarily mean better. And you have to be ready for it. The larger the news market, the more pressure and challenges that there are. You need to be ready to know how to deal with that."

NEGOTIATING A CONTRACT

When you get a job offer, you will most likely be asked to sign a contract. If this is your first job, you won't have a lot of room to negotiate. That doesn't mean you should just accept what is offered without carefully reviewing the contract. In fact, it wouldn't hurt to get that contract reviewed by an attorney to make sure you understand all of the clauses.

SAG-AFTRA, a labor union that represents broadcast journalists and media professionals, will review your contract for free even if you are not a member or the job offer isn't from a union station.

Bob Butler, SAG-AFTRA national broadcast vice president, says it's important you understand what you're signing even if you can't negotiate. You need to know whether the salary you're being offered is standard for the market, and you need to understand non-compete rules.

"A typical non-compete clause may say if they lay you off or at the end of your two-year contract, you have to wait one year before you can take a similar job in the same market," Butler explains. "You're not allowed to compete with the company if they let you go."

Butler says if you break a non-compete rule, the company can sue you. If a court rules any part of the non-compete is illegal, the company has the right to amend it so that it is legal.

Butler says you should also be aware of termination clauses and liquidated damages in your contract. Some termination clauses state the company can end your employment whenever it wants without cause. Liquidated damages means if you break the contract early, you will owe the station money.

Even if you can't negotiate a higher salary, Butler says you can negotiate other things such as moving expenses and professional development. You may also be able to negotiate an "out clause," which would allow you to leave after a specified length of time for a job in a larger market.

Reporter Elisa Navarro signed a two-year contract when she was hired at KXXV in Waco, Texas. She didn't negotiate any outs because she never intended to leave the station before her contract was up. But then she got a job offer from "the one station in the entire country" where she wanted to work.

"I didn't want to take any chances because this job wasn't going to be there when my contract was up in six months," Navarro says. "I felt like it was a train I had to jump on because it was going to go whether I jumped on it or not."

She talked to her news director and general manager and had their full support. But she still had to pay to get out of the contract. It ended well for Navarro, but Butler says that isn't always the case. You could wind up burning bridges—something that could follow you around for the rest of your career.

STARTING YOUR NEWS CAREER

Once you get that job, be ready for a whole new learning experience. It will be exhilarating, exhausting and challenging both mentally and physically. Don't be hard on yourself. Learn from the process, and grow from it. Be ready for things to change quickly.

On Bryan Lenocker's first day as a weekend assignment editor at KFSN in Fresno, the news director told him a producer had just quit. He asked if Lenocker wanted that job.

During the job interview Lenocker had mentioned he wanted to produce but took the assignment editor position because no producer position was available at the moment:

> I try to never say 'no' to a project or a new opportunity. This business should be all about helping people grow and learn. If I had said no to some things, who knows where I'd be and what I'd be doing. Don't let your fear of the unknown prevent you from saying 'yes.'"

"Nothing will prepare you for it," says producer Alex White:

> My first week I went home bawling, crying my eyes out to my mom saying, 'I can't do this. Why did they think I could do this?' You just learn so much about what you can handle. People won't fault you for making mistakes if you learn from them. You might make it twice, but you won't make it three times.

White's advice: Accept that things will be hard and scary at first. You'll have a lot of growing pains, and that's part of life.

> **Mentor Moment: Nick King, Sports Reporter/Anchor, 3TV CBS5, Phoenix**
>
> "Things will go right more often than they go wrong. But the times when things go wrong, while perhaps cringeworthy in the moment, are often more memorable in the long run. So long as you can learn from each of those experiences, it's best to accept that they will happen, and embrace them. The first time the screen goes black while you're talking, or the wrong video pops up, or the teleprompter starts speeding past where it's supposed to be, or you lose your train of thought, or mispronounce a word, or you get the time of a game wrong and show up as it's ending, or run out of breath while you're talking because you were literally running to the set after finishing editing a video at the last possible second, it's a nightmare. All those things have happened to me and will likely happen to you at some point. Eventually, you gain poise in these moments and handle it in stride because you've been there before."

Patience is key. Patience with yourself and your learning curve. It's also crucial to remember that each day is a stepping stone. It's a piece to your whole career. It is *not* your whole career.

You must think of the big picture. Give all you can to each job you do and pay attention to the jobs of others. That will help you understand why decisions are made.

Remember, do not take newsroom decisions personally. A newsroom can be a brutal place. Everyone is working on a tight deadline. It's stressful trying to be creative in that setting. That stress is often what feeds news people, but not everyone handles the stress well.

We're not giving a pass to tantrums or rude behavior. Just don't take it personally.

For example, if a reporter thinks his or her story should be the lead but the producer does not, don't take it personally. After the show, talk with the producer to understand his or her news philosophy.

If an anchor constantly changes words in the producer's scripts, ask that anchor (away from a deadline) for writing and producing advice.

Remember, in Chapter 11, KNXV producer Kianey Carter says she did this, and it not only helped make her a better producer and writer, it helped build a relationship with that anchor.

Fox News correspondent Alicia Acuna remembers a time at a new job when she was spurned by a couple of co-workers. It went on for a while, and she was miserable. Then, one day, she realized something.

"I remembered, somehow, somewhere inside of me that they didn't hire me," Acuna recalls. "Somebody else did. And they really didn't have any say over whether I did my job because there was a reason somebody hired me. I had to remember that. It was something that I held onto."

After that, Acuna says the tide turned slowly and those mean colleagues began to treat her better.

While you're busy doing your job, you need to keep an eye on how the whole building works. Get involved in the station softball team, the community clean-up or holiday party planning committees. Become friends with colleagues in other departments. Become a student of sales and promotions and human resources, not to get involved in gossip, but to get a better understanding of other decisions that affect the station as a whole.

You may see things you don't understand or like. You may notice someone leaves early on certain days or comes in late. Don't get bugged by it unless somehow it negatively impacts your job. If it has nothing to do with you, let it go. You have no idea what's going on in that person's life or what kind of understanding that person has with his or her boss.

Now, what if after a while you've given all of yourself to the position for which you were hired and you just do not like it? Have a candid conversation with your boss that is more about growth and less about whining.

Mentor Moment: Chad Hypes, News Director

"I have worked with a ton of people who switched jobs within the newsroom, from producer to reporter, reporter to meteorologist, etc. That only happens when people take the time to learn how each position contributes to the overall newsroom. You never know what you might like or what you might be

> good at if you don't try. Worst case scenario, you are building your resume and showing that you are a team player. So many people get caught up in specialization at their first job. You will have plenty of time for that later!"

Remember Alex White, who said her first few weeks were emotional and rough? Three years later, she's feeling much more confident and rewarded as a newscast producer.

"The biggest change from the first day to the third year is my confidence level," White says. "I have really taken the time to learn the ins and outs of the industry and talk with the people who hold all of the different positions so we can be a more cohesive unit."

> **Mentor Moment: Nick King, Sports Reporter**
>
> "This is not an easy business to survive in. The first job, I was making $19,500 a year. The second job, $21,500. I was a sports anchor on TV four to five days a week, and I had to split a $450 a month apartment to survive. With every job I took, I was moving to a new city, far from friends and family, where I didn't know a single person. Sports jobs in general are diminishing by the day. It's getting harder to find a gig. But, if you love journalism, and you'll know before long, it is worth it. Every step of the way."

AGENTS, CONSULTANTS AND RECRUITERS

Agents can be helpful to someone moving up the ranks in the business. They are likely not going to work with a college student or someone coming into the industry. But, after some time working on your craft, an agent could be someone to consider.

You will need to find a balance of how much you can afford versus how much this person can offer working on your behalf. Signing with an agent can cost you anywhere from 5 to 10% of your paycheck as well as a one-to-three-year contract.

Many stations hire consultants, and those consultations are free to station employees. Usually, that person works with *all* of the TV stations owned by that company. If you want to have a consultant look at your work and help you progress, start by talking with your news director. The station or company ownership may also have a mentorship program.

Remember, professional organizations can also help. Yes, you may pay for the membership. Ask your accountant if it can be written off as a business expense. Some are free. There are also groups on Facebook that mentor for free. If you want mentorship and advice, you must be proactive in getting it.

WHY YOUR MENTORS LOVE THEIR JOBS

Throughout this book, you have heard from dozens of mentors. Together their experience in the broadcast and digital news industries totals more than 800 years. That's a lot of wisdom. They all have different reasons for doing the jobs they do and for staying in this business. We want to conclude this chapter with their voices. They hope their experiences can help you with yours.

> **Mentor Moment: Adrian Luevano, Sports Reporter**
>
> "People say all the time, 'Oh, you're such a go-getter because you do this and this.' But to me, it's just natural. It's what I do. I just go out there and just do the work. I want to do it. This job is fun. I would go to these sports games no matter what. But I'm getting paid for this."

> **Mentor Moment: Alicia Acuna, FOX News Correspondent**
>
> "Let yourself be a human being. Be informed. If you think you're the smartest person there, then start asking questions, because everybody can teach you something. It's really easy to get caught up in your own ego in this business, especially if your face is on television or online. Don't believe your own press. You're still responsible for telling other people's stories, and it's really important to remember the weight of the responsibility of telling someone else's story. It does not belong to you."

Mentor Moment: Boyd Huppert, Reporter, KARE11, Minneapolis

"It's a front-row seat. Two weeks ago, I covered the George Floyd memorial service. His death is changing the course of history, and I was given the privilege of writing part of it. I love every step of the process: the gathering, the interpreting, the writing and the presenting."

Mentor Moment: Brandon Mercer, Digital Content Director

"I love seeing people engage with content, and I love the energy of a team delivering it. It's addictive."

Mentor Moment: Brett Akagi, Owner, Akagi Media, Kansas City

"I've seen more change in the industry in the last 10 years than I saw in the previous 20. Then COVID-19 came along in 2020 and put nearly everything into turmoil. The result? Some changes have been good, like being able to work remotely, technology and software advancements for remote work, creative storytelling under very restrictive conditions, an appreciation for working in a newsroom with teammates and storytelling using innovative graphics. The bad changes include downsizing staff, permanent layoffs and companies shutting down. I was laid off because of COVID. I was told by HR and my GM the job loss wasn't a reflection of my work. The reason wasn't personal or professional. It was because the economy was so bad. My wife, who was upset at the time, told me if I were to give advice to students, tell them 'Don't get into journalism or if you do, marry rich.' It's funny and sad. I understand how she feels. However, I also know that democracy is at its best when journalists are doing journalism. We need good and great journalists, especially in these divisive and turbulent times. Without us, democracy is diminished."

Mentor Moment: Bryan Lenocker, Executive Producer, WABC, New York

"There are so many people out there who need help, or have stories to tell. We literally can give a voice to those people. People turn to us when they need help or want to know what is happening in their community. This past year we helped cover stories of people and businesses struggling to survive. We covered stories about loved-ones desperate for information as COVID spread in our area. I have always felt what we do is important."

Mentor Moment: Carmaine Means, Photographer/Drone Pilot, CNN, Chicago

"I talked to one of my best friends who works in New York at the network. Guess what he did two weeks ago? He was setting up a shoot for Cicely Tyson. It was her last interview she shot with Gayle King. I mean, he shot her last interview and it looked fantastic. And that's why I get up and do this job every day. It's a way for people to impact you but also for you to impact other folks. And that was her last interview. How many times does a photographer get to say I met Cicely Tyson or I met America Ferrera? The images that you've captured are going to stay around forever. How can you not love that? That's just awesome. Right?"

Mentor Moment: Chad Hypes, News Director

"I love the teaching, coaching and training. I love seeing people get better, seeing them try new things, and seeing them move on to bigger markets. I love hearing people say that we prepared them well for their next market. This business is unique in that each day is different. We get to inform people, help people, and empower people. Your stories can make a difference in people's lives. That's pretty powerful!"

Mentor Moment: Chad Nelson, Director of Photography, KARE11, Minneapolis

"The reason I am in this business is pretty simple for me. I want to tell great stories to help keep the memories of people alive. Years ago, I started telling people to have a personal mission statement and how much that has helped me. It doesn't have to be great at first, and you can modify it over time. But it's something that you can go back to when you are having a tough time. 'Good storytelling brings people to life; great storytelling keeps them alive forever.' When I am not feeling the story or just having a bad day, I take a deep breath and recite this to myself, and I'm right back in the game."

Mentor Moment: Chris Alvarez, Sports Reporter, KGO, San Francisco

"The TV business is a small world. Be kind to everyone because you never know where that next opportunity may be coming from and your character and work ethic will be just as important if not more important than how talented you may be."

Mentor Moment: Da Lin, MMJ, KPIX, San Francisco

"If your goal is to be 'on TV,' best not to waste your time because you'll hate this job. Think of the job not as a privilege but a responsibility. This job is stressful and demanding. You're constantly on deadline. And get ready to work on most holidays. I worked this last Thanksgiving, Christmas, and New Year's Day. Also, the workday is long. The list of challenges in the business goes on. So, if you don't love the different aspects of this business for the right reason, you'll get burned out and leave very fast."

Mentor Moment: Dion Lim, News Anchor, KGO, San Francisco

"Being in TV journalism is a gift. Along with the highest highs of being on a red carpet at the Oscars are the days when you're covered in ash, reporting on a neighborhood that has been charred to the ground from a wildfire. You get to experience the fullest life possible and witness history. This is much cooler than just showing your face on TV and sure as heck beats crunching numbers at a desk all day and doing the same thing every single day. This career path is exciting and every day is different."

Mentor Moment: Greg Vandegrift, University of St. Thomas Professor and Freelance Reporter, KARE 11, Minneapolis

"I have continued because I get such joy out of storytelling. I still get a kick out of writing a simple, efficient line that marries the video in a powerful but subtle way. When a story works, I get great satisfaction."

Mentor Moment: Jeff Lenk, News Director

"I just love having a job where I go in and feel excited about what I'm doing every day. And I go in knowing that every day is going to be different. We as journalists have the power to affect change and do things to make our community a better place, whether that's bringing attention to positive things that are happening or exposing negative things that are harming people and doing what we can to change that situation."

Mentor Moment: Jobin Panicker, Reporter, WFAA, Dallas

"I am still in this business because I still love the process of storytelling. I love creating. I love telling stories that evoke emotion. Every newsroom has its good and bad. No newsroom is perfect. We must control what we can, and I learned that I can truly only control my news product. And now that I am in market number five and 13 years in the business, I can happily say the compensation is a competitive wage, finally."

Mentor Moment, Joe Little, MMJ/Director of Storytelling, KNSD, San Diego

"I do this because I love telling stories. Even when I have bad days, I know tomorrow gives me another chance to tell someone's story even better."

Mentor Moment: John Colucci, Senior Director, Social Media, Sinclair Broadcast Group

"The most important thing I look for in a digital content producer candidate is how comfortable they are with being flexible to whatever happens in the newsroom and juggling multiple tasks at once. Most folks should come equipped with that mindset already, as anything can happen in a newsroom. That's part of the fun, the chaos, really. But in most stations, you don't have a dedicated social media person or a dedicated person who just writes web stories—you're doing it all."

Mentor Moment: Kevin Olivas, Recruiter, Sinclair Broadcast Group

"Be versatile! Just about everyone is going to need to be a one-person band now when it comes to journalism. Newscast producers will also need to be comfortable with gathering stories with their own equipment, and putting themselves on camera to explain stories, even if their video appearance ends up being on a station's app or its social media as opposed to the news broadcast."

Mentor Moment: Luis Felipe Godinez, News Director, Univision 19, KUVS, Sacramento

"It doesn't pay well. It's deadline driven. It's very time consuming, and it's something you have to have a vocation for. Understand you are not a celebrity. The main driver should be making a difference and really affecting someone's life."

Mentor Moment: Nancy Bauer Gonzales, News Director, KTNV, Las Vegas

"I love it. I don't know that I'll ever retire. I'll probably get kicked out again. I've loved it since I was in second grade. I just love the churn of news. There's nothing I like more than to sit in my office, which is really close to the newsroom, and I can hear what everybody's saying. The conversations are so fun. They're so good. Somebody's mad about somebody. Somebody's debating something. And I think this industry is going to be alive and well."

Mentor Moment: Nick King, Sports Anchor/Reporter, 3TV CBS5, Phoenix

"In the last decade, I've learned more about people and the world than I ever could have imagined. I've lived in Virginia, Missouri, California, and now Arizona, and traveled to many more states while working. I've met people from all walks of life and had the opportunity to ask them questions about how they got to this point in life, what motivates them, and what they want to accomplish. I've been given a front row seat at so many unforgettable games, from high school on up to the pros. Every single day is a new adventure."

Mentor Moment: Randy Forsman, Newscast Director, KCRA, Sacramento

"Have you heard the saying, 'Find a job you enjoy doing, and you will never have to work a day in your life.'? Every day feels like that for me. Being a director has lent such a powerful sense of purpose and continues to challenge me each and every day."

Mentor Moment: Stan Heist, Director of News Training and Development, Sinclair Broadcast Group

"We have an awesome responsibility, and we have to cherish that above all else. But I do also value and firmly believe that we can do our jobs in a compelling way to add meaning to help people better understand the world."

REMINDERS ON JOB OPPORTUNITIES

- Be willing to start in a small to medium market.
- Be versatile.
- Humility and hard work will take you far.
- Join professional organizations.
- Keep up with local, national and world news.
- Exemplify professionalism in demeanor, language and dress.
- Own up to mistakes. Learn from them to keep from repeating them.

TRY THIS

1. Create a LinkedIn account with your resume. Connect with people from different news markets, universities and public offices.
2. Connect to people and organizations on Twitter, Facebook and Instagram.
3. Go through your classwork and add samples to your website or reel.
4. Make sure your YouTube channel is updated and ready for hiring managers to see.

NOTE

1 https://tvnewscheck.com/business-revenue/article/nexstar-remains-firmly-atop-station-groups/

Key Terms

Active Interview An interview that is conducted while the interviewee is performing a task related to the topic.

Analytics Information that helps you track and measure social media engagement.

Attribution Sourcing a soundbite, quote or other piece of information.

Backtime The act of timing a newscast from the end by subtracting the estimated length of each news story.

Beat check Calls, texts and email inquiries routinely made to news sources to find out whether anything newsworthy is happening.

Bite Short for soundbite.

Block A segment of the newscast.

B-roll Video that helps visually illustrate a news story. The term originated from film and was used to differentiate B-roll from A-roll. (A-roll was video with sound; B-roll was for the video of the story.)

Bridge A reporter's stand-up that is placed in the middle of a news package that facilitates a transition from one part of the story to the next.

Byline The writer's name on a web story.

CG Abbreviation for "character generator" graphics that appear on the screen. Usually refers to the lower-third location or interviewee name used in news stories.

Chroma Key Also known as the green screen which allows visuals to be superimposed behind a person.

Closeup shot (CU) A tight shot of either a person's face, subject or action.

Cold open Video headline at the beginning of a newscast or story.

Copy A reader story where there is no video.

Copyright The legal right a company or individual has over each piece of video, sound or product.

Cutaway shot A shot of something that isn't directly related to the action to help in editing.
Day-turn A story completed in one day.
Director The person who has technical control of the newscast.
DMA Designated Market Area. It is the geographic area in which local television viewing is measured.
Embed (a video) To add a video to a webpage or website either with a link or an embed code.
Executive producer Newsroom manager who supervises the producers, writers and reporters.
Extreme closeup (XCU) Super tight shot. For example, only the person's eyes fill the frame. Extreme closeups will get you out of editing quandaries.
Fake News Untrue information shared and presented in a way that makes it appear as factual.
Front time The act of timing a newscast from the beginning by adding the estimated length of each news story.
Headlines Short attention-grabbing video teases that run at the very beginning of a newscast.
Headroom The space between the top of the subject's head and the top of the frame.
IFB Abbreviation for "interruptible feedback" or "interruptible foldback." Allows direct communication to the talent by interrupting programming sound so the message can be heard in the talent's ear.
Incue The first few words of any pre-recorded video or interview.
Intro The script an anchor reads to introduce a reporter's packaged story.
Jump cut A cut in video editing in which two shots of the same subject are used from the same position and give the effect of the subject jumping through time.
Key light A large, soft light.
Kicker A light-hearted story that is often used to end a segment or newscast on a positive note.
Lead One or two sentences at the beginning of a story that is meant to grab the viewer, listener or reader's attention.
Legalese Language used by law enforcement or lawyers that is not conversational.

Live Content happening in real-time.

Live Shot A live remote with a reporter or of a live scene using cellular, microwave, satellite or social media.

LiveU Portable cellular backpack streaming technology used for live video transmission. Also known as TV-U.

Logging Transcribing interviews in preparation for writing a news story.

Look-live or As-live A recorded "live shot" done in one take without edits.

Lower-third Also known as a CG, Super or Matte. It's the identifying graphic that appears in the lower-third of the screen.

Match cut In editing, action that continues across two shots from different camera angles.

Medium shot (MS) In between a closeup shot and a wide shot.

MMJ Multimedia journalist. A term used to denote a solo journalist who shoots, writes and edits stories without a support crew.

Moments Little surprises or gold nuggets that a reporter weaves through a story. The foundation to good storytelling.

MOS Abbreviation for "man-on-the-street." Interviewing multiple random people about a specific topic. Known as a POS (people-on-the-street) or vox pop in some newsrooms.

Nat sound (NATS) Natural sound that is used to enhance a news story.

News Director Manager in charge of the newsroom and its employees.

Open Source Video, pictures, graphics or sound found on the internet that is free to use, but still may be copyrighted so you may still need to get permission to use it.

OTS Abbreviation for "Over-The-Shoulder" graphic that appears while an anchor reads a script on camera.

OTT Over-The-Top: Streaming content offered directly to viewers over the internet without the use of cable, broadcast or satellite operators. For example, Netflix, Roku, YouTube, Apple-TV.

Outcue Three or four words for when a soundbite or package will end.

Pacing The pace and tempo of a newscast or news story.

Package (PKG) A self-contained news story produced by a reporter that includes a voice track, interview clips, a stand-up and b-roll.

Pad Extra video after story ends to avoid going to black. Usually 10-seconds but NEVER counted in the total running time of a story.

Pan Moving the camera horizontally. Avoid panning.
Parroting Lead into the soundbite and the soundbite are similar. Avoid this.
PIO Abbreviation for "Public Information Officer." The communications director for public agencies who is assigned to work directly with the media.
POS People-on-the-street (see MOS).
Post To put your story on the website and/or on social media.
Producer The person who decides the order and treatment of stories in a newscast. The producer usually writes the headlines and teases and times the newscast.
Promo Sometimes called a "topical." A short 15- or 30-second announcement often promoting an upcoming story or program.
Q-rating Measurement of familiarity and appeal of a news anchor
Ratings The measurement of how many people or households are watching a specific broadcast.
Reader A copy story without any video.
Reporter sandwich One-point lighting with the reporter placed between the camera and the key light. The darker side of the interviewee's face is closest to the camera.
Room sound Also known as room tone. The recording of ambient sounds at a location to fill gaps when editing a news package.
Rundown The outline of stories running in a newscast.
Scanner traffic Emergency crews talking on the two-way radio while out in the field.
Sequence Two or more shots of the same action from varying angles, focal points and distances.
Sidebar A term that originates from print journalism. It is a smaller story that accompanies the main story on the same topic.
Slot Position in the rundown where a story is to air.
Slug The story name or title.
SOT Abbreviation for "Sound on Tape."
Stand-up A reporter's appearance on camera in a news package or live.
Story focus A short three- or four-word phrase that sums up what the story is about.
Sweeps Industry term for "ratings." Typically, measured in February, May, July and November.

Talent On-air presenter.

Toss When the anchor or reporter passes the newscast to another anchor or reporter.

Tripod A three-legged stand that supports a camera. Also called "sticks."

TRT Abbreviation for "Total Running Time."

VO Voice over—a brief news story read live by the news anchor who voices over the video.

Voice Track Narration in a package.

VOSOT Voice over with sound on tape. Also called soundbites or bites. Read live by the news anchor with the addition of an interview clip (or SOT).

Wallpaper video B-roll video that is used in a news story that has no connection or a vague connection to the words.

Wide shot (WS) A shot that allows the viewer to see the entire scene. It is often used as an establishing shot.

XLR Abbreviation for "external line return." It's the three pronged (or three holed) electrical connector used in audio/video/lighting equipment.

No No No Words

These are words or phrases you'll want to avoid using. You will hear police officers, public officials, doctors, scientists, academics and other experts use this stilted terminology because it's the language of their profession. Your job is to cut through the legalese or medical lingo and make the information understandable and relatable for your audience.

Accident Implies judgment or exoneration. Use "crash" instead.
Allegedly Doesn't protect the writer legally. Attribute to a reliable or official source instead.
Apprehend Police jargon. Just say "arrest."
Apparently Infers rumor and that the information may not be believable.
Armed gunman Redundant. A gunman is already armed.
Arson fire Redundant. Arson stands on its own.
Blaze Use "fire."
Bound (as in northbound, southbound, etc.) Cop talk. Say: "driving north" or "driving south."
Brandished Instead, say what the person was doing: "angrily waving the gun around."
Brutal murder All murders are brutal. Just use "murder" or "homicide."
Collision Crash is more conversational.
Completely or totally destroyed Redundant. Destroyed means completely gone and stands on its own.
Completely or totally engulfed Redundant. Engulfed means totally and stands on its own.
Could of (also "should of" and "would of") Could have, should have, or would have.
Currently "Right now" is more conversational.
Dead body Redundant. A body means dead. If alive, it's a person, not a body.

Deceased Use "dead." Avoid the euphemism passed away.
Due to Use "because of."
Ejected Use "thrown out" or "thrown from."
Ensued Happened.
Evacuate (a person) You evacuate a building or an area as in, "Police evacuated the neighborhood." If you say, "Fifty people were evacuated," you're talking about bodily functions.
Evading Police jargon. Use: "running from," "speeding away" or "trying to get away."
Exited Cop talk. Use "got out."
Female Use "woman" or "girl."
Fled on foot Use "ran."
Gone missing or went missing A person is either missing or gone. Do not use both together.
Gonna (also wanna) Do not use substandard spellings. Use "going to" and "want to."
Handicapped Do not use to describe a person. Handicapped-accessible parking is OK when talking about a parking spot or placard. Consult AP Stylebook.
How do you feel? Avoid asking this cliché and ineffective question when a subject is dealing with a painful event.
Incarcerated Use "locked up," "in jail," "behind bars," "in prison."
Incident This is police jargon. Instead use descriptive words such as "crash," "fight," etc.
Male Use "man."
Murder Use "homicide," which is the legal term for slaying or killing according to AP.
Myself Never used as a subject pronoun. Use "I" or "me." No: "Send your response to Kim and *myself*." Yes: "Send your response to Kim and *me*."
Near miss A miss is a miss.
Occurred It happened.
Officials Be specific about the person you are quoting: "Lieutenant John Dix says" or "the fire chief says."
Only time will tell Trite and doesn't say anything of use. Instead, say what will happen next.
Passed away AP says use "died." "Don't use euphemisms like passed on or passed away except in a direct quote."
Past history History means "the past." Use "history."

Pontiff Refers to any bishop. Use "pope."
Possibly Implies rumor and that the information may not be accurate.
Residence Home or apartment.
Resident Use "lives there."
Responded to the scene Police jargon. Use "went there," "got there" or "drove there."
Seems Implies rumor and that the information may not be believable.
Slaying or was slain Use "killed."
Stable condition Not a medical state. Use "undetermined," "good," "fair," "guarded," "serious," "critical," "grave." "Critical but stable" would be accurate.
Suffocated to death Suffocation means death. Use "suffocated."
Suspect A suspect is a specific, named person who is known to police and is wanted, charged or in jail—not an unknown, mysterious person.
Sustained injuries Was hurt (injured by itself is OK).
Terminate Fired or lost a job.
Totally involved or completely involved Police jargon. Use "fire" or describe what you see.
Totally submerged or partially submerged Submerged means "completely under." If it's not submerged, say partially underwater.
Tragedy/Tragic This is an opinion. Explain what happened and let the viewer/reader determine whether it was a tragedy.
Transported Use "driven" or "taken."
Two Twins A twin implies two. A set of twins is correct. Please note that "set" is a singular entity.
Undetermined Use "It is not known at this time" or "is unknown."
Utilize Just say "use."
Vehicle It's a car, truck or motorcycle. Call it what it is.
Very A weak word that diminishes the meaning of the adjective or adverb.
Victim People become victimized through no power of their own. Find another way that doesn't rob the person of dignity and power.
Whether or not Redundant. Just say "whether."
Wounded "Hurt" is a more conversational word.

Works Cited

Acuna, Alicia. Personal Interview. December 15, 2020.
Akagi, Brett. Zoom Interview. December 16, 2020.
Alvarez, Chris. Email Interview. December 11, 2020
American Bar Association. *How Courts Work*. n.d. Web. January 31, 2021.
AP Stylebook. n.d. Web. January 31, 2021.
Argen, Lisa. Personal Interview. January 2, 2021.
Bauer Gonzales, Nancy. Zoom Interview. January 8, 2021.
Best Practices for Facebook and Instagram. Facebook. n.d. Web. January 31, 2021.
Brown, Fred, ed. (2020). *Media Ethics: A Guide for Professional Conduct*. Indianapolis: Society of Professional Journalists. Print.
Buchanan, Michael, Terry Getz, and David Hotz. "East Tennessee Tornado Outbreak on May 18, 1995." *National Weather Service*. Web. January 31, 2021.
Buchanan, Tim. Email Interview. February 7, 2021.
Butler, Bob. Telephone Interview. May 26, 2021.
Butler, Bob. "Navigating a Career in Broadcasting" *Workshop*. Fresno State. April 28, 2018.
Carr, Michael. Zoom Interview. January 14, 2021.
Carter, Kianey. Personal Interview. July 28, 2020.
Clavijo, Alliz. Personal Interview. August 3, 2020.
Colucci, John. Personal Interview. January 12, 2021.
Copyright Law and U.S. Government Works. Copyrightlaws.com. Web. May 31, 2021.
De los Santos, Theresa. Personal Interview. January 13, 2021.
Finchman, Kelly. "What Every Young Journalist Should Know About Using Twitter." *Poynter*. September 21, 2012. Web. January 31, 2021.
Forsman, Randy. Personal Interview. January 2, 2021.
Freedman, W. (2011). It Takes More Than Good Looks to Succeed at Television News Reporting. A Wealth of Wisdom, LLC, p. 55, ebook.
Galvan, Louis. "Alleged Sausage Attacker Set Free DA Decides Not Enough Evidence to Try Man Held in Bizarre Robbery Case," The Fresno Bee. September 11, 2008. Web. January 31, 2021
Gill, Kathy. What is the Fourth Estate? ThoughtCo. January 16, 2020. Web. January 31, 2021.
Godinez, Luis Felipe. Personal Interview. January 3, 2021.
Hebert, Cyndee. Personal Interview. January 12, 2021.
Hernandez, Victor. Personal Interview. May 24, 2020.
Heist, Stan. Personal Interview. August 3, 2020.

Hill, Desiree. Personal Interview. January 14, 2021.
Hollowood, Ella, and Alexi Mostrous. "Fake News in the Time of C-19." Tortoise Media. March 23, 2020. Web. January 31, 2021.
How do I Create a Facebook Page? Facebook Help. n.d. Web. January 31, 2021.
How to use Hashtags. Twitter Support. n.d. Web. January 31, 2021.
History.com editors. When is Veterans Day? 9 Nov. 2020. Web. January 31, 2021.
Holiday, Ryan (2016). *Ego is the Enemy*, New York Penguin Random House. Print.
How to Manage Multiple Accounts. Twitter Support. n.d. Web. January 31, 2021.
Hsu, George. Personal Interview. January 12, 2021.
Hudgins, Ryan. "Man Saves Family from Fire." KMPH FOX 26. September 26, 2015.
Huppert, Boyd. Zoom Interview. July 6, 2020.
Huppert, Boyd. Storytelling workshop. California State University, Fresno, February 20, 2016.
Hypes, Chad. Personal Interview. December 28, 2020.
Journalist's Toolbox. Web. January 31, 2021.
King, Nick. Personal Interview. January 2, 2021.
Lenk, Jeff. Personal Interview. December 22, 2020.
Lenocker, Bryan. Personal Interview. January 5, 2021.
Light, Sarah. Personal Interview. May 24, 2020.
Lim, Dion (2019). *Make Your Moment The Savvy Woman's Communication Playbook for Getting the Success You Want*. McGraw-Hill. Print.
Lim, Dion. Personal Interview. August 1, 2020.
Lin, Da. Personal Interview. January 3, 2021.
Little, Joe. Telephone Interview. September 3, 2020.
Little, Joe. "NPPA News Video Workshop." Gaylord College of Journalism & Mass Communication. Norman, Oklahoma. March 21, 2019. Lecture.
Luevano, Adrian. Personal Interview. September 4, 2020.
"Man Rubbed With Spices, Other Beaten With Sausage," The Fresno Bee. September 7, 2008. Web. January 31, 2021.
McGrew, Scott. Personal Interview. June 11, 2020.
McSpadden, Kevin. "You Now Have a Shorter Attention Span Than a Goldfish." Time. May 14, 2015. Web. January 31, 2021.
Means, Carmaine. Zoom Interview. January 29, 2021.
Mercer, Brandon. Zoom Interview. September 4, 2020.
Milstein, Jake. Personal Interview. September 6, 2020.
National Weather Service will STOP YELLING and Use Lower-Case Letters in Alerts, Weather.com, April 11, 2016. Web. https//weather.com/news/news/national-weather-service-to-use-lower-case-letters
Navarro, Elisa. Telephone Interview. February 10, 2021.
Nelson, Chad. Personal Interview. August 27, 2020.
Olivas, Kevin. Email Interview. January 2, 2021.
Panicker, Jobin. Zoom Interview. September 10, 2020.
Potts, Tracie. Personal Interview. July 27, 2020.

Potts, Tracie. "Journalists of Color Are Part of the Story of Racism in America. That Raises Tough Questions on the Job." Center for Health Journalism. June 22, 2020. Web. January 31, 2021

"Religion & Public Life, In U.S., Decline of Christianity Continues at Rapid Pace An Update on America's Changing Religious Landscape." Pew Research Center. October 17, 2019. Web. January 31, 2021.

Student Reporting Labs Tutorials. PBS News Hour. n.d. January 31, 2021

Powell, Tracie. "Do's and Don'ts of Covering Protests." Poynter. June 8, 2020. Web. January 31, 2021.

Prato, Lou (1999) "Easy to Do, But Often Worthless." American Journalism Review. April 1999. Web. January 31, 2021.

Public Records Letter Generator. Student Press Law Center. n.d. Web. January 31, 2021.

Rose, Les. "Tips and Tricks." The Road Less Traveled. n.d. January 31, 2021.

Rose, Les. Zoom Interview. August 18, 2020.

Ruiz, Don Miguel (1997). *The Four Agreements*. Amber-Allen Publishing. Print.

Safety Tips for Journalists. Facebook. n.d. Web. January 31, 2021.

Salm, Lauren. "70% of Employers are Snooping Candidates' Social Media Profiles." Career Builder. June 15, 2017. Web. January 31, 2021.

Sample Demand for Cure or Correction; Alleged Violation of Brown Act. California News Publishers Association. n.d. Web. January 31, 2021.

Sidlow, F. and Pierce, T. (2016). *Are Broadcast Journalism Graduates Job Ready? A Survey of Skills Desired by TV News Directors*. Presented at the Broadcast Education Association Super Regional Conference, Columbia, South Carolina, October 13, 2016.

Siegal, A. and Connolly, W. (2015). *The New York Times Manual of Style and Usage The Official Style Guide Used by the Writers and Editors of the World's Most Authoritative News Organization*, 5th Ed. Crown.

Slater, Robin. Telephone Interview. January 13, 2021.

SPJ Code of Ethics, Revised Sept. 6, 2014. Web. January 31, 2021.

Tompkins, Al. (2018). *Aim for the Heart Writing, Reporting, Photojournalism, Producing, Ethics and Resources for Journalists*, 3rd ed. Sage Thousand Oaks.

Tompkins, Al. Telephone Interview. February 1, 2021.

Tompkins, Al. "Monday Edition Bob Dotson's Essential Storytelling Tools," Poynter, July 1, 2007. Web. January 25, 2021.

Tran, Will. Personal Interview. January 5, 2021.

Vandegrift, Greg. Telephone Interview. June 29, 2020.

Vandegrift, Greg. License Plates. KARE-11, April 25, 2017. Web. January 31, 2021. www.youtube.com/watch?v= kV3FnvdJuWM.

Vandegrift, Greg. A Work of Art. KARE-11. April 25, 2017. Web. January 31, 2021 https //youtu.be/zA0UQVZ0zqw.

Vanek, Adam. "Open Letter to American Judges Association and American Bar Association." MADD. n.d. Web. February 21, 2021.

Wallenstein, Andrew. "Q Scores Stats Reveal Who's More Popular Digital Stars vs. Mainstream Celebs." Variety, June 21, 2016. Web. January 31, 2021.

White, Alex. Personal Interview. December 4, 2020.

Index

Note: page numbers in italic type refer to Figures; those in bold type refer to Tables.

30-degree rule 158, *158*
180-degree rule 158–160, *159*

abbreviations 40
abortion 295
accident, as a "NO, NO, NO" word 60
accountability 292
accuracy 5, 46, 49, 80, 207, 291
acronyms 40
action reaction 161
active interviews 29, 170–171
active writing 41–42, 42–43, 44, 52–53, 208
actual malice 298
Acuna, Alicia 13, 109, 240, 242, 246–247, 252, 292, 312, 326, 328
ad-libbing 201, 239, 243, 246–249, 250, 275, 318
AE (assignment editors) 185; and breaking news 199–200; and interviewing 75; role and responsibilities 4, 30–31
age, references to 41
agents 327–328
Air Force, Air Force Reserve 67
Akagi, Brett 292–293, 295, 306, 329
allegedly, as a "NO, NO, NO" word 57
Alvarez, Chris 258, 276–277, 278, 279, 331
ambient sound 168; *see also* sound
analogy 232
analytics 16

anchors: anchor intro 140–141, *141*, *142*; "anchor read" 188; anchor script 249; anchor tags 35, 125, 148, *148*; *see also* news anchors; sports anchors; weather anchors
anticipation, and shooting 160–161
apostrophes 56–57
apparently, as a "NO, NO, NO" word 58–59
archives 31
Argen, Lisa 9, 205, 279–280
Army 67
arraignment 65
as-live shots 133, 252–253; *see also* look live
assignment editors (AE) *see* AE (assignment editors)
Associated Press 37; AP style book 40, 41, 54, 60, 61, 72, 295, 296
attribution 40, 46, 57; digital content writing 209
audio 30, 80, 97–99, 165–168 176, 177; audio booths 149, *149*; video chat interviews 88; *see also* sound
Avalos, Gina 101, 102
AWB (auto white balance) 165

background 169–170
background sound 97–99, 177; *see also* audio
backlighting 164–165, *165*

backtiming, the day 122–123, 137; in newscasts 189, 197
bail 65
Bauer Gonzales, Nancy 13, 53, 185, 208, 210, 316, 334
beat check 64
bias 292
Blitzer, Wolf 270
BLM (Black Lives Matter) movement 77–78, 119, 235, 241, 242, 244, 266
blocks 188
Boyle, Danny 165
brands, as a "NO, NO, NO" word 71–72
breaking news 199–202; live reporting 250–252; news anchors 259–260
breathing, and voice 261, 264–265
brevity: in news writing 49; in pitching your story 21; and slugs 35–36
bridges, stand-up 131–132
broadcast formats 177
broadcast news producers 31; role and responsibilities 4–5; *see also* newscast producers
B-roll 115, 176, 176; logging 137–138, **138**; video chat interviews 88–89
Butler, Bob 311, 323
bylines 145; digital content 208

California News Publishers Association 299
camera angles 158
cameras 120; *see also* shot types
capital letters 37–38
careers *see* job opportunities
Carr, Michael 293, 307, 310
Carter, Kianey 4, 77–78, 182, 186, 187, 195, 197, 199, 200–201, 326
cell phone 3, 7, 89, 245, 253
CG ("character generator" graphics) 102–103, 103, 108–109, 114, 114, 141, 195; legislators 71–72
character-driven interviews 105–106

checklist, for breaking news live shots 250–251
children, names of 44–45
chroma key 9; *see also* green screen
city government 70
civil law 67
clarity 49
Clavijo, Allizbeth 220, 308
clean shots 243
cliches 232
clicks 203
closed courtroom 298–299
closed questions 83
closeup (CU) 134, 137, 155, 156, 157
clothes, news anchors 267–268; men 268–269; women 271–273
Coast Guard 67
cold calling 23
cold opens 194
collision, as a "NO, NO, NO" word 60
Colucci, John 203, 204, 213, 214, 216, 220, 258, 333
commas 39, 54–56
communication skills 23–24
community 4, 193; knowledge of 63–64; news anchors' engagement with 282–284; as sources for stories 13, 15
CONFLICT, and newsworthiness 18
conflicts of interest 292
ConnectedTV *see* OTT (Over-The-Top streaming devices)
consent 80, 296–297
consultants 327–328
contempt of court 297
content, and storytelling 233–235
contract negotiation 323–324
contractions 38–39, 56
conversational writing 19, 38–41
Coomey, Marion 23
copy 95
copyright issues 206–207
coronavirus pandemic *see* COVID-19 pandemic

county government 70
COVID-19 pandemic 3; fake news 300–301; impact on broadcast news 119, 120; news reporting of 192–193, 233–235; reporters' equipment 119; video chat interviews 85
credibility, of news anchors 258–260
criminal cases 65–67
cross dissolves 177; *see also* editing
CTV *see* OTT (Over-The-Top streaming services)
CU (closeup) 134, 137, 155, 156, 157
cultural understanding 320–321
curiosity 12, 75, 276, 290
cutaways 138, 159; video chat interviews 88, 88

DA (district attorney) 65
Dateline 36, 208
dates 44, 56; digital content writing 208
days of the week, in writing 44
day-turns 78, 229
dB (decibel) 177
de los Santos, Theresa 216, 301, 319
deadlines 137; digital content 215; missing 124–125; and writing 46–47
deception, and interviews 85
defamation 46, 298
defendant 65, 67
demo reels 315–318
Democratic Party 71, 72
demonstration stand-ups 131, 131
designated market area (DMA) 313–314
diamond shaped model of video storytelling 121–122, 122; *see also* storytelling
diaphragm, the 261
Dietz, Lexi 132
digital content producers 31; role and responsibilities 5
digital news, as source for stories 14

digital producers 203–204, 222; making money on digital content 219–220; permission to share pictures and video 206–207; role and responsibilities 204–205; social media 211–218; writing the web story 207–210
director/production crew: role and responsibilities 10–11
directors; *see also* director/production crew; news directors
disability: handicapped, as a "NO, NO, NO" word 60–61
disinformation 82, 218, 244; *see also* misinformation
district attorney (DA) 65
DMA (designated market area) 313–314
Dotson, Bob 83
drone journalism 235–236
due to, as "NO, NO, NO" words 61

early evening news 187
editing 172; ethical 114–115; getting organized for 173–174; PKG (package) 127–128, 150; process of 174, 175, 176, 176–177
editors: role and responsibilities 7–8; *see also* assignment editors (AE)
Einstein, Albert 56
embedded 114
embeds: digital content writing 210
emergency responders 69
emotion 243; and facial expression 265–267
empathy 74, 260
emphasis 38, 45, 265
employment *see* job opportunities in broadcast news
ending, of stories 43
energy, and live reporting 242
entertainment stories 15
equipment 30, 118–119, 120–121; journalist's toolbox and "go" bag 118–120

ethical issues 289–291, 292–295, 302; Codes of Ethics 114, 291–292
evading, as a "NO, NO, NO" word 61–62
executive producers 5, 31
external hard drive 119, 135, 150, 173, 177
extreme closeup (XCU) 137–138, 155, 157
extreme wide shot (XWS) 157
eye-level shots 170

face closeup 155, 156
Facebook 113, 204, 212–213, 215–216, 218, 233, 284; *see also* social media
FaceTime interviews 233–234
facial expressions 265–267
facial hair 270
failures, in live reporting 238–239, 246–248
fair comment 298
fake news 300–301, 302
false light 297
Federal Privacy Protection Act 297
female, as a "NO, NO, NO" word 60
file organization, in editing 173
file video 96
fire departments 69
First Amendment of the United States Constitution 63–64, 296, 299
flash frame 177
flow 190–191
Floyd, George 194, 266–267, 329
focus statements 26, 27–28, 30
FOIA (Freedom of Information Act) 300
format, of stories 36, 117, 177, 182, 184, 189, 193, 195, 207, 208
Forsman, Randy 10–11, 250, 334
framing 155–158, 157, 158; solo stand-ups 133, 133–134; video chat interviews 86
Freedman, Wayne 109, 110, 131, 155, 230, 231–232, 243
Freedom of Information Act (FOIA) 300

front time 189
full-screen graphics 100–101, 101

gatekeeper 82
"go" bags 118–120
Godinez, Luis Felipe 126, 191, 320–321, 333
Google: Analytics 220; Fact Check Explorer 301; Image Search 301; Maps 102; Search 14
grammar 49; social media 211
graphics: stand-up with 130, 130; VO (voiceover) 99–103, 100, 101, 102, 103; *see also* CG ("character generator" graphics), lower thirds
green screen 9; *see also* chroma key
grieving families, and interviews 85

hair 270
Hall, Ted 271
handicapped, as a "NO, NO, NO" word 60–61
hands closeup 155, 156
"handshake shots" 143–145, 227
hashtag symbol 39
hashtags 217
haters, and social media 218
headlines 207, 208
headphones 167–168
headroom 134, 156
heartburn, and voice health 263
Hebert, Cyndee 16, 38, 127, 190, 193, 234, 242, 257, 312–313
Heist, Stan 234, 317, 319, 334
Hernandez, Victor 4, 15, 20, 21, 76
Hill, Desiree 268, 321
history 182, 191–192
homicide 61
Hsu, George 261, 263
Hudgins, Ryan 105–106
Hulnick, Eric 312
HUMAN INTEREST, and newsworthiness 16–17
Hunter, Holly 201–202

Huppert, Boyd 6, 76, 84, 88, 89, 132, 143–144, 160, 170–171, 221–222, 227–228, 228–229, 230, 231, 232, 233, 329
Hurt, William 201–202
Hypes, Chad 11, 14, 36, 79, 119, 202, 215, 307, 314, 317, 318, 322, 326–327, 330

IFB (Interruptible Feedback) connections 198, 201, 245, 248, 249
IMPACT, and newsworthiness 17
incident, as a "NO, NO, NO" word 61
incue 113, 139
independence, of journalists 291–292
information sources 192–193; *see also* research
Instagram 204, 212–213, 216–217, 284; *see also* social media
interactivity 241–242
internships 308–310
Interruptible Feedback (IFB) connections 198, 201, 245, 248, 249
interviews and interviewing 74–76, 89–90; active 29; active interviews 170–171; challenging interviews 84–85; character-driven 105–106; compelling 24, 25; conducting the interview 79–84; and deception 85; first question 80–81; grieving families 85; job interviews 321–323; logging **139**, 139–140; MOS (man-on-the street) interviews 26, 28–29; with officials 24; on-set interviews 275; preparation for 78–79; reasons for 76–78; shooting 168–171, 169170; video chat interviews 85–86, 87, 88, 88–89, 233–234; VOSOT 105–106
intrusion 297
inverted pyramid style of writing 37
irregular verbs *see* verbs

jewelry 269, 272–273
job opportunities 305–307, 335; agents, consultants and recruiters 327–328; applying for a job 312–315; building your digital/ social media brand 307–308, 315; contract negotiation 323–324; demo reels 315–318; internships 308–310; interviews 321–323; mentors' perspectives on their careers 328–334; networking 310–312; personal websites 318–320; resumes 320–321; starting your career 324–327
Journalist's Toolbox website, SPJ 119–120
jump cuts 114, 158, 176 *see also* editing

key light 164
kickers 15
King, Gayle 330
King, Nick 9, 207, 214, 256–257, 270, 276, 277, 278, 279, 325, 327, 334
kitbag *see* "go bag"
Korean War veterans 111, *111*

language proficiency 320–321
larynx, the 262, 262–264, 264
Lasorda, Tommy 13, 14
late night news 187
Latino community, and racism 126
lavalier microphones 118, 121, 148, 167, 178, 240, 253
law enforcement 68–69
law, the 65–67; *see also* legal issues
lead room 156, 157, 158
leadership skills: newscast producers 183
leads 93–95, 107, 140
legal issues 57, 296, 302; closed courtroom 298–299; contempt of court 297; contract negotiation 323–324; defamation 298; FOIA (Freedom of Information Act) 300;

open meeting/open record 299; privacy 296–297; shield laws 297; and writing 45–46; see also law, the
legalese 139
legislative officials 70–71
Lenk, Jeff 212, 315–316, 332
Lenocker, Bryan 184, 190, 191, 300, 324, 330
Light, Sarah 5, 206, 207, 220–221
lighting 121, 162–165, 164, 165; key light 164; reporter sandwich 163–164, 164; video chat interviews 86, 87
Lim, Dion 8, 93–94, 215, 239, 251, 259, 260, 267, 273, 282, 283, 285, 331–332
Lin, Da 38, 128, 134, 213, 235, 241, 245, 331
LinkedIn 319 see also social media
links, in digital content writing 210
liquidated damages 323
literary devices 230–233
Little, Joe 29, 118–119, 122, 122, 123, 124, 129, 130, 133, 133–134, 154–155, 172, 240–241, 333
live reporting 238–240, 254–255; anchor questions 249–250; as-live/look-live 252–253; breaking news 250–252; digital live shot 253; good live shots 240–245; problems and failures 238–239, 246–248; setting up the live shot 245–246; writing the script 249
live signals 245
LiveU technology 119
location 171; live reporting 240
locator graphics 102–103, 103
logging 127–128, 135–140, 136; interviews (SOTs or soundbites) **139**, 139–140; sound 136–137; and storytelling 229; video (B-roll) 137–138, **138**; see also SLVWE

look-live shots 133, 252–253; see also as-live shots
lower thirds 51; see also graphics
Lucas, George 165
Luevano, Adrian 305–306, 309, 328

MADD (Mothers Against Drunk Driving) 60
makeup: men 270–271; women 273–274
Malat, Jonathan 132
male, as a "NO, NO, NO" word 60
man-on-the street (MOS) interviews 26, 28–29; see also person-on-the-street (POS) interviews
maps 101–102, 102
Marine Corps, Marine Corps Reserve 68
market size 313–314
match cuts 176; see also editing
Matsch, Richard 13
McGrew, Scott 8, 81, 260, 295, 301, 313
Means, Carmaine 7, 120, 154, 162–163, 235–236, 330
media: digital content writing 210
medium shot (MS) 137
medium shots 134, 155, 157
men news anchors: personal appearance 267–271
Mercer, Brandon 205, 210, 219, 220, 221, 329
metaphor 232; see also literary devices
meteorologists see weather anchors
#MeToo movement 285
metrics: digital content 220–222
microphones 121, 148, 166–167; lavalier microphones 118, 121, 148, 167, 178, 240, 253; shotgun microphones 167; stick microphones 148, 241
mid-afternoon news 186
midday news 186
military: structure and roles 67–68
Milstein, Jake 290, 314

misappropriation 297
misinformation 82, 85, 218, 244, 300; *see also* disinformation
mix-minus 248
MMJs (multimedia journalists): equipment 118–119, 120–121; role and responsibilities 6, 7, 117–118; time management 118, 121–125, 122; toolbox and "go" bag 118–120
mobile technology 120
MOJO (mobile journalism) 120
moments, in storytelling 228–230; logging of 137
morning news 186
MOS (man-on-the-street) interviews *see* man-on-the street (MOS) interviews
Mothers Against Drunk Driving (MADD) 60
MS (medium shot) 137
MSJs (multi-skilled journalists) 6, 117; *see also* MMJs (multimedia journalists)
multimedia journalists (MMJs) *see* MMJs (multimedia journalists)
murderer, as a "NO, NO, NO" word 61
Murphy's Law 124

names: spelling of 51, 80; and writing 44–45; *see also* CG ("character generator" graphics)
National Guard 68
National Press Photographers Association (NPPA) 154–155, 227, 292
National Weather Service 37
NATS (natural sound) 126–128, 145–147, 146, 166, 167, 168, 174, 176, 194; logging 136–137; *see also* sound
Navarro, Elisa 211, 324
Navy, Navy Reserve 68
negative action 161

Nelson, Chad 75, 84, 160, 162, 167, 228, 331
networking 310–312
news anchors 183, 193, 199, 201, 255–257, 285–286; anchor intro 140–141, 141, 142; "anchor read" 188; anchor script 249; anchor tags 35, 125, 148, 148; breaking news 259–260; and capital letters 37, 38; clothes 267–269, 271–273; community engagement 282–284; credibility of 258–260; facial expressions 265–267; as influencers 257–258; and interviewing 75; live on the anchor set 274–275; on-set interviews 275; personal protection 285; questions from 249–250; role and responsibilities 8; and social media 258, 284–285; voice health 261–265, 262, 264
news directors 5, 75, 183–184, 189, 201; role and responsibilities 11
news value 16, 19, 21; *see also* newsworthiness
newscast producers 31, 181, 202; breaking news 199–202; building a newscast 187–197, 188, 194, 196; daily work 184–185; live newscasts 198–199; ratings periods 197–198; role and responsibilities 182–184
newscast themes 185–187
newscasts 187; attention to detail 195–196, 196; community connection 193; flow 190–191; forwarding the story 192; helpful information 192–193; live 198–199, 238–255; pacing 190; perspective 191–192; priority 189–190; reassurance 192; rundown 188, 188–189; teases 193–195, 194; timing 196–197

newsworthiness 15–19
Nielsen Global Media 313–314
"NO, NO, NO" words 57–62, 72
non-compete clauses 323
Non-question questions 83
NPPA (National Press Photographers Association) 154–155, 227, 292
numbers: writing style 40–41

occur, as a "NO, NO, NO" word 59–60
off-camera shots 169
Olivas, Kevin 38, 46, 63–64, 82, 108, 181, 183, 212, 217, 306–307, 317, 322–323, 333
OMB (one-man band) *see* MMJs (multimedia journalists)
"On Cam" 99
open meeting/open record 299
open-ended questions 83
open-source materials 210
opposing themes 231; *see also* literary devices
OTS (Over-The-Shoulder) graphics 100, 100
OTT (Over-The-Top streaming devices) 14; streaming services 210–211
"out clauses" 323–324
outcue 113, 139
Over-The-Shoulder (OTS) graphics 100, 100
over-the-shoulder shots 155, 156
Over-The-Top streaming devices (OTT) *see* OTT (Over-The-Top streaming devices)

pacing 137, 190
package (PKG) *see* PKG (package)
pad 103, 104
Panicker, Jobin 6, 126, 332
panning 162
parroting 107–108, 139
passive voice, in writing 53
personal appearance 267–274
personal protection: news anchors 285

person-on-the-street (POS) interviews 26, 28; *see also* MOS
perspective 182, 191–192
photographers: role and responsibilities 7; *see also* shooting
photojournalists 154; and interviewing 75, 84
pictures: digital content writing 210
Pinterest 204; *see also* social media
PIOs (public information officers) 64
pitching your story 21–26, 25, 27–28, 28–32
PKG (package) 35, 93, 117–118, 152–153, 195; basics of 125–127; edit 127–128, 150; equipment 118–121; journalist's toolbox and "go" bag 118–120; logging 127–128, 135–140, 136, **138, 139**; package script 141–142, 142, 143, 151, 151; shooting 127–134, 130, 131, 133, 135; time management 118, 121–125, 122; voice track 127–128, 148–150, 149; workflow 127–128; writing 127–128, 140–148, 141, 142, 143, 146, 147, 148, 150–152, 151, 152
planning meetings 185
Police Department 68
police scanners 64
political parties 71–72
POS (person-on-the-street) interviews *see* person-on-the-street (POS) interviews
positive action 161
Potts, Tracie 6, 81, 83, 107, 125, 200, 234, 239, 243, 250, 266–267
Pregnant I model 122, 122, 123, 172; *see also* storytelling
pre-interview 22–23
press freedom 296
priority 189–190
privacy 296–297
problems, in live reporting 238–239, 246–248

"process journalism" 217
process language 191
producers 3; *see also* broadcast news producers; digital content producers; executive producers
projecting the voice 261
PROMINENCE, and newsworthiness 16
promos 195
pronunciation and pronouncers 45; news anchors 258–259
props 99
PROXIMITY, and newsworthiness 19–20
public disclosure of private facts 296–297
public engagements by news anchors 283–284
public information officers (PIOs) 64
punctuation 39–40, 49–50, 54–57; social media 211

Q-rating 282
questions: open and closed 83
quotes: full-screen graphics 101; punctuation 55–56; quotation marks 39–40, 56

racism: Latino community 126; *see also* BLM (Black Lives Matter) movement
Ramsey, Jon Benet 13
ratings 16
ratings periods 197–198; *see also* sweeps
reader 34, 99
reassurance 192
recording, permission for 80
recruiters 327–328
Reilly, Mike 119
RELEVANCE, and newsworthiness 18
repetition 161
reporter sandwich 163–164, 164; *see also* lighting
reporters 3; freezing 248; preparedness 245–246; role and responsibilities 6, 7; tag-outs 35; toolbox and "go"

bag 118–120; *see also* live reporting; PKG (package)
Republican Party (GOP/Grand Old Party) 71, 72
research: for interviews 78, 79; *see also* information sources
resident, as a "NO, NO, NO" word 59
resume 320–321; reel 249, 279, 305, 312, 314, 318–319
"reveals" 229
revenue, from digital content 219–220
room tone 168
Rose, Les 160, 161, 163RTDNA(Radio Television Digital News Association) Code of Ethics 114, 291
Ruiz, Don Miguel 282
rule of thirds 156–157, 157
rule of threes 231–232
rundown 32; building of 188, 188–189

safety: live reporting 244–245; news anchors 285
SAG-AFTRA union 323
scanners 64
schools, as sources for stories 13
semicolons 39
sequences 134, 135, 155, 156, 176, 176
Sheriff's Department 69
shield laws 297
silence: interviews and 83, 166
shooting 154–155; 180-degree rule 158–160, 159; action reaction 161; anticipating 160–161; background 169–170; framing 155–158, 157, 158; interviews 168–171, 169170; lighting 162–165, 164, 165; location 171; panning and zooming 162; PKG (package) 127–134, 130, 131, 133, 135; sequencing 155, 156; shot types 155, 156, 157, 160, 168, 169, 170;

355 Index

sound 165–168; and storytelling 228–229; tripod use 121, 129, 162
shotgun microphones 167 *see also* microphones
side angle shots 155
sidebars 212
Sidlow, Faith 121
"sizzle" 230
Skold, Marti 280–282
slash symbol 39
Slater, Robin 270, 273–274
slot, making 4, 124, 245
slugs 35–36, 188
SLWVE (Shoot, Log, Write, Voice Track, Edit) acronym 127–128
smart phones *see* cell phone
Snapchat 204 *see also* social media
social media 193, 195, 204, 211–218, 230; building your personal digital/social media brand 307–308, 315; and communication skills 23; digital content producers 5; fake news 300–301; and haters 218; and news anchors 258, 284–285; as sources for stories 14, 15; "surprises" and "teases" 229; verification 301; *see also* digital producers
Society of Professional Journalists (SPJ) *see* SPJ (Society of Professional Journalists)
solo video journalist *see* MMJs (multimedia journalists)
SOT (sound on tape) 35, 107–112, 110, 111, 112, 195; logging 137, **139**, 139–140
sound 30, 165–166; background sound in VOs 97–99, 177; headphones 167–168; live reporting 240–241; logging 136–137; microphones 148, 166–167; *see also* audio; NATS (natural sound); SOT (sound on tape); VOSOT (Voice overwith Sound On Tape)
soundbites 35, 107–112, 110, 111, 112; logging 137, **139**, 139–140; and package writing 145–147, 146, 147; *see also* SOT (sound on tape)
sources, of stories 12–15, 32, 189, 192–193
Space Force 68
spelling 49, 50–52
SPJ (Society of Professional Journalists) 291, 293; Journalist's Toolbox website 119–120
sports anchors 276–279; clothes 268; role and responsibilities 9–10
stand-ups 129–131, 130, 131; as-live or look-live open and close 133; solo 133, 1330134; stand-up bridges 131–132; stand-up close 133
state government 70–71
State Police 69
steady bags 119
Steele, Brittney 134
Stephens, Kim 50, 198, 217, 238–239, 247, 312
stick microphones 148, 241
sticks 162; *see also* tripod
stories: ending of 43; forwarding of 192; newsworthiness of 15–20; pitching of 21–26, 25, 27–28, 28–32; sources of 12–15, 32, 189, 192–193; story formats 34–35
story focus 25, 26, 27–28, 28–31, 227–228
storytelling 227–228, 236; importance of content 233–235; literary devices 230–233; models, diamond 121–122; pregnant I 122, 123, 172; moments 228–230; stealing from the pros 230
Student Press Law Center 300
subject/verb placement 42–43
sunshine laws 299

"surprises" 83, 229; in digital 194; in storytelling 228–230, 233
suspect, as a "NO, NO, NO" word 57–58
sweeps *see* ratings periods

tag-outs 35, 145
talent 188
"talking ear" shots 168, 169 *see also* framing
"talking heads" 171
TDs (technical directors) 189
teases 193–195, 194, 229
Teleprompter 95, 201, 243; writing formats 37, 38
termination clauses 323
thirds, rule of 156–157, 157
threes, rule of 231–232
tight shots 160
TikTok 204; *see also* social media
time 43–44; digital content writing 208
time management 118, 121–125, 122
timeliness 190; and newsworthiness 18–19
timeslots, and newscast themes 185–187
timing 189, 196–197; TRT (Total Running Time) 113, 195; VO (voiceover) 103–104
Tompkins, Al 52, 77, 166, 289, 293–294
topicals 195
toss 140
Total Running Time (TRT) 113, 195
Tran, Will 150, 214, 242, 243, 257, 296
transparency 292
trespass 297
tripods 121, 129, 162 *see also* sticks
TRT (Total Running Time) 113, 195
TVU technology 119
Twitter 204, 212–213, 213–215, 233, 284; *see also* social media
two-shot 188, 274

undetermined, as a "NO, NO, NO" word 59
United States Constitution, First Amendment 63–64, 296, 299
unusual shots 155, 156
UNUSUALNESS, and newsworthiness 17
U.S. Congress 71
U.S. House of Representatives 71
U.S. Senate 71
Utsler, Max 109

Vandergrift, Greg 124, 127, 135, 136, 137, 139, 140, 145, 146–147, 234, 332
Vanek, Adam 60
verbs, tense of 52–54, **54**
verification 301
victim, as a "NO, NO, NO" word 58
video: editing 172–174, 175, 176, 176–177, 178; and editing 176; logging 137–138, **138**; photographers 7; shooting 154–171, 156, 157, 158, 159, 164, 165, 169, 170, 177–178
video chat interviews 85–86, 87, 88, 88–89, 233–234
visuals 20
VJ (video journalist) *see* MMJs (multimedia journalists)
VO (voiceover) 18, 35, 93, 104, 106, ; graphics 99–103, 100, 101, 102, 103; the lead 93–95; reader 99; timing 103–104; writing to your video 95, 95–99, 98
vocabulary 50; "NO, NO, NO" words 57–62; social media 211
vocal cords 262, 262–264, 264
voice health 261–265, 262, 264
voice track 177; PKG (package) 127–128, 148–150, 149
voicebox 262, 262–264, 264
VOSOT (Voice over with Sound On Tape) 35, 93, 105–106, 106–107, 115; best interviews 106; finishing

of 112, 112; scripting 113–114, 114; soundbites 107–112, 110, 111, 112; writing of 107–108

wallpaper video 96, 172
weather anchors 279–282; role and responsibilities 9
web story writing 150–152, 151, 152, 207–210
websites: digital content producers 5; personal 318–320; *see also* digital producers
White, Alex 75, 187, 309–310, 311, 321, 324–325, 327
white balance 165
wide shot (WS) 137
wide shots 155, 156, 157; video chat interviews 89
WOCHU (Wide shot or medium shot, Over the shoulder, Closeup of face, Hands closeup, Unusual shot or wide angle) 155, 171
women news anchors: personal appearance 271–274
Woods, Tiger 278
wording 49–50; social media 211
workflow 175; PKG (package) 127–128
workplaces, as sources for stories 13
World War II veterans 110–111, 111
wounded, as a "NO, NO, NO" word 60
Wright, Robert 105–106, 113

writing 34–36, 49–50, 62; active writing 41–42, 42–43, 44, 52–53, 208; conversational 19, 38–41, 49; deadlines 46–47; ethical 114–115; legal issues 45–46; literary devices 230–233; live shot script 249; names 44–45; "NO, NO, NO" words 57–62; now, new, next 41–42; passive voice 53; PKG (package) 127–128, 140–148, 141, 142, 143, 146, 147, 148; pronunciation and pronouncers 45; punctuation 39–40, 49, 54–57; into SOTs 110–112, 111; spelling 49, 50–52; of teases 193–195, 194; verb tense 52–54, **54**; to video 95, 95–99, 98; web story 150–152, 151, 152, 207–210; writing like we speak 36–38
WS (wide shot) 137

XCU (extreme closeup) 137–138, 155, 157
XLR cables 118
XWS (extreme wide shot) 157

YouTube 204, 218, 230, 234, 318

Zelich, Mark 170–171
Zoom 233–234; *see also* video chat interviews
zooming 162

Made in the USA
Las Vegas, NV
01 September 2025